Thomas Nicolas Burke, P. H. Moran

English Misrule in Ireland

A Course of Lectures in Reply to James Anthony Froude

Thomas Nicolas Burke, P. H. Moran

English Misrule in Ireland
A Course of Lectures in Reply to James Anthony Froude

ISBN/EAN: 9783337157654

Printed in Europe, USA, Canada, Australia, Japan

Cover: Foto ©ninafisch / pixelio.de

More available books at **www.hansebooks.com**

THE IRISH-AMERICAN LIBRARY.

VOL. I.

ENGLISH MISRULE IN IRELAND.

A COURSE OF LECTURES,

DELIVERED BY THE

VERY REV. THOMAS N. BURKE, O.P.,

IN REPLY TO

JAMES ANTHONY FROUDE, ESQ.

With an Appendix,

CONTAINING A REVIEW OF THE SO-CALLED "BULL" OF ADRIAN IV., BY THE MOST REV. P. H. MORAN, BISHOP OF OSSORY; AND "AN ANALYSIS OF THE REBELLION OF 1641," BY MATHEW CAREY.

NEW YORK:
LYNCH, COLE & MEEHAN, 57 MURRAY STREET,
1873.

ENTERED ACCORDING TO ACT OF CONGRESS, IN THE YEAR 1872, BY
LYNCH, COLE & MEEHAN,
IN THE OFFICE OF THE LIBRARIAN OF CONGRESS, AT WASHINGTON.

POOLE & MACLAUCHLAN,
PRINTERS AND BOOKBINDERS,
205-213 *East 12th St.*

INTRODUCTION.

THE idea of an "IRISH-AMERICAN LIBRARY," similar to the "Library of Ireland," which Davis originated for his and our native land, suggested itself to us many years ago, and would have been put into practical execution before now, but that circumstances did not permit us to subtract from other and more pressing duties the time and personal attention that were required to make the experiment not only successful, but worthy of the National idea it would represent. The necessity of some such collection of works relating to our people,—in their connection with their native and adopted countries,—has, however, never been absent from our mind. And recent events have so strongly demonstrated the urgency of that need, that our resolution was at once taken to do what lay in our power to supply the want, and at least to make a beginning of what may hereafter be a work of some consequence to our people in this New World. The Irish-American element, at the present day, in this Republic, is second to no other in importance as a component portion of the community. Its status in the history of the country, from the earliest dates of which we have any authentic or reliable records, has never been insignificant. Yet, with the exception of two volumes (both the work of men who, however able, were very imperfectly acquainted with the subjects on which they treated), we have met no work that even pretended to deal with the connection of the Irish race with this Republic, or preserve to futurity the record of what Irish-Americans have done, and are doing, for the advancement of the land in which so many of them have found citizenship and hospitable welcome. Yet this deficiency does not spring from lack of material fit for authentic history. Probably no other portion of the community possesses a richer store of materials for a creditable history than can be produced by the Irish branch of the great Celtic family, which has been transplanted to this North American Continent. But, unfortunately, this mass of information,—invaluable to us as an essential portion of our title-deeds to the citizenship of the United States,—has lain undeveloped and unused; hidden away in family records, or only finding access to the light in the uncertain and perishable form of newspaper publications. The knowledge of many important facts relating to the share which Irishmen and their immediate descendants have had in the establishment of this Republic, and its subsequent progress to prosperity and greatness as a nation, is rapidly passing away with the men of the last generation, who were familiar with the story. And it is only occasionally, when some accidental circumstance elicits a detail of those facts, that the world is apprised how, in one of the greatest revolutions by which the political relations of human society have ever been influenced, the children of that little island in the far-off ocean, which England has been so assiduously, but vainly, endeavoring to shut out from the gaze of mankind, played an important part, and left their mark worthily upon the past of their adopted country. As an instance of the historical losses to which we have been liable from the want of any permanent form of record appertaining to our people in this country, we may cite the writings and speeches of the adopted son of the great WASHINGTON—the late GEORGE WASHINGTON PARKE CUSTIS. That eminent gentleman,—one of the best representatives of that generation,—the first-born of the Republic,—whose patriotism, genius, and high integrity made the American name illustrious, and compelled the respect and admiration of even hostile critics,—that eminent gentleman thought so highly of our people, for the share they had taken in the emancipation of his native land, that he lost no opportunity of giving expression to his favorable opinion; and, in his latter days, he claimed as one of his most cherished titles, that by which he had distinguished himself as "The Old Orator of Ireland." Yet in his Biography (published some years since, by one of his surviving descendants) not one word is mentioned of all that he has said or written in behalf of the country and the people in whose fate he took so deep an interest; and for the testimony which he so nobly bears to the part played by the Irish, in the great struggle for the independence of these States, we are indebted to the columns of an extinct and almost forgotten journal, and to the painstaking care and research of a patriotic Irish-American, Michael Hennessy, Esq., of Brooklyn, who, with a zeal and perseverance that merit the grateful recognition of his fellow-countrymen, has collected and made available a vast amount of references and authorities, which, to the student of Irish history, are invaluable, and in this country would be unattainable, were it not for the excellent literary taste and patriotic spirit which impelled Mr. Hennessy to devote himself to the congenial work of concentrating and preserving them.

There are many interesting narratives now existing in no more permanent form than that of an occasional newspaper file, or "scrap-book," that would in a few years, perhaps, be of the highest value to the descendants of the men by whom those events of history have been acted out. To rescue from oblivion, and place within the reach of all our people, as much as possible of those records relating to our race in this hemisphere, shall be the mission of "THE IRISH-AMERICAN LIBRARY." There are also many splendid contributions, of oratory, song, and poetic fiction, with which Irish genius has enriched the literature of America; and with some of these we design, also, to lighten, and, as it were, beautify, the dryer but more important details of current history. The successive volumes of the "Library" shall be issued as rapidly as the matter comprising them can be properly collated and arranged.

In selecting for the first issue of this series the lectures of Father Burke in refutation of the sophistries of the English historian Froude, we have been influenced not merely by the intrinsic merit and beauty of those discourses, and their value as a defence of our national character, but also by the consideration of that tendency of the American mind which impels it to deal immediately and directly with what is *present*, and to leave the remote past for more leisurely consideration. The value of these lectures, both as a defence of our people against a most flagrant attack, and as a future source of reference in relation to many important portions of our history, will be materially enhanced by the Appendix which we have added, and which contains all the most authentic historical quotations relating to the matters which Mr. Froude has so artfully misrepresented or mystified.

The importance and reliability of these historical notes may be judged from the fact that it was from the works from which they are extracted (most of which have long been out of print,) O'Connell principally composed his celebrated "Memoir on Ireland," which has since been a hand-book for Irish national reference. We have endeavored to place those portions of them which bear upon the subject-matter of the Froude controversy in the shape most available for the general mass of readers, who may not have leisure or opportunity to hunt up these references for themselves; in which view they add materially to the value of the work; and may, perhaps, be productive of further good by stimulating some readers to a more careful study of the facts of Irish history,—a correct knowledge of which is so essential in repelling attacks on our national reputation, such as that projected by our latest English assailant, and so happily met and defeated by the great Irish Dominican.

ENGLISH MISRULE IN IRELAND.

FIRST LECTURE.

(Delivered in the Academy of Music, New York, Nov. 12, 1872.)

NORMAN INVASION AND MISRULE.

LADIES AND GENTLEMEN: It is a strange fact that the old battle that has been raging for seven hundred years should continue so far away from the old land. The question on which I am come to speak to you this evening is one that has been disputed at many a council board—one that has been disputed in many a Parliament, one that has been disputed on many a well-fought field, and is not yet decided—the question between England and Ireland. Among the visitors to America, who came over this year, there was one gentleman, distinguished in Europe for his style of writing, and for his historical knowledge,—the author of several works, which have created a profound sensation, at least for their originality. Mr. Froude has frankly stated that he came over to this country to deal with England and the Irish question, viewing it from an English standpoint; that, like a true man, he came to make the best case that he could for his own country; that he came to state that case to the American public, as to a grand jury, and to demand a verdict from them, the most extraordinary that ever yet was demanded of any people,—namely, a declaration that England was right in the manner in which she has treated my native land for seven hundred years.

It seems, according to this learned gentleman, that we Irish have been badly treated (that he confesses); but he puts in as a plea that we only got what we deserved. It is true, he says, that we have governed them badly; the reason is, because it was impossible to govern them rightly. It is true that we have robbed them; the reason is, because it was a pity to leave them their own,—they made such a bad use of it. It is true that we have persecuted them; the reason is, persecution was the fashion of the time and the order of the day. On these pleas there is not a criminal in prison to-day, in the United States, that should not immediately get his freedom by acknowledging his crime, and pleading some extenuating circumstances.

Our ideas about Ireland have been all wrong, it seems. Seven hundred years ago, the exigencies of the time demanded the foundation of a strong British empire. In order to do this, Ireland had to be conquered; and Ireland was conquered. Since that time (according to Mr. Froude,) the one ruling idea in the English mind has been to do all the good they could to the Irish. Their legislation and their action have not been always tender, but they were always beneficent; they were sometimes severe; but they were severe to us for our own good: and the difficulty of England has been, that the Irish, during all these long hundreds of years, have never understood their own interests, nor known what was for their own good! *Now*, the American mind is enlightened; and henceforth no Irishman must complain of the past in this new light in which Mr. Froude puts it before us; and the amiable gentleman tells us, moreover, that, what has been our fate in the past, he greatly fears we must reconcile ourselves to in the future.

Mr. Froude comes to tell us his version of the history of Ireland, and he also comes to solve Ireland's difficulty, and to lead us out of all the miseries that have been our history for hundreds of years. When he came, many persons questioned what was the reason or motive of his coming. I have heard people speaking all around me, assigning to the learned gentleman this motive or that. Some persons said he was an emissary of the English Government; that they sent him here because they were beginning to be afraid of the rising power of Ireland in this great nation; that they saw here eight millions of Irishmen by birth, and perhaps fourteen millions Irish by immediate descent; they knew enough of the Irish to know that the Almighty God blessed them always with an extraordinary power, not only to preserve themselves, but to spread themselves; and that, in a few years, not fourteen, but fifty millions of Irish blood and of the Irish race would be in this land. According to those who thus surmised, England wants to check the sympathy of the American people for their Irish fellow-citizens; and it was considered that the best way to effect this was to send a learned man with a plausible story to this country,—a man with a singular power of viewing facts in the light in which he wished himself to view them, and in that light to put them before others;—a man with an extraordinary power of so mixing up these facts, that many simple-minded people will look upon them as he puts them before them; and whose mission it was to alienate the mind of America from Ireland to-day, by showing what an impracticable, obstinate, accursed race we are.

Others, again, surmised that the learned gentleman came for another purpose. They said: "England is in the hour of her weakness; she is tottering fast, and visibly, to her ruin. The disruption of that old empire is visibly approaching. She is to-day cut off, without an ally in Europe. Her army is a cipher; her fleet—according to Mr. Reed, the best authority on this great question—is nothing to be compared with the rival fleet of the great Russian power that is growing up beside her. With France paralyzed by her late defeat, England lost her best ally. The three Emperors, the other day, they said, contemptuously ignored her, and settled the affairs of the world without as much as mentioning the name of that kingdom that was once so powerful. Her resources of coal and iron are failing; her people are discontented; and she shows every sign of decay." Thus did some persons argue that England was anxious for an American alliance; for they said: "What would be more natural than that the old and tottering empire should wish to lean upon the strong, mighty, vigorous young arm of America?"

I have heard others say that the gentleman came over on the invitation of a little clique of sectarian bigots in this country; men who,—feeling that the night of religious bigotry and sectarian bitterness is fast coming to a close before the increasing light of American intelligence and education,—would fain prolong the darkness by an hour or two, by whatever help Mr. Froude could lend them. But I protest to you, gentlemen, to-night, that I have heard all these motives assigned to this learned man, without giving them the least attention. I believe Mr. Froude's motives to be simple, straightforward, and patriotic. I am willing to give him credit for the highest motives; and I consider him perfectly incapable of lending himself to any base or sordid proceeding, from a base or sordid motive.

But, as the learned gentleman's motives have been so freely criticised, and, I believe, in many cases misinterpreted, so, my own motives in coming here to-night, to answer him, may, perhaps, be misinterpreted or misunderstood,

unless I state them clearly and plainly. As he is said to come as an emissary of the English Government, I may be said to appear here, perhaps, as an emissary of rebellion or revolution. As he is supposed by some to have the sinister motive of alienating the American mind from the Irish citizenship of these States, so I may be suspected of endeavoring to excite religious or political hatred. Now, I protest that these are not my motives. I come here to-night, simply to vindicate the honor of Ireland and her history. I come here to-night lest any man should think that, in this our day,—or in any day,—Ireland is to be left without a son who will speak for the mother that bore him. . . . . .
. . . . And I hold that Mr. Froude is unfit for the task which he has undertaken, for three great reasons. First of all, because I find, in the writings of this learned gentleman, that he solemnly and emphatically declares that he despairs of ever finding a remedy for the evils of Ireland, and that he gives it up as a bad job. Here are his words, written in one of his essays a few years ago:

"The present hope is that by assiduous justice, that is to say, by conceding everything that the Irish please to ask, we shall disarm their enmity, and convince them of our good will. It may be so. There are persons sanguine enough to hope that the Irish will be so moderate in what they demand, and the English so liberal in what they will grant, that at last we shall fling ourselves into each other's arms, in tears and mutual forgiveness. I do not share that expectation. It is more likely that they will push their importunities, till at last we turn upon them, and refuse to yield further. There will be a struggle once more; and either the emigration to America will go on, increasing in volume till it has carried the entire race beyond our reach, or, in some shape or other, *they will again have to be coerced into submission.*"

Banish them or coerce them! There is the true Englishman speaking! My only remedy, he emphatically says, my only hope, my only prospect of a future for Ireland is, let them go to America: have done with the race altogether, and give us Ireland, at last, such as we have labored to make it for seven hundred years,—a desert and a solitude. Or, if they remain at home, they will have to be coerced into submission. I hold, that that man has no right to come to America, to tell the American people, or the Irish in America, that he can describe the horoscope of Ireland's future. He ought to be ashamed to do it, after uttering such words as those.

The second reason why I say he is unfit for the task of describing Irish history, is because of his contempt for the Irish people. The original sin of the Englishman has ever been his contempt for the Irish. It lies deep, though dormant, in the heart of almost every Englishman. The average Englishman despises the Irishman, and looks down upon him as a being almost inferior in nature. Now, I speak not from prejudice, but from an intercourse of years, for I have lived among them. I have known Englishmen,—amiable, gentle, religious, charming characters,—who would not, for the whole world, wilfully nourish in their hearts a feeling of contempt for any one—much less express it in words: and yet I have seen even these manifest in a thousand forms that contempt for the Irish which seems to be a part of their very nature. I am sorry to say that, in respect to this feeling, I can make no exception of Catholic or Protestant among the English. I mention this not to excite animosity, not to create bad blood or bitter feeling. No: I protest this is not my meaning. But I mention this because I am convinced it lies at the very root of that antipathy and hatred between the English and Irish, which seems to be incurable. And I verily believe, that, until that feeling is destroyed, you never can have a cordial union between the two countries; and the only way to destroy it is to raise Ireland, so by justice and by home legislation, that her people will attain to such a position, as to enforce and command the respect of their English fellow-citizens.

Mr. Froude, himself (who, I am sure, is incapable of any ungenerous sentiment, towards any man, or any people,) is an actual living example of that feeling of contempt of which I speak. In November, 1865, this learned gentleman addressed a Scottish assembly, in Edinburgh. The subject of his address was the effect of the Protestant Reformation upon the Scottish character. According to him, it made the Scots the finest people on the face of the earth. Originally fine, they never got the last touch,—that made them, as it were, archangels among men,—until the holy hand of John Knox touched them. On that occasion the learned gentleman introduced himself to his Scottish audience in the following words:—

"I have undertaken to speak, this evening, on the effects of the Reformation in Scotland, and I consider myself a very bold person to have come here on any such undertaking. In the first place, the subject is one with which it is presumptuous for a stranger to meddle. Great national movements can only be understood properly by the people whose disposition they represent. We say, ourselves, about our own history, that only Englishmen can properly comprehend it. It is the same with every considerable nation. They work out their own political and spiritual lives through tempers, humors, and passions peculiar to themselves: and the same disposition which produces the result is required to interpret it afterwards."

Did the learned gentleman offer any such apology for entering so boldly on the discussion of Irish affairs? Oh, no! There was no apology necessary. He was going to speak only of the "mere Irish." There was no word to express his fear that, perhaps, he had not understood their character, or the subject of which he was about to treat. There was no apology to the Irish in America,—the fourteen millions before whom he so boldly told his story, endeavoring to hold them up as an irreligious, licentious, contentious, obstinate, ungovernable race. None at all. It was not necessary; they were only Irish! If they were Scotch, how the learned gentleman would have come with a thousand apologies for his presumption in venturing to approach such a delicate subject as a delineation of the sweet Scotch character, or anything connected with it!

What, on the other hand, is his treatment of the Irish? I have in this book before me the words that came from his pen: and I protest, as I read them, I felt every drop of my Irish blood boiling in my veins. I felt how bitter was the taunt when he said:—"They may be good at the voting booths, but they are no good to handle the rifle!" He compares us, in this essay, to a pack of hounds; and he says:—

"To tell Ireland to go in peace and freedom would be the same as if a gentleman addressed his hounds, and said, 'I give you your freedom: now, go out and act as you please.' It is needless to say that, after worrying all the sheep in the neighborhood, they would end by tearing each other to pieces."

I deplore this feeling. The man who is possessed by it can never understand the philosophy of Irish history.

Thirdly, Mr. Froude is utterly unfit for the task of delineating or interpreting the history of the Irish people, because of the more than contempt,—the bitter hatred and detestation,—in which he holds the Catholic clergy and the Catholic religion. In this book before me, he speaks of the Catholic Church as an "Old Serpent, whose poisonous fangs have been drawn from her;"—as a "Witch of Endor, mumbling curses to-day because she cannot burn at the stake and shed blood as of old." He most unfairly charges the Church with and makes her responsible for the French massacre of St. Bartholomew's Day; for the persecutions and deaths which originated from the revolt of the Netherlands, against the Duke of Alva, under Philip II.; for every murder and butchery that has been committed, he says, with the virus of the most intense prejudice, that the Catholic Church lies at the bottom of them all, and is responsible for them. The very gentlemen that welcomed him and surrounded him when he came to New York, gave him plainly to understand that, where the Catholic religion is involved, where a favorite theory is to be considered, or a favorite view has to be proved, they do not consider him as a reliable or trustworthy witness or historian. . . . . Not, I again declare, that I believe this gentleman to be capable of a lie. I do not. I believe he is incapable of it. But wherever prejudice such as his comes in, it distorts the most well-known facts for its own purpose. Thus, the gentleman wishes to exalt Queen Elizabeth by blackening the character of Mary Queen of Scots; and in doing this he has been convicted, by a citizen of Brooklyn, of putting his own words as if they were the words of ancient chronicles, and ancient laws and deeds and documents; and the taunt has been flung at him: "Mr. Froude has never grasped the meaning of inverted commas."

Henry VIII., of blessed memory, has been painted by this historian as a most estimable man,—as chaste as a monk. Bless your souls! you are all mistaken about him! A man that never robbed anybody! burning with zeal for the public good! His putting away his wife, and taking young Anna Boleyn to his embraces!—oh! that was a chaste anxiety for the public welfare. All the atrocities of this monster in human shape melt away under Mr. Froude's eyes; and Henry VIII. rises before us in such a form, that even the

Protestants of England, when they saw him as described by Mr. Froude, cried out:—"Oh, you have mistaken your man!" One fact will show you how this gentleman writes history. When Henry VIII. declared war against the Church,—when England was distracted by his tyranny,—one day hanging a Catholic because he would not deny the supremacy of the Pope, and the next day hanging a Protestant for denying the Real Presence in the Blessed Sacrament; —during this time, when the ministers who remained faithful to the Pope were most odious to the tyrant; and such was the slavish acquiescence of the English people, that they began to hate their clergy, in order to please their king,—a certain man, whose name was Hun, was lodged a prisoner in the Lorillard Tower, and he was found in his cell, hanged by the neck, and dead. There was a coroner's inquest held over him, and the twelve—I can call them nothing but the twelve blackguards—that were on the jury,—in order to express their own hatred, and to please the powers that were, brought in a verdict of wilful murder against the Chancellor of the Bishop of London, a most excellent priest. When the Bishop heard of this verdict, he applied to the Prime Minister to have the verdict quashed; just the same as if they found a verdict of wilful murder against you, who were not yet born. He brought the matter before the House of Lords, in order that the character of his Chancellor might be fully vindicated. The King's Attorney-General took cognizance of it; and by a solemn decree the verdict of the coroner's jury was set aside; and these twelve men were declared to be twelve perjurers. Now, listen to Mr. Froude's version of that story. Writing the history of England, he comes to that fact; and he says:

"The clergy at that time were reduced to such a state of immorality and wickedness, that, Hun being found dead in his cell, a coroner's jury actually found a verdict of murder against the Chancellor of the Bishop of London; and the Bishop was obliged to apply to Cardinal Wolsey for a special jury to try the Chancellor, because, if they took any ordinary twelve men, they would be sure to find him guilty:"

—leaving the reader under the impression, that the man was guilty of a murder, of which he was as innocent as Abel; and that if he were placed before any twelve of his countrymen, they would find him guilty on the evidence. This is the impression this "candid writer" leaves, knowing the facts as well as I know them.

Well, now, we come to consider the subject of his first lecture; and, indeed, I must say, I never personally experienced the difficulty of hunting a will-o'-the-wisp through a marsh, until I came to follow this learned gentleman in his first lecture. I say this, not disrespectfully to him at all; but he covered so much ground, and at such unequal distances, that it is impossible to follow him with anything like order. He began by telling how Minister Rufus King wrote a letter about certain Irishmen; and he went on to say how, —in the time of America's great Revolutionary struggle,— the Catholics of Ireland sympathized with England, while the Protestants of Ireland were breast-high for America. All these questions—which belong to our own day,—I will leave aside for the present; and when I come, towards the close of my lectures, to speak of them, then I shall have great pleasure in taking up Mr. Froude's assertions and examining them.

But,—coming home to the great question of Ireland,—what does this gentleman tell us? He tells us that, seven hundred years ago, Ireland was invaded by the Anglo-Normans: and the first thing, apparently, he wishes to do is to justify this invasion, and to establish the principle that the Normans were right in coming to Ireland. How does he do this? He begins by drawing a terrible picture of the state of Ireland before the invasion. He says—they were cutting each other's throats; the whole land was covered with bloodshed; there was in Ireland neither religion, morality, nor government; and, therefore, the Pope found it necessary to send the Normans to Ireland, as one would send a policeman into a saloon where the people were killing each other. This is the first justification—that in Ireland, seven hundred years ago,—just before the Norman invasion,—there was neither morality, religion, nor government. Let us see if he is right.

The first proof Mr. Froude gives that there was no government in Ireland, is a most insidious statement. He says:—

"How could there be any government in a country where every family maintained itself according to its own ideas, right or wrong, and acknowledged no authority?"

Well, if this be true, according to the modern use of the word "family," certainly Ireland was in a deplorable state; every family governing itself according to its own notions, and acknowledging no authority. What does he mean by the word "family"? Speaking to Americans in this nineteenth century, the word "family" means every household in the land. We talk of a man and his family,—the father and mother, and three or four, five or six children, as the case may be. This is our idea as to the word family; and using the word in this sense, I fully admit that, if every family in Ireland were governed by their own ideas, admitting no authority, Mr. Froude has established his case. But what is the fact? What is the meaning of the word "family," as applied in Ireland, seven hundred years ago. The "family," in Ireland, meant the sept, or tribe—all that had the same name. They owned whole counties, a large extent of territory. The men of the same name were called the men of the same family; as for instance, the McMurroughs, of Leinster; the O'Tooles, of Wicklow; the O'Byrnes, of Kildare; the O'Conors, of Connaught; the O'Briens, of Munster; the O'Neills and O'Donnells, of Ulster. The family meant a nation; the family mean two or three counties of Ireland, governed by one Chieftain; all the men of one sept: and it is quite true that every such family governed itself in its own independence, and acknowledged no superior. That is quite true. There were five great families in Ireland: the O'Conors, in Connaught; the O'Neills, in Ulster; the McLaughlins, in Meath; the O'Briens, in Munster; and the McMurroughs, in Leinster. Under these five great heads there were many septs, or smaller families, each counting from five hundred or six hundred to a thousand fighting men: but all acknowledging, in the different Provinces, the sovereignty of these five great royal houses. These five houses, again, elected their monarch, or supreme ruler, called the "Ard-righ," who dwelt in Tara. I ask, if the family thus meant a whole sept or tribe, having a regularly constituted head, is it fair to say that Ireland was in a state of anarchy because every family governed itself? Is it fair of this gentleman thus to try and hoodwink the American jury, to which he has made his appeal, by describing the Irish family, which meant a sept or tribe, as a family of the nineteenth century, which means only the head of the house and the mother and children?

Again, he says, the Irish people lived like the New-Zealanders of to-day, in underground caves: and then he declares *boldly*—" I, myself, opened one of these underground lodging-houses of the Irish people." Now, mark! this gentleman lives in Ireland; and, a few years ago, he opened an ancient rath in Kerry,—one of those Danish raths;—and there he discovered a cave and some remains of mussel-shells and bones. At the time of that discovery he had the most learned archæologist in Ireland with him: and they put their heads together about it; but Mr. Froude has written in this very book before me that what these places were intended for,—what use they were applied to,—baffled conjecture: no one could tell it. Well, if it baffled conjecture then, and they could not tell what to make of it—if it so puzzled him then, what right has he to come out here in America, and say they were the ordinary dwellings of the Irish people?

In order to understand the state of Ireland before the Norman invasion, I must ask you to consider, first, the ancient Irish Constitution which governed the land. Ireland was governed by septs or families. The land, from time immemorial, was in possession of these families or tribes. Each tribe elected its own Chieftain; and to him they paid the most devoted allegiance and obedience; so that the fidelity of the Irish clansman to his chief was proverbial. The chief, during his lifetime, convoked an assembly of the tribe; and they elected from among the members of the family the best and the strongest man to be his successor: and they called him the Tanist. The object of this was that the successor of the King might be known, and that, at the King's death, there might be no riot or bloodshed, or contention for the right to succeed him. Was not this a wise law? An elective monarchy has its advantages. The best man comes to the front because he is chosen by his fellow-men. When they came to select a successor to their Prince, the King's eldest son had no right, because he was the King's son, to succeed his father; he might be a booby or a fool. So, they wisely selected the best and strongest and bravest and wisest man; and he was acknowledged to have the right of succession; he was the Tanist, according to the ancient law of Ireland. Well, these families, as I have said, in the various Provinces, owed and paid allegiance to the King of the

Province, who was one of the five great families, called "the Five Bloods of Ireland." Each Prince had his own Judge, or Brehon, who administered justice in solemn court for the people. These Brehons, or Irish judges, were learned men. The historians of the times tell us, they could speak Latin as fluently as they could Irish. They had an established code of law, had colleges where they studied that law; and it was only when they graduated in their studies that they came home to their respective septs, or tribes, and were established as Brehons or Judges over the people. Nowhere in the history of Ireland do we read that any man rebelled or protested against the decision of a Brehon Judge. Then the five monarchs, in the five Provinces, elected the "Ardrigh" or High King. With him, they sat in council on national matters, and on all matters that concerned the whole people, within the halls of imperial Tara. There St. Patrick found them in the year 432, minstrels and bards, and Brehons, princes, crowned monarchs, and High King:—there did he find them, discussing, like wise and prudent men, the affairs of the nation, when he preached to them the Faith of Christ. While this Constitution remained, the clansmen paid no rent for their land. The land of the tribe or family was held in common—it was the common property of all; and the Brehon or Judge divided it, giving to each man what was necessary for him, with free right of pasturage over the whole. They had no idea of slavery or serfdom among them. The Irish clansman was of the same blood as his Chieftain. The O'Brien that sat in the saddle, at the head of his men, was related by blood to the Gallowglass O'Brien that fought in the ranks. There was no such thing as slavery among them; no such thing as the Chieftain looking down upon the people; no such thing as cowed, abject submission on the part of the people to every worthless decree. The Chieftain was one of themselves; and the men stood in the ranks as freemen, perfectly equal, one with another. We are told even by Gerald Barry, the lying historian, who sometimes, though rarely, told the truth, that, when the English came to Ireland, nothing astonished them more than the free and bold manner in which the humblest man spoke to his Chieftain, and the condescension and equality with which the Chieftain treated the humblest soldier in his tribe. This was the ancient Irish Constitution. Does this look like anarchy? No! It cannot be said, with truth, that there was anarchy in a land where the laws were so well defined, where everything was in its proper place. Mr. Froude says that there was, because that the Chieftains were fighting amongst themselves. And so they were. But he immediately adds, that there was fighting everywhere throughout Europe, after the breaking up of the Roman Empire. If there was fighting going on in every land,—if the Saxon was cutting the Norman's throat, in England,—what right has he to say that Ireland, beyond all nations, was given up to anarchy, because Chieftain drew the sword against Chieftain, frequently, or from time to time?

So much for the question of government. Now for the question of religion. The Catholic religion flourished in Ireland for six hundred years and more before the Anglo-Normans invaded her coasts. For the first three hundred years after the introduction of Christianity into Ireland, the religion of the Irish was the glory of the world and the pride of God's holy Church. Ireland, for these three hundred years, was the island-mother home of saints and scholars. Men came from every country of the then known world to light the lamp of knowledge and sanctity at the sacred fire that burned upon the altars of Ireland. Then came the Danes; and for three hundred years more our people were harassed by incessant wars. The Danes, as Mr. Froude remarked,—apparently with a good deal of approval,—had no respect for Christ or His religion. The first thing they did was to pull down the churches, and set fire to the monasteries. They slaughtered the monks and holy priests and Bishops of Ireland. The people were left without religious instruction, for in time of war men have not much time to think of religion. For three hundred years Ireland was subjected, year after year, to the incursions of the Danes; until on Good Friday morning, 1014, Brian Boroihme defeated them at the great battle of Clontarf. But it was not until the twelfth century,—on the 23d of August, 1103,—that they were finally driven out of the country, by the defeat of Magnus, their King, on Lough Strangford, in the North of Ireland.

The consequence of those Danish wars was that the Catholic religion,—though it remained in all its vital strength, and in all the purity of its faith, among the Irish people,—was sadly shorn of that sanctity which adorned it for the first three hundred years of Ireland's Christianity. Vices sprang up among the people. They were accustomed to war, war, war, night and day, for three centuries. Where is the people on the face of the earth that would not be utterly demoralized by fifty years of war, not to speak at all of three hundred? The wars of the Roses in England did not last more than thirty years; but the people were so demoralized by their effects that,—almost without a single struggle,—they changed their religion at the dictate of the blood-thirsty and licentious tyrant, Henry VIII. But no sooner were the Danes gone, than the Irish people assembled their Bishops and Princes in Council. We find, almost the very year after the final expulsion of the Danes, a Council was held: and here gathered their bishops and priests and almost all the chieftains of the land, the heads of the leading septs or families: and they framed wise laws, endeavoring to repair all that Ireland lost in the Danish invasion; and strict laws of Christian morality were enforced. Again we find a Council assembled, with the Papal Legate Cardinal Paparo at its head, in the year 1164, five years before the Normans invaded us. Now, we find the same Cardinal Paparo, the very year before the Norman invasion, presiding at a Council of the Bishops of Ireland. We find the people making laws for their government, and preparing to observe them faithfully. We find the Irish Bishops and Archbishops supported by the swords and the power of the Chieftains. We find the Pope's Legate travelling fearlessly into Ireland, whenever his master sent him, without let or hindrance; and when he arrived he was received with all the devotion and chivalrous affection which the Irish have always evinced towards the representatives of their religion and their God. It is worth our while to see what was the result of all these Councils, what was the result of this great religious revival, which was taking place in Ireland during the few years that elapsed between the end of the Danish and the beginning of the Norman invasion. We find three great Irish Saints reigning together in the Church. We find St. Malachi, Primate of Armagh. We find him succeeded by St. Celsus; and he again by St. Gregorius, whose name is in the Martyrology of Rome. We find, in Dublin, St. Laurence O'Toole, of glorious memory. We find Felix and Christian, two Bishops reigning in Lismore, in Waterford. And we find every man of them filling not only Ireland, but enshrined by the whole Church of God for their learning and the brightness of their sanctity. We find, at the same time, Catholicus, in Down; Augustin O'Daly, in Waterford; Dionysius, Marianus, Johannes Scotus, Gregorius and others;—all Irish monks, famous for their learning, famous for their sanctity,—in the great Benedictine Monastery of Ratisbon. We find, moreover, just before the Normans arrived, in 1168, a great Council was held in Athboy. Thirteen thousand representatives of the nation,—thirteen thousand warriors on horseback, with their Chieftains,—attended that Council, that they might hear whatever the Church commanded, and obey it. What was the result of all this? I am not speaking from any prejudiced point of view. It has been said that if Mr. Froude gave the history of Ireland from an outside point of view, Father Burke would give it from an inside view. I am only quoting English authorities: and in this interval, I find Langfranc, Archbishop of Canterbury, writing to Brian, King of Munster, to congratulate him upon the religious spirit and peaceful disposition of his people. Furthermore, St. Anselm,—one of the greatest English saints, and Archbishop of Canterbury under William Rufus,—has written as follows to Murchertach O'Brien, King of Munster:—

"I give thanks to God for the many good things we hear of your Highness, and especially for the profound peace which the subjects of your realm enjoy. All good men who hear this give thanks to God, and pray that He may grant you length of days."

The man who wrote that, perhaps, was thinking of the awful corruption,—the impiety and darkness of the most terrible kind,—which covered the whole land of England under the reign of the ferocious "Red King," William Rufus. Yet, the Irish were irreligious, we are told by Mr. Froude!—and a good judge he must be of religion; for he says it is a well-known fact, that religion is a thing of which one man knows as much as another; and none of us know anything at all. He tells us that the Irish were without religion at that very time, when the Irish Church was forming itself into the ancient model of sanctity, which it was before the Danish invasion; when, until the time, two years before the Normans came, Ireland was at peace, and Roderic,

King of Connaught, was acknowledged "Ard-righ," by every Prince and every Chieftain in the land.

As to the charge that Ireland was without morality, I will answer it by one fact: A King in Ireland stole another man's wife. His name—accursed—was Dermot McMurrough, King of Leinster. Every Chieftain in Ireland,—every man in the land,—rose up and banished him from Irish soil, as unworthy to live in the land. If this was the immoral people,—if this was the bestial, animal, depraved race which Mr. Froude describes to us, on lying Norman authorities, may I ask you, could not Dermot turn round and say to the Chieftains: "Why do you make war upon me? have I not as good a right to be a blackguard as anybody else?"

Now comes Mr. Froude, and says that the Normans were sent to Ireland to teach the Irish the Ten Commandments. In the language of Shakspere, I say, "I thank thee, Jew, for teaching me that word." Of these Ten Commandments, the most important, in relation to human society, are: "Thou shalt not steal." "Thou shalt not kill." "Thou shalt not covet thy neighbor's wife." The Normans, according to Mr. Froude's own showing, had no right or title to one square inch of the soil of Ireland. They came to take what was not theirs, what they had no right or title to. They came, as robbers and thieves, to teach the Ten Commandments to the Irish people; amongst them the Commandment—"Thou shalt not steal."

Henry landed in Ireland in 1171. He was after murdering the holy Archbishop of Canterbury, St. Thomas á Becket. They scattered his brains at the foot of the altar, before the Blessed Sacrament, at the Vesper hour. His blood was upon the hands of this monster,—he who came to Ireland to teach the Irish—"Thou shalt not kill!" What was the action of this "reformer" when the adulterer was driven from the sacred soil of Erin, as one unworthy to profane it by his tread. He went over to Henry II., and got from him a letter permitting any of his subjects that chose to embark for Ireland, there to reinstate the adulterer and tyrant in his kingdom. They came, then, as proved, as helpers of an adulterer, to teach the Irish "Thou shalt not covet thy neighbor's wife!" Mr. Froude tells us they were right—that they were apostles of purity and honesty and clemency; and Mr. Froude "is an honorable man."

"Ah! but," he says, "my good Dominican friend, remember, that, if they came, they came because the Pope sent them." King Henry, in the year 1174, produced a letter which he said he got from Pope Adrian IV., permitting him to go to Ireland, and urging him, according to the terms of that letter, to do whatever he thought right and fit to promote the glory of God and the good of the people. The date that was on the letter was 1154, consequently it was twenty years old. During twenty years nobody had ever heard of that letter except Henry, who had it in his pocket, and an old man, called John of Salisbury, who went to Rome and got the letter in a hugger-mugger way, from the Pope. It has been examined by a better authority than mine—by one who has brought to bear upon it all the acumen of his great knowledge. It bears,—according to Reimer, the most acceptable authority amongst English historians,—the date of 1154. Pope Adrian was elected on the 3d of December, 1154. As soon as the news of his election had arrived in England, John of Salisbury was sent by King Henry to congratulate him, and get this letter. He was elected on the 3d of December. It must have been a month later before the news arrived in England. In those days no letter could come so far, at least, under a month. John of Salisbury set out; and it must have been another month before he arrived in Rome; consequently it must have been the beginning of March, 1155, when he arrived in Rome; yet the letter of the Pope is dated 1154! It was found inconvenient, this date of Reimer's; and by whatever authority he did it, it seems he changed the date afterwards to 1155.

"But," says Mr. Froude, "there is a copy of this letter in the archives at Rome. How do you get over that?" Well, the copy has no date at all. As Baronius, the historian, and the learned Dr. Mansuerius declare—a rescript or document that has no date,—the day it was executed, the seal and the year,—is invalid—just so much paper;—so that even if Adrian gave it, it was worth nothing. Again, learned authorities tell us that the existence of a document in the archives does not prove the authenticity of that document. It may be kept there as a mere record. It was said that Henry kept this letter a secret, because his mother, the Empress Matilda, did not wish him to act on it. But if he had the letter, when he came to Ireland, why did he not produce it? That was his only warrant for coming to Ireland. He came there and invaded the country, and never breathed a word about having that letter, to a human being. There is a lie on the face of it.

But Mr. Froude says that Alexander III., Adrian's successor, has mentioned that rescript or document in a letter. The answer I give on the authority of Dr. Lynch, the author of "Cambrensis Eversus," as well as the Abbé McGeoghegan, one of the greatest Irish scholars, and one of the best archæologists; and Dr. Moran, the learned bishop of Ossory—that Alexander's letter was a forgery, as well as that of Adrian IV. There are many learned men who admit the genuineness of both Adrian's and Alexander's rescripts; but there are an equally large number who deny it; and I prefer to believe with them that it was a forgery.

Alexander's letter bore the date of 1172. Let us see is it likely that Pope would give a letter to Henry, whom he knew well, asking him to take care of the Church and set everything in order? Remember, Adrian did not know him, but Alexander knew him well. Henry, in 1159, supported the anti-Pope, Octavianus, against Alexander. Henry, in 1166, supported the anti-Pope, Guido, against Alexander. According to Mathew of Westminster, Henry obliged every man in England,—from the boy of twelve years up to the old man,—to renounce their allegiance to the true Pope, and go over to an anti-Pope. Was it likely, then, the Pope would give him a letter to settle ecclesiastical matters in Ireland? Alexander himself wrote to Henry, and said to him,—instead of referring to a document giving him permission to settle Church matters in Ireland;—

" Instead of remedying the disorders caused by your predecessors, you have oppressed the Church, and you have endeavored to destroy the canons of apostolic men."

Is this the man that Alexander would send to Ireland to settle affairs, and make the Irish good children of the Pope?

According to Mr. Froude, the Irish never loved the Pope till the Normans taught them. What is the fact? Until the accursed Normans came to Ireland, the Papal Legate always came and went when and wherever he would, at his own will. No Irish king obstructed him; no Irishman's hand was ever raised against a Bishop, much less against the Papal Legate. But the very first Legate that came to Ireland, after the Norman Invasion, in passing through England, Henry took him by the throat, and imposed upon him an oath that, when he went to Ireland, he would not do anything that would be against the interest of the King. It was an unheard-of thing that a Bishop, Archbishop, or Cardinal should be persecuted, until the Anglo-Normans brought with them their accursed feudal system, and concentration of power in the hands of the king, an account of which I shall come to presently. Bitterly did Laurence O'Toole feel it. This great heroic, patriotic saint of Ireland, when he went to England, the very moment he arrived he was made a prisoner, as a man to be feared; for the King had left an order, that whenever he was found in England, the Saint should never be allowed to set his foot in Ireland again. And this is the man that was sent over as the apostle of morality to Ireland! the man that is accused of violating the betrothed wife of his own son, Richard I.!—the man whose crimes cannot bear repetition!—who was believed by Europe to be possessed by a devil! and of whom it was written that when he got into a fit of anger, he used to tear off his clothes, and sit down naked on the ground, and chew straw like a beast! Is it likely that the Pope, who knew him so well, and suffered so much from him, sent him to Ireland;—the murderer of Bishops, the robber of churches, and the destroyer of ecclesiastical and every other form of liberty that came before him? No, no! Never will I believe that the Pope of Rome was so short-sighted, so blind, so unjust as, by the stroke of his pen, to abolish and destroy the liberties of the most faithful people that ever bowed down in allegiance to him.

But let us suppose even that Pope Adrian gave the Bull. I hold still that it was of no account, for it was obtained by false pretences. It was obtained by falsely representing to the Pope that the Irish were in a state of ignorance and immorality, which did not exist. Secondly, this rescript from the Pope, if it was obtained, was obtained under a lie, and was null and void, being obtained under false pretences. But more than this; the Pope gave Henry, in that rescript, only power to go to Ireland and fix everything; to do everything for the glory of God and the good of the people. Unless he did this (and he never did it and never intended to do it,) the rescript was null and void. But suppose that rescript had actually been given; what power did it give Henry? Did it make him master of Ireland? Did it give him power over the land of Ireland? All that that Bull of the Pope says is that he should do what is necessary for the glory of God and the good of the people. By calling on the Irish Chieftains to accept Henry,—at most he established only what is called a "*haute suzerainty*" of Ireland. Now, you must know that, in the early Middle Ages, there were two kinds of sovereignty; there was the sovereign, the acknowledged head of the people. They were his, and he governed them, like the Kings and Emperors of to-day in Europe. But, besides this, there was the sovereign, who only claimed the *title* of King, who only claimed the homage of the Chieftains of the land, but who left them in perfect liberty, and recognized the perfect independence of the land. He received the tribute of their homage and nothing more. This was all the fealty that the Pope ever permitted Henry to claim in Ireland, if he permitted him to claim so much. The proof lies here, that, when Henry came over to Ireland, he never said to the Irish that they should give up their independence. Not at all. On the contrary, he left Roderic O'Conor King of Connaught, and dealt with him as a king with his fellow-king. He acknowledged his royalty and nationality; and he only demanded of him the allegiance and homage of a feudal prince to a feudal king, leaving him as a ruler perfectly independent.

Again, let us suppose that Henry intended to conquer Ireland, and bring it into slavery. Did he succeed? Nothing of the kind. When he came to Ireland, the kings and princes of the Irish people said to him:—"We are willing to acknowledge your high sovereignty over us, as Lord of Ireland. We are the owners of the land. You are the

Lord of Ireland; and there is an end of it." The King was acknowledged by the people by the simple title of "Lord of Ireland;" nothing more. If he intended anything more— if he intended to invade and conquer the country, he never effected his purpose. For the Normans, for centuries, held only that part of Ireland which before was held by the Danes. The Irish, who are naturally straightforward, and always generous, in the hour of their triumph permitted the Danes to remain in Dublin, Wexford, Wicklow, and Waterford. Consequently, the Danes held the whole of the eastern seaboard towns. From the Hill of Howth round to Waterford harbor was in their possession. The Normans who came over were regarded by the Irish as cousins to the Danes; and they only took the Danish territory;—nothing more. They took precisely all that the Danes had before; all that the Irish had given to the Danes, who were understood to be perfectly independent. At most, it seems to us that the Irish were willing to share the land with them, willing to receive them with a certain hospitality, and to divide the country with them.

Now, Mr. Froude's second justification of the Norman invasion is that Ireland was a prey to the Danes, who invaded the island; and that the Irish were rendered ferocious by these continual contests; leaving the impression that the Danish wars in Ireland were only a succession of ferocious individual combats, between tribe and tribe, between man and man; when the fact is, the Danish wars were magnificent national trials of strength, between two of the bravest races that ever met each other, foot to foot and hand to hand on the battlefield. The Danes were unconquerable. They conquered the Saxons in England. The Frenchman in France was unable to stand his ground against them. Still, for three hundred years, the Celt of Ireland disputed every inch of the island with them, filled every valley in the land with their dead bodies; and at last drove them back into the North Sea, and freed his native land from their dominion forever. Yet this magnificent national contest is represented by this historian as a mere ferocious onslaught, daily renewed, between man and man, in Ireland!

The Norman arrived: and we have seen how he was received. The Butlers and Fitzgeralds went down into Kildare; the De Burgs, or Burkes, and the De Berminghams went down into the province of Connaught. The people offered them very little opposition. They gave them a portion of their lands, and welcomed them amongst them, and began to love them as if they were their own flesh and blood. Now the Norman, in England, hated and despised the Saxons. So thoroughly did he despise them, that his name for the Saxon was "villein" or "churl." He did not allow the Saxons to sit at the same table with him; and he would not intermarry with the Saxons for long years. The proud, steel-clad Normans, ferocious in passion, bold as lions, formed, by their Crusades and Saracenic wars, to be the bravest men then living on the face of the earth, never allowed the Saxons to interfere in any of their disputes. Gerald Barry, when he was speaking of the Saxons, said: "I am a Welshman, and I am proud to be a Welshman; but the Saxons are the vilest and basest race on the face of the earth." I am only giving his own words; I do not say that I share his sentiments. "They fought one battle," he goes on to say: "they allowed the Normans to overcome them, and consented to be slaves forevermore to the Normans." And he wrote a book, in which he says, that they are by no means to be compared to the Celtic race; "not to be compared in bravery or in intelligence to the magnanimous race of the Celts." Now, the Normans went down into Ireland, among the Irish people. When they went outside the English portion of the country, or the "Pale," and got amongst the Irish people, what is the first thing that we see? The very first thing, I answer, is that the Normans began to forget their Norman-French and their English, and learned to talk the Irish. They took Irish wives and were glad to get them, they adopted Irish names and Irish customs; until we find, two hundred years after the Norman invasion, these proud descendants of William FitzAdelm, Earl of Clanricarde, changing their names from De Burg, or Burke, to McWilliam, or sons of William; and they called themselves in Irish, "McWilliam Oughter," and "McWilliam Eighter," or the Upper and Lower McWilliams. In the days of Lionel, Duke of Clarence, they called themselves by that name, and adopted the Celtic laws and Celtic customs.

Concerning the four hundred sad years that followed the Norman invasion, down to the accession of Henry VIII., Mr. Froude has nothing to say, except that Ireland was in a constant state of anarchy and confusion; and it is too true. It is perfectly true. Chieftain warred against chieftain. It was comparative peace before the invasion; but when the Normans came in, they divided the Irish by craft and cunning. The ancient historian Strabo, speaking of the Gael, says: "The Gauls always march openly to their end, and they are therefore easily circumvented." So when the Normans came, and the Saxons, they sowed dissensions among the Irish people. They stirred them up against each other, and the bold, hot blood of the Celt was always ready to engage in contest and in war. What was the secret of that incessant and desolating war? There is no history more painful to read than the history of the Irish people, from the day that the Normans landed, until the day when the great issue of Protestantism was put before the nation, and when Ireland, for the first time, united as one man.

. . . . . . My friends, the true secret of that history is the constant effort of the English to force upon Ireland the feudal system, and consequently to rob the Irish of every inch of their land and to exterminate them. I lay this down as the one secret, the one thread by which you may unravel the tangled skein of our history for the four hundred years that followed the Norman invasion. The Normans and Saxons came with the express purpose and design of taking every foot of land in Ireland and exterminating the Celtic race. It is an awful thing to think of; but we have the evidence of history for the fact. First of all, Henry II., whilst he made his treaties with the Irish kings, secretly divided the whole of Ireland into ten portions, and allotted each of these ten portions to one of his Norman knights. In a word, he robbed the Irish people and the Irish chieftains of every single foot of land in the Irish territory, and gave it to the Normans. It is true they were not able to take possession. It was as if a master robber were to divide the booty before it is taken. It was far easier to assign property not yet stolen than to put his fellow-thieves in possession of it. There were Irish hands and Irish battle-blades in the way for many a long year; nor has it been accomplished to this day.

In order to root out the Celtic race, and to destroy us, mark the measures of legislation which followed. First of all, my friends, whenever an Englishman was put in possession of an acre of land, he got the right to trespass upon his Irish neighbors', and to take their land as far as he could; and they had no action in a court of law to recover their land. If an Irishman brought an action at law against an Englishman for taking half of his field, or for trespassing upon his land, according to the law, from the beginning, that Irishman was put out of court; there was no action; the Englishman was perfectly justified in what he did. Worse than this; they made laws declaring that the killing of an Irishman was no felony. Sir John Davis, Attorney-

General, in the time of James I., tells us how, upon a certain occasion, at Waterford, in the 29th year of Edward I., of England, a certain Edward Butler brought an action against Robert de Almey to recover certain goods that Robert had stolen from him. The case was brought into court. Robert acknowledged that he had stolen the goods; that he was a thief. The defence he put in was that Edward, the man he had plundered, was an Irishman. The case was tried. Now, my friends, just think of it! The issue that was put before the jury was, whether Edward, the plaintiff, was an Irishman or an Englishman. The jury found that Edward was an Englishman. That was enough; Robert, the thief, was obliged to give back the goods. But if the jury found that Edward was an Irishman he might keep the goods;—there was no action against him.

We find upon the same authority,—Sir John Davis,—a description of a certain jail-delivery at Waterford, where a man named Robert Walsh had killed the son of Ivor McGilmore. He was arraigned and tried for manslaughter; and, without the slightest difficulty, acknowledged it. "Yes," he said, "I did kill him; but you have no right to try me for it: for he was an Irishman!" Instantly he was let out of the dock, on condition—as the Irishman, at the time, was in the service of an English master—that he should pay whatever the master could claim for the loss of his services; whatever was their value: but for the murder, he was let go scot-free. "Not only," says Sir John Davis, "were the Irish considered aliens, but they were considered enemies: insomuch that though an Englishman might settle upon an Irishman's land, there was no redress; but if an Irishman wished to buy an acre of land from an Englishman, he could not do it." So they kept the land they had; and they were always gaining by plunder. They could steal; while we could not even buy.

NORMAN INVASION AND MISRULE. 37

If any man made a will, and left an acre of land to an Irishman, the moment it was proved that he was an Irish man, the land was forfeited to the Crown of England—even if it was only left in trust to him: of which we have two very striking examples. We read that, in the first year of Henry VI., a certain Edward Butler, of Clonboyne, in the county of Meath, left some lands in trust for charitable purposes; and he left them to his two chaplains, Conor O'Mulrooney and John McCann. It was proved that the two priests were Irishmen; and though the land was left to them in trust for charitable purposes it was forfeited to the Crown, because the two men were Irishmen. Later, a certain Mrs. Catherine Dowdall, a pious woman, made a will when she was dying, leaving some land, near Swords, in the county of Dublin, to a priest named John O'Bellane: and the land was forfeited to the Crown because, as it was set forth, "the said John O'Bellane being one of the King's Irish enemies."

In the year 1367, Lionel, Duke of Clarence, third son of Edward III., came to Ireland and held a Parliament in Kilkenny, which passed certain laws. Some of these laws were as follows: "If any man speak the Irish language, or be found keeping company with the Irish, or adopting Irish customs, his lands shall be taken from him and forfeited to the Crown of England." If an Englishman married an Irish woman, what do you think was the penalty? He was sentenced to be half hanged; to have his heart cut out before he was dead; then to have his head struck off; and every rood of his land passed to the Crown of England. "Thus," says Sir John Davis, the great English authority, "it is evident that the constant design of English legislation in Ireland was to possess the Irish land, and to extirpate and exterminate the Irish people."

Now, citizens of America, Mr. Froude came here to appeal

to you for your verdict ; and he asks you to say : " Was not England justified in her treatment of Ireland, because the Irish people would not submit ? " Now, citizens of America, I ask you, would not the Irish people be the vilest dogs on the face of the earth if they submitted to such treatment as this ? Would they be worthy of the name of men, if they submitted to be robbed, plundered, and degraded ? It is true that, in all this legislation, we see the same spirit of contempt of which I spoke in the beginning of my lecture. But remember who it was that these Saxon churls were thus despising; and ask yourselves what race was it they treated with so much contumely and so much contempt, and attempted in every way to degrade, whilst they were ruining and robbing them ? What race were they ? Gerald Barry, speaking of the Irish race, says the Irish came from the grandest race that he knew of on this side of the world, " and there are no better people under the sun." By the word " better," he meant more valiant or more intellectual. Those who came over from England, by even the English who went before them, were called Saxon hogs, or churls, while the Irish called them *bodach Sassenagh*. These were the men who showed, in the very system by which they were governed, that they could not understand the nature of a people who refused to be slaves. They were slaves themselves. Consider the history of the feudal system under which they lived. According to the feudal system of government, the King of England was lord of every inch of land in England. Every foot of land in England was the king's ; and the nobles, who had the land, held it from the king—but they held it under feudal conditions, the most degrading that can be imagined. For instance : if a man died and left his heir, a son or daughter, under age, the heir or heiress, together with the estate, went into the hands of the king. He might perhaps leave a widow, with ten children. She would have to support all the children herself, whatever way she could, out of her dower; but the estate and the eldest son or the eldest daughter went into the hands of the king. Then during the minority of the heir, the king could spend the revenues or rent of the estate, without the knowledge of any one, or could sell the castle and the estate, and no one could demand an account of him; and when the son or daughter came of age, he then sold them in marriage to the highest bidder. We have Godfrey de Mandeville buying for twenty thousand marks, from King John, the hand of Isabella, Countess of Gloster. We have Isabella de Lingera, another heiress, offering a hundred marks to King John—for what do you think?—for liberty to marry whoever she liked, and not to be obliged to marry the man he would give her to. . . . . If a widow lost her husband, the moment the breath was out of him, the lady and the estate passed to the king; and he might squander the estate, or do whatever he liked with it; and then he could sell the widow. We have a curious example of this. We have Alice, Countess of Warwick, paying King John one thousand pounds sterling, in gold, for leave to remain a widow as long as she liked. This was the slavery called the feudal system, of which Mr. Froude is so proud, and of which he says: "It lay at the root of all that is noble and good in Europe." The Irish could not stand it, —small blame to them! But when the Irish people found that they were to be hunted down like wolves,—found their lands were to be taken from them, and that there was no redress,—over and over again the Irish people sent petitions to the King of England, to give them the benefit of English law, and they would be amenable to it. But they were denied, and told that they should remain as they were: that is to say, England was determined to exterminate them, and get every foot of Irish soil. This is the one leading idea or principle which animated England in her treatment of Ireland throughout those four hundred years, and it is the only clue you can find to that turmoil and misery, and constant fighting which was going on in Ireland during that period.

Sir James Cusack, an English commissioner sent over by Henry VIII., wrote to his Majesty these quaint words: "The Irish be of opinion amongst themselves that the English wish to get all their lands, and to root them out completely." He just struck the nail on the head. Mr. Froude himself acknowledges that the land question lay at the root of the whole business. Nay, more, the feudal system would have handed over every inch of land in Ireland to the Norman king and his Norman nobles; and the O'Briens, the O'Neills, the O'Donnells, and the O'Conors, were of more ancient and better blood than that of William, the bastard Norman. . . . . . . The Saxon might submit to feudal law, and be crushed into a slave, a clod of the earth; the Celt never would. England's great mistake—I believe, in my soul, that the great mistake, of all others the greatest,—lay in this, that the English people never realized the fact that, in dealing with the Irish, they had to deal with the proudest race on the face of the earth.

During all these years the Norman nobles, the Ormondes, the Desmonds, the Geraldines, the De Burghs, were at the head and front of every rebellion. The English complained of them, and said they were worse than the Irish rebels; that they were constantly stirring up disorders. Do you know the reason why? Because they, as Normans, were under the feudal laws, and therefore the king's sheriffs could come down on them, at every turn, with fines and forfeitures of the land held from the king. So, by keeping the country in disorder, they were always able to defy the sheriffs; and they preferred the Irish freedom to the English feudalism: therefore, they fomented and kept up these discords. It was the boast of my kinsmen of Clanricarde that, with the blessing of God, they would never allow a king's writ to run in Connaught. Dealing with this period of our history, Mr. Froude says that the Irish Chieftains, and their septs or tribes, were doing this or that—the Geraldines, the Desmonds, and the Ormondes. I say, slowly, Mr. Froude; the Geraldines and the Ormondes were not Irish Chieftains; so do not father their acts upon the Irish; the Irish Chieftains have enough to answer for, during these four hundred years. I protest to you that, in this most melancholy period of our sad history, I have found but two cases, two instances, that cheer me; and both were the action of Irish Chieftains. In one we find that Turlough O'Conor put away his wife; she was one of the O'Briens. Theobald Burke, one of the Earls of Clanricarde, lived in open adultery with the woman. With the spirit of their heroic ancestors, the Irish Chieftains of Connaught came together, deposed him, and drove him out of the place. Later on, we find another Chieftain, Brian McMahon, who induced Sorley McDonnell, chief of the Hebrides, or Western Islands, to put away his lawful wife, and marry a daughter of his own. The following year they fell out; and McMahon drowned his own son-in-law. The chiefs, O'Donnell and O'Neill, came together with their forces, and deposed McMahon, in the cause of virtue, honor, and womanhood. I have looked in vain through these four hundred years for one single trait of generosity or of the assertion of virtue among the Anglo-Norman chiefs; and the dark picture is only relieved by these two gleams of Irish patriotism and Irish zeal in the cause of purity and of outraged honor.

Now, Mr. Froude opened another question in his first lecture. He said that, during all this time, while the English monarchs were engaged in trying to subjugate Scotland, and trying to subdue their French Provinces, the Irish were rapidly gaining ground, hemming the English in, and crippling the Pale, year by year. The English power in Ireland was frequently almost annihilated; and the only thing that saved it was the love of the Irish for their own independent way of fighting, which, though favorable to freedom, was hostile to national unity. He says, speaking of that time, "Would it not have been better to have allowed the Irish Chieftains to govern their own people? Freedom to whom?—freedom to the bad, to the violent! It is no freedom!" I deny that the Irish Chieftains, with all their faults, were, as a class, bad men or violent men. I deny that they were engaged, as Mr. Froude says, in cutting their peoples' throats; that they were a people who would never be satisfied. Mr. Froude tells us emphatically and significantly, that "the Irish people were satisfied with their Chieftains;" but the people are not satisfied if their throats are being cut. The Irish Chieftains were the bane of Ireland by their divisions; the Irish Chieftains were the ruin of their country by their want of union, and want of generous acquiescence in the rule of some great and noble head that would save them by uniting them. The Irish Chieftains, even in the days of the heroic Edward Bruce, did not rally around him as they ought. In their divisions is the secret of Ireland's slavery and ruin through those years. But with all that, history attests that they were still magnanimous enough to be the fathers of their people, and to be the natural leaders, as God intended them to be, of their septs, families, and namesakes. And they struck whatever blows they did strike, in what they imagined to be the cause of right, justice, and liberty; and the only blow that came in the cause of outraged purity, came from an Irish hand, in those dark and terrible years.

I will endeavor to follow this gentleman in his subsequent lectures. Now a darker cloud than that of mere invasion is lowering over the horizon of Ireland; now comes the demon of religious discord—waving the sword of religious persecution over the distracted and exhausted land. And we shall see whether this historian has entered into the spirit of the great contest that followed, and that, in our day, has ended in a glorious victory for Ireland's Church; which will be followed, as assuredly, by a still more glorious victory for Ireland's Nationality.

SECOND LECTURE.

(Delivered at the Academy of Music, New York, Nov. 14, 1872.)

THE TUDORS IN IRELAND.

LADIES AND GENTLEMEN: We now come to consider the second lecture of the eminent English historian who has come amongst us. It covers one of the most interesting and terrible passages in our history. It takes in three reigns,—the reign of Henry VIII., the reign of Elizabeth, and the reign of James I.: I scarcely consider the reigns of Edward VI. and of Philip and Mary worth counting. The learned gentleman began his second lecture with a rather startling paradox. He asserted that Henry VIII. was a hater of disorder. Now, my friends, every man in this world has a hero. Whether consciously or unconsciously, every man selects out of history some character or other which he admires: until at length, from constantly thinking of the virtues and excellences of his hero, he comes almost to worship him. Before us all lie the grand historic names that are written upon the world's annals: and every man is free to select the character that he likes best, and to choose his hero. Using this privilege, Mr. Froude has made the most singular selection of his hero that ever you or I heard of: his hero is Henry VIII. It speaks volumes for the integrity of Mr. Froude's own mind; it is a strong argument that he possesses a charity the most sublime, when he has been enabled to discover virtues in the historical character of one of the greatest monsters that over cursed the earth. He has, however, succeeded in this, which, to us, appears an impossibility. And he has discovered, amongst many other shining virtues in the character of the English Nero, a great love for order, and a great hatred of disorder. Well, we must stop at the very first sentence of the learned gentleman, and try to analyze it, and see how much there is of truth in this word of the historian, and how much there is which is only an honorable, and, to him, a truthful figment of his imagination.

All order in the State is based upon three grand principles, my friends, namely,—the supremacy of the law; the respect for, and the liberty of, conscience; and a tender regard for that which lies at the fountain-head of all human society, namely,—the sanctity of the marriage-tie. The first element of order in every State is the supremacy of the law. In this supremacy lies the very quintessence of human freedom, and of all order. The law is supposed to be (according to the definition of Aquinas), the judgment pronounced by profound reason and intellect, thinking and legislating for the public good. The law, therefore, is the expression of reason;— reason backed by authority; reason influenced by the noble motive of the public good. This being the nature of law, the very first thing that we demand for this law is that every man bow down to it and obey it. No man in the community can claim exemption from obedience to the law; least of all, the man who is at the head of the community; because he is supposed to represent, before the nation, that principle of obedience, without which all national order and happiness perish among the people. Was Henry VIII. an upholder of law? Was he obedient to the law? I deny it: and I have the evidence of all history to back me up in the denial. I brand Henry VIII. as one of the greatest enemies of freedom and of law that ever lived in this world; consequently one of the greatest promoters of disorder. I will only give you one example; out of ten thousand, I have only selected one. When Henry broke with the Pope, he called upon his subjects to acknowledge him—bless the mark!—as the spiritual head of the Church. There were three Abbots of three charter-houses in London,—namely, the Abbot of London proper, the Abbot of Axiolam, and the Abbot of Bellival. These three men refused to acknowledge Henry as the supreme spiritual head of the Church. He had them arrested, had them tried, and had a jury of twelve citizens of London to sit upon them. Now, the first principle of English law, the grand palladium of English legislation and freedom, is the perfect liberty of the jury. The jury, in any trial, must be perfectly free: not only free from all coercion from without, but free even from any prejudice. They must be free from any prejudging of the case; must be perfectly impartial, and perfectly free to record their verdict. These twelve men refused to convict the three Abbots of high treason; and they grounded their refusal upon this: "Never," they said, "has it been heard in England that it was high treason to deny the spiritual supremacy of the king. It is not law; and, therefore, we cannot find these men guilty of high treason." What did Henry do? He sent word to the jury that if they did not find the three Abbots guilty, he would visit them with the same penalties that he had prepared for their prisoners! He sent word to the jury that they should find them guilty! I brand him, therefore, as having torn in pieces the charter of English liberty, Magna Charta, and as having trampled upon the first grand element of English law and jurisprudence, namely, the liberty of the jury. Citizens of America! would you, any one of you, like to be tried by a jury, if you knew that the President of the United States had informed that jury that they were bound to find you guilty or else he would put them to death? Where would there be liberty,—where would there be law,—if such a transaction were permitted? And this was the action of Mr. Froude's great admirer of order—his hero, Henry VIII.

The second grand element of order is respect for conscience. The conscience of a man, and consequently of a nation, is supposed to be the great guide in all the relations in which the people or the individual stand to God. The conscience of man is so free that the Almighty God Himself respects it; and it is a theological axiom that if a man does a wrong act, thinking he is doing right, the wrong will not be attributed to him by Almighty God. Was this man a respecter of conscience? Again, out of ten thousand acts of his, I will select one. He ordered the people of England to change their religion; ordered them to give up that grand system of dogmatic teaching which is in the Catholic Church, where every man knows what to believe and what to do. And what religion did he offer them instead? He did not offer them Protestantism, for Henry VIII. never was a Protestant; and, to the last day of his life, if he could only have laid his hands on Martin Luther, he would have made a toast of him. He heard Mass up to the day of his death; and after his death there was a solemn High Mass over his inflated corpse,—a solemn High Mass, that the Lord might have mercy on his soul. Ah! my friends, some other poor soul, I suppose, got the benefit of that Mass. What religion did he offer the people of England? He simply came before them and said : " Let every man in the land agree with me; whatever I say, that is religion." More than this, his Parliament, a slavish Parliament,—every man afraid of his life, —passed a law making it high treason not only to disagree with the King in anything that he believed, but making it high treason for any man to dispute anything that the King should ever believe in the future time. He was not only the enemy of conscience; he was the annihilator of conscience. He would allow no man to have a conscience. "I am your conscience," he said to the nation; "I am your infallible guide in all things that you are to believe, and in all things that you are to do; and if any man sets up his own conscience against me, that man is guilty of high treason, and I will stain my hands in his heart's blood." This is the great lover of order!

The third great element of order is that upon which all society is based. The great key-stone of the arch of society is the sanctity of the marriage tie. Whatever else is interfered with, that must not be touched; for Christ, our Lord, has said, "Those that God has joined together let no man put asunder." A valid marriage can only be dissolved by the angel of death. No power in heaven or on earth—much less in hell—can dissolve the validity of a marriage. Henry VIII. had so little respect for the sanctity of the marriage tie that he brutally put away from him a woman to whom he was lawfully married, and took in her stead (while she was yet living,) a woman who was supposed to be his own daughter. He married six wives. Two of them he repudiated—divorced; two of them he beheaded; one of them died in childbirth;—and the sixth and last one—Mistress Catherine Parr—had her name down in Henry's book, at the time of his death, in the list of his victims; and she would have had her head cut off, if the monster had lived for a few days longer. This is all matter of history. And now, I ask the American public, is it fair for Mr. Froude, or any other living man, to present himself before an American audience,—an audience of enlightened and cultivated people, that have read history as well as the English historian, and ask them to swallow the absurd paradox that Henry VIII. was an admirer of order and a hater of disorder.

But Mr. Froude says: "Now, this is not fair. I said in my lecture that I would have nothing to do with Henry's matrimonial transactions." Ah! Mr. Froude, you were wise. "But at least," he says, "in his relations to Ireland, I claim that he was a hater of disorder;" and the proof he gives is the following: First of all he says that one of the curses of Ireland was absenteeism,—the absentee landlords; and he is right. Now, Henry, he says, put an end to that business in the simplest way imaginable; he took the estates away from the absentees and gave them to other people. My friends, it sounds well, very plausible—this saying of the English historian. Let us analyze it a little. During the "Wars of the Roses," between the Houses of York and Lancaster, which preceded the Reformation in England, many of the English families and Anglo-Norman families that were settled in Ireland, went over to England and joined in the conflict. It was an English question and an English war; and the consequence was that numbers of the English settlers retired from Ireland and left their estates, —abandoned them entirely. Others again,—from disgust, or because they had large English properties,—preferred to live in their own country, and retired from Ireland to live in England. So that, when Henry VIII. came to the throne of England, the English "Pale," as it was called, comprised only about one-half of the counties of Louth, Westmeath, Dublin, Wicklow, and Wexford,—nothing more; only one-half of each of these counties. Henry, according to Mr. Froude, performed a great act of justice, when he took from these absentees their estates, and gave them—to whom? To other Englishmen, his own favorites and friends. Now, the historical fact is this, that, as soon as the English retired, and abandoned their estates, the Irish people came in and repossessed themselves of their own property. Mark, my friends, that even if the Irish people had no title to that property, the very fact of the English having abandoned it gave them a sufficient title; because, "*bona derelicta sunt præmia capientis*,"—that is to say, things that are abandoned belong to the man that first gets hold of them. But much more just was the title of the Irish people to that land, because it was their own, because they were unjustly dispossessed of it by the very men who abandoned it now. And therefore they came in with a twofold title, namely, "the land is ours because there is nobody to claim it, the owner having retired; and even if there were, the land is ours because it was always ours, and we never lost our right to it." When, therefore, Henry VIII., the "lover of order," dispossessed the absentees of their estates, and sent over other Englishmen, and handed over these estates to men who would live in Ireland, and on the land, Mr. Froude claims great credit for him, and says, that in so doing he acted well for the Irish people. But the doing of this involved the driving of the Irish people a second time out of their own property. That was the whole secret of Henry's wonderful beneficence to Ireland, in giving us "resident landlords!" Just picture it to yourselves, in this way, my friends. There are a great many here who are owners of property,—I suppose the most of you. Just suppose the Government of the United States, or the President, turning you out of your property, taking your houses and lots and lands from you, and giving them to some friend of his own; and then saying to you: "Now, my friend, you must remember, I am a lover of order; I am giving you 'a resident landlord!'"

Henry, as soon as he ascended the throne, sent over the Earl of Surrey, in the year 1520. Surrey was a brave soldier, a stern, rigorous man; and Henry thought that, by sending him over, and backing him with a grand army, he would be able to repress the disordered elements in the Irish nation. That disorder reigned in Ireland, I am the first to admit; but in tracing that disorder to its cause, I claim that the cause was not in any inherent love for disorder in the Irish character, though they were always very fond of a fight; I admit that attribute;—but I hold and claim that the great cause of all the disorder and turmoil of Ireland was, first, the strange and inhuman legislation of England for four hundred years previously; and secondly, the presence of the Anglo-Norman lords in Ireland, who fostered and kept up disturbances in the country in order that they might have an excuse for not paying their feudal dues and duties to the king.

Surrey came over and tried the strong hand for a time; but he found,—brave as he was, and accomplished General as he was,—he found that the Irish were a little too many for him; and he sent word to Henry: "This people can only be subdued by conquering them utterly,—by going in amongst them with fire and sword. And this you will not be able to do because the country is too large, and so geographically difficult, that it is impossible for an army to penetrate into its fastnesses, to subjugate the whole population." Then it was that Henry took up the policy of conciliation—when he could not help it. Mr. Froude makes it a great virtue in this monarch that he endeavored to conciliate the Irish. He did it because he could not help it.

And now, my friends, there is one passage in the correspondence between Surrey and Henry the Eighth that speaks volumes; and it is this: When the Earl of Surrey arrived in Ireland he found himself in the midst of war and confusion. But the people who were really at the source of all that confusion he declares to be not so much the Irish, or their Chieftains, as the Anglo-Norman and English lords in Ireland. Here is the passage in question. There were two Chieftains of the McCarthys,—Conor Og McCarthy and McCarthy Ruadh, or the Red McCarthy. Surrey wrote of these two men, to Henry VIII., and he says:—"These are two wise men, and more conformable to order than some of the Englishmen here." Thus out of the lips of one of Ireland's bitterest enemies, I take the answer to Mr. Froude's repeated assertion that we Irish are so disorderly, and such lovers of turmoil and confusion, that the only way to reduce us to order is to sweep us away altogether.

The next feature of Surrey's policy, when he found he could not conquer Ireland with the sword, was to set Chieftain against Chieftain. And so he writes to Henry:—"I am endeavoring," he says, "to perpetuate the animosity between O'Donnell and O'Neill in Ulster." Here are his words:—"It would be dangerful to have them both agree and join together." It would be *dangerous!* Well might Mr. Froude say, that, in the day in which we, Irish, shall be united, we shall be invincible, and no power on earth shall keep us slaves. " It would be. dangerful to have them both join together; and the longer they continue at war, the better it will be for your Grace's subjects here." Now, mark the spirit of that letter, and you mark the whole genius of England's treatment of Ireland. He was not speaking of the Irish as subjects of the King of England. He has not the slightest consideration for the unfortunate Irish, whom he was pitting against each other. " Let them bleed," he says; "the longer they continue at war,—the greater number of them that are swept away,—the better it will be for your Grace's subjects here." The spirit of the legislation, the spirit of the law, was intended only to protect the English settler, and to exterminate the Irishman. This Sir John Davies himself, Attorney-General of King James I., declares lay at the root of all England's legislation for Ireland for four hundred years, and was the cause of all the misery and all the evils of Ireland.

Surrey retired after two years; and then, according to Mr. Froude, Henry tried " Home Rule " in Ireland. Here again the learned historian tries to make a point for his hero; and Irishmen, he says, admire the memory of this man. "He tried 'Home Rule' with you. He found that you were not able to govern yourselves; and he was obliged to take the whip and drive you." Let us see what kind of "Home Rule" did Henry try. One would imagine that "Home Rule," in Ireland, meant that Irishmen should manage their own affairs, should have the making of their own laws; it either means this, or it means nothing. It is "a delusion, a mockery, and a snare," unless it means that the Irish people have a right to assemble in their own Parliament, to govern themselves by legislating for themselves, and by making their own laws. Did the "Home Rule" of Henry VIII. mean this? Not a bit of it. All he did was to make the Earl of Kildare Lord Lieutenant, or Lord Deputy,— to place an Irishman—that is to say an Anglo-Norman Irishman—at the head of the State, for a few years. And in this consisted the whole scheme of the "Home Rule" attributed by Mr. Froude to Henry VIII. He did not call upon the Irish nation and say to them, "Return members to Parliament, and I will allow you to make your own laws." He did not call upon the Irish Chieftains, the natural representatives of the nation,—the men in whose veins flowed the blood of Ireland's Chieftaincy, for thousands of years; he did not call upon the O'Briens, the O'Neills, the McCarthys, and the O'Conors, and say to them, "Go, and assemble; make your own laws; and, if they are just laws, I will set my seal upon them; and let you govern Ireland through your own legislation." No; but he called on a clique of Anglo-Norman lords,—the most unruly, the most warlike, the most restless pack that ever you or I read or heard of in all history,—and he said to these men: "Take and govern the country; I vest the government in your hands."

No sooner did Henry leave these men to govern Ireland,

than they began to make war upon the Irish. Kildare was made Lord Deputy in 1522; and the very first thing those Anglo-Norman lords did was to assemble an army and lay waste all the territory of the Irish Chieftains around them. They killed the people, burned the villages, and destroyed everything. Then, after a time, they fell out among themselves,—these Norman lords. The great family of the Butlers, the Earls of Ormonde, became jealous of Kildare, who was a Fitzgerald, and began to accuse him to the King of treasonable actions. In 1524, the Earl of Kildare entered into an undoubtedly treasonable correspondence with Francis I., King of France, and Charles V., Emperor of Germany. He was called to England for the third time to answer for his conduct; and, in 1534, Henry put him in prison. Then his son, Lord Thomas Fitzgerald,—called "Silken Thomas," —a brave, hot-headed, rash young Norman noble,—revolted, because his father was a prisoner in England, and it was told him that the old Earl was about to be put to death. Henry declared war against him, and he declared war against the King of England. The consequence of this war was that the whole province of Munster and a great part of Leinster were ravaged;—the people were destroyed; towns and villages were burned; until, at length, there was not as much left in nearly one-half of Ireland as would feed man or beast. So that this "Home Rule." of Henry resulted in the rebellion of his Norman lords; and the treason of Kildare ended in the ruin of nearly one-half the Irish people.

Perhaps you will ask me, did the Irish people take any part in that war, so as to justify the treatment they received? I answer, they took no part in it; it was an English business from beginning to end; and the Irish Chieftains took little or no interest in that war. We read that only O'Carroll, O'Moore, of Offaly; and O'Conor—only three Irish Chieftains sided with the Geraldines and drew the sword against Henry;—three Chieftains of rather small, unimportant septs, who by no means represented the Irish people of Munster or any other Province. And yet upon the Irish people fell the avenging and destroying hand of Henry the Eighth's army.

Mr. Froude goes on to say, "The Irish, somehow or other, yet seemed to like Henry VIII." Well, if they did, I don't admire their taste. He pleased them, says Mr. Froude, and they got fond of him; and then he adds the reason why: and it was that Henry never showed any disposition to dispossess the Irish people of their lands or to exterminate them. Now, I take him up on that. Is it true or is it not? Fortunately for the Irish Historian, the State papers are open to us as well as to Mr. Froude. What do the State papers of the reign of Henry tell us? They tell us that project after project was formed, during the reign of this monarch, to drive the whole Irish nation into Connaught, or west of the Shannon. That Henry VIII. wished it; that the Irish Council, that (according to Mr. Froude) governed Ireland by "Home Rule," wished it; and that the people of England desired it. And one of those State papers is in these words:—

"Considering these premises brought to pass, there shall no Irish be on this side of the waters of Shannon, unprosecuted, unsubdued, and unexiled. Then shall the English Pale be fully the distance of two hundred miles in length and more."

More than this, we have the evidence of the State papers of the time, that Henry VIII. meditated and contemplated an utter extirpation,—the utter sweeping away and destruction of the whole Irish race. We find the Lord Deputy and Council, in Dublin, writing to his Majesty; and here are their words. They tell him that his project is impracticable; they say:

"The land is large: by estimation as large as England: so that to inhabit the whole with new inhabitants would be an enterprise so great, that there is no prince christened that might commodiously spare so many subjects to depart out of his realms; but to encompass the destruction and total subjection of the land would be a marvellous and stupendous achievement from the great difficulties, both by lack of inhabitants and the great hardiness of these Irish, who can endure both hunger, and cold, and thirst, and evil lodging, far more than the inhabitants of any other land. And it would be unprecedented, the conquest of this land. We have not heard nor read of any country that was subdued by such a conquest, the whole inhabitants of which had been utterly extirpated and banished."

Great God! is this the man that Mr. Froude tells us was the "friend of Ireland," that never showed any design to take their lands or to dispossess them of their possessions! This is the man—the model "admirer of order," the "hater of disorder!" Surely, he was bound to create magnificent order; for, if a people are troublesome, and you want to reduce them to quiet, the best way, and the simplest way, is to kill them all. Just like some of those people in England —nurses, we read of, a few years ago,—that were farming out children; and, when a child was a little fractious, they gave it a nice little dose of poison; and they called that "quieting" it.

Do you know the reason why Henry VIII. pleased the Irish,—for there was no doubt about it,—that they were more pleased with him than with any other English monarch, up to that time? The reason is a very simple one. He had his own designs; but he concealed them. He was meditating, like an anticipated Oliver Cromwell, the ruin and destruction of the Irish race. But he had good sense; he kept it to himself; and it only came out in the State papers. But he treated the Irish with a certain amount of courtesy and politeness. Henry, with all his faults, was a learned man, an accomplished man, a man of the very best manners,—a man that, with a bland smile, would give you a warm shake of the hand. It is true, the next day he might have your head cut off; but still he had the manners of a gentleman. And it is a singular fact, my friends, that the two most gentlemanly Kings in England were the two greatest scoundrels, perhaps, that ever lived,—Henry VIII. and George IV. Henry had dealt with the Irish people with a certain amount of civility and courtesy. He did not come in amongst them, like all his predecessors, saying: "You are the King's enemies; you ought all to be put to death; you are without the pale of law; you are barbarians and savages: and I will put you under my heel." Henry came and said: "Now let us see if we cannot arrange our difficulties; let us see, if we cannot live in peace and quiet;" and the Irish people were charmed with the man's manner. Ah! my friends, there was a black heart under that smiling face; but it was also true,—a fact that Mr. Froude acknowledges,—that Henry VIII. had a certain amount of popularity with the Irish people; which proves that, if England only knew how to treat us with a certain amount of kindness, they would, long since, have won the heart of Ireland, instead of alienating and embittering it by the injustice as much as by the cruelty of their laws. . . .

. . . . And this is what I meant on last Tuesday night, when I said that the English contempt of Irishmen is really the evil that lies deep at the root of all the bad spirit that exists between the two nations; for the simple reason that the Irish people are too intellectual, too strong, too energetic, too pure of race, and of blood too ancient and too proud, to be despised.

And now, my friends, Mr. Froude, in his second lecture, gave us a proof of the great love the Irish people had for Henry VIII. He says they were so fond of that King that actually, at his request, Ireland threw the Pope overboard. I use the gentleman's own words: "Ireland threw the Pope overboard!" No, Mr. Froude, fond as we were of your glorious hero, Henry VIII., we were not so enamored of him, we had not fallen so deeply in love with him as to give up the Pope for him. What are the facts of the case? Henry, about the year 1530, got into difficulties with the Pope, which ended in his denying his authority and supremacy as the head of the Catholic Church. He then picked out an apostate monk,—a man who gave up his faith,—a man without a shadow of either conscience, character, or virtue,—and he had him consecrated as the first Protestant Archbishop of Dublin. He was an Englishman named Brown—George Brown;—and Henry sent him over to Dublin, in the year 1534, with a commission to get the Irish nation to follow in the wake of the English, and to "throw the Pope overboard" and acknowledge the supremacy of Henry. Brown arrived in Dublin. He called the Bishops together—the Bishops of the Catholic Church; and he said to them: "You must change your allegiance. You must give up the Pope, and take Henry, King of England, in his stead." The Archbishop of Armagh, in those days, was an Englishman whose name was Cromer; and the moment the old man heard these words, he rose up from the Council Board and said: "What blasphemy is this I hear? Ireland will never change her faith; Ireland never will renounce her Catholicity; and she would have to renounce it by renouncing the head of the Catholic Church." . . . . And all the Bishops of Ireland followed the Primate, all the priests of Ireland followed the Primate; and George Brown wrote the most lugubrious letter home to his protector, Thomas Cromwell, telling him: "I can make nothing of this people; and I would return to England, only I am afraid the King would have my head taken off."

Three years later, however, Brown and the Lord Deputy summoned a Parliament, and it was at this Parliament of 1537, according to Mr. Froude, that "Ireland threw the Pope overboard." Now, what are the facts? A Parliament was assembled; and, from time immemorial, in Ireland, whenever a Parliament was assembled, there were three delegates, called proctors, from every Catholic diocese in Ireland, who sat in the House of Commons, in virtue of their office;—three priests from every diocese in Ireland. When this Parliament was called, the first thing they did was to banish the proctors and deprive them of their seats in the House. Without the slightest justice, without the slightest show or pretence of either right, or law, or justice, the proctors were excluded; and so the ecclesiastical element—the Church element—was completely precluded from that Parliament of 1537. Then, partly by promises, partly by bribes, partly by threats, this venal Parliament of the "Pale,"—this English Parliament,—this Parliament of the rotten little boroughs that surrounded Dublin, and the five half-counties that we have seen,—willingly took an oath that Henry was the head of the Church; and Mr. Froude calls this the apostasy of the Irish nation! With that strange want of knowledge (for I can call it nothing else,) of our religion, he imagines that Ireland remained Catholic, even though he asserts that she gave up the Pope. They took, he says, the oath—Bishops and all—and thereby acknowledged the supremacy of Henry VIII. But, nevertheless, they did not become Protestants; they still remained Catholics; and the reason why they did not take the same oath to Elizabeth, was because Elizabeth insisted on their taking the Protestant religion as well as the oath of supremacy. I answer him, at once, and will set him right upon this question. The Catholic Church teaches, and has always taught, that no man is a Catholic who is not in communion of obedience with the Pope of Rome. Henry VIII., who was a learned man, had too much theology, and too much logic, and too much sense to become what is called a Protestant. He never embraced the doctrines of Luther; and he held on to every iota of Catholic doctrine to the last day of his life, save and except that he refused to acknowledge the Pope. But, in the day that Henry VIII. refused to acknowledge the Pope, he ceased to be a Catholic. And to pretend or to hint that the Irish people were so ignorant as to imagine that they could "throw the Pope overboard," and still remain Catholic, is to offer to the genius and intelligence of Ireland a gratuitous insult. . . . .

. . . . . It is true that some of the Bishops apostatized: I can call it nothing else. They took the oath of supremacy to Henry VIII., and their names,—living in the execration of Irish history,—are: Eugene McGinnis, Bishop of Down and Conor; Roland Burke (I am sorry to say), Bishop of Clonfert; Florence Kirwan, Bishop of Clonmacnoise; Mathew Saunders, Bishop of Ossory; and Hugh O'Carolan, Bishop of Clogher. Five bishops only apostatized, the rest of Ireland's episcopacy remained faithful;—and George Brown, the apostate Archbishop, acknowledges in a letter, written at this time, that of all the priests of the diocese of Dublin he could only find three that would take the oath to Henry VIII. There was a priest down in Cork,—he was an Irishman, rector of Shandon; his name was Dominic Tyrrell. He was offered the Bishopric of Cork, if he took the oath; and he took it. There was a man named William Myah; he was offered the Diocese of Kildare if he took the oath; and he took it. There was another, Alexander Devereux, Abbot of Dunbrody; he was offered the Diocese of Ferns, in the county of Wexford, in order to induce him to swear allegiance to the English King: and he did it. These are all the names that represent what Mr.

Froude calls the national apostasy of Ireland. Out of so many hundreds, eight men were found wanting; and Mr. Froude turns round, quietly and calmly, and tells us that the Irish Bishops and people "threw the Pope overboard."

He makes another assertion, and I regret he made it. I regret it, because there is much in the learned gentleman that I admire and esteem. He asserts that the Bishops of Ireland, in these days, were immoral men; that they had families; that they were not like the venerable men whom we see in the episcopacy of to-day. Now, I answer, that there is not a shred of testimony to bear up Mr. Froude in this wild assertion. I have read the history of Ireland— national, civil, ecclesiastical—as far as I could; and nowhere have I seen even an allegation, much less a proof, of immorality against the Irish clergy, or their Bishops, at the time of the Reformation. . . . . But, perhaps, when Mr. Froude said this, he meant the apostate Bishops. If so, I am willing to grant him whatever he chooses in regard to them, and whatever charge he lays upon them, the heavier it is, the more pleased I am to see it coming from that source.

The next passage in the relation of Henry VIII. to Ireland, goes to prove that Ireland did not "throw the Pope overboard." My friends, in the year 1541, a Parliament assembled in Dublin, and declared that Henry VIII. was "King of Ireland." They had been four hundred years and more fighting for that title; and at length it was conferred by the Irish Parliament upon the English monarch. Two years later, in gratitude to the Irish Parliament, Henry called all the Irish Chieftains over to a grand assembly at Greenwich; and on the 1st day of July, 1543, he gave the Irish Chieftains their English titles. O'Neill, of Ulster, got the title of Earl of Tyrone; the glorious O'Donnell, the title of Earl of Tyrconnell; Ulic McWilliam Burke was called the Earl of Clanricarde; Fitzpatrick got the name of Baron of Ossory; and they returned to Ireland with their new titles. Henry, free, open-handed, generous fellow, as he was—he was really very generous—gave those Chieftains not only the titles, but a vast amount of property; only it happened to be stolen from the Catholic Church. He was an exceedingly generous man with other people's goods. In order to promote the authorized reformation—not Protestantism, but his own reformation—in Ireland, Henry gave to these Irish Earls, with their English titles, all the abbey lands and convent and church lands that lay within their possessions. The consequence was that he enriched them; and to the eternal shame of the O'Neill and O'Donnell, McWilliam Burke and Fitzpatrick of Ossory, they had the cowardliness and weakness to accept those gifts at his hand. They came home with the spoil of the monasteries, and their English titles. And now, mark. The Irish people were as true as steel in that day when the Irish Chieftains proved false to their country and their God. Nowhere in the previous history of Ireland do we read of the Clans rising against their Chieftains. Nowhere do we read of the .O'Neill or O'Donnell dispossessed by his own people. But on this occasion, when they came home, mark what followed. O'Brien, Earl of Thomond, when he arrived in Munster, found half his dominions in revolt against him. McWilliam Burke, Earl of Clanricarde, when his people heard that their leader had accepted the Abbey lands, the first thing they did was to depose him, and set up against him another man, with the title of The McWilliam Oughter de Burgh. Con O'Neill, Earl of Tyrone, when he came home to Ulster, was taken by his own son, and clapped into jail; and he died there, all his people abandoning him. O'Donnell, Earl of Tyrconnell, came home, and his own son and all his people rose against him and drove him out from the midst of them. Now, I say, in the face of all this—Mr. Froude is not justified in stating that "Ireland threw the Pope overboard." These Chieftains did not renounce the Catholic religion; they only renounced the Papal supremacy. They did not come home Protestants; they only came home schismatics, and very bad Catholics; and Ireland would not stand them.

Henry died in 1547; and I verily believe that, with all the badness of his heart, had he lived a few years longer, he would not have been a curse, but a blessing to Ireland; for the simple reason that those who came after him were worse than himself. He was succeeded by his child-son, Edward VI., who was under the care or guardianship of the Duke of Somerset. Somerset was a thoroughgoing Protestant. Somerset did not believe in the Papal supremacy; he did not believe in the Blessed Sacrament, nor in anything that savored of the teachings of the Catholic Church. He was opposed to them all. As soon as Henry was dead, and young Edward had been proclaimed King, he sent over to Ireland orders to put the laws in force against the Catholic Church. Consequently the churches were pillaged; the Catholic priests were driven out; and as Mr. Froude puts it, "the emblems of superstition were pulled down." The emblems of superstition, as Mr. Froude calls them, were the figure of Jesus Christ crucified, the statues of His Blessed Mother, and the pictures of His Saints. All these things were pulled down and destroyed. The crucifix was trampled under foot. The ancient statue of Our Lady of Trim, in the county of Meath, was publicly burned. The churches were rifled and sacked; and, as Mr. Froude eloquently says, "Ireland was taught the lesson that she must yield to the new order of things or stand by the Pope." "Irish traditions and ideas," Mr. Froude says, "became inseparably linked with religion." Glory to you, Mr.

Froude. He goes on to say in eloquent language: "Ireland chose her place on the Pope's side, and chose it irrevocably; and from that time the cause of the Catholic religion and Irish independence became inseparably and irrevocably one."

Edward VI. died after a short reign; and then came Queen Mary, known in England by the title of "Bloody Mary." She was a Catholic; and without doubt, she persecuted her Protestant subjects. But Mr. Froude, speaking of her in his lecture, says: "There was no persecution of Protestants in Ireland, because there were no Protestants to be persecuted." And he goes on to say: "Those who were in Ireland, when Mary came to the throne, fled." Now, my friends, I must take the learned historian to task on this. The insinuation is, that if the Protestants had been in Ireland, the Irish Catholic people would have persecuted them. The impression he desires to leave on the mind is that we, Catholics, would be only too glad to imbrue our hands in the blood of our fellow-citizens, on the question of religion, or difference in doctrine. He does this to convey the impression, as much as to say that, if the Protestants were in Ireland, whatever chance they might have in any other country, they had no chance at all in Ireland.

Now, what are the facts,—the historical facts? The facts are that, during the reign of Edward VI., and during the latter years of his father's reign, certain apostates from the Catholic Church were sent over to Ireland as Bishops; —men, whom even English history convicts and condemns for almost every crime. As soon as Mary came to the throne, these gentlemen did not wait to be ordered out; they went out of their own accord. It was not a question, at all, of the Irish people; it was not a question for Ireland; it was a question between the Queen of England and certain English Bishops that were foisted upon the Irish Church. They thought it the best of their play to clear out at once; and I verily believe that they acted very prudently. But so far as regards the Irish people, I claim for my native land that she never persecuted on account of religion. I am proud, in addressing an American audience, to be able to put in this high claim for Ireland. The genius of the Irish people is not a persecuting one. There is not a people on the face of the earth so attached to the Catholic religion as the Irish race: but there is not a people on the face of the earth so unwilling to persecute or to shed blood in the cause of religion as the Irish. And, here are my proofs: Mr. Froude says that the Protestants fled out of Ireland as soon as Queen Mary came to the throne; but Sir James Ware, in his "Annals," tells us that the Protestants were being persecuted in England under Mary, and that they actually fled over to Ireland for protection. He gives even the names of some of them. He tells us that John Harvey, Abel Ellis, Joseph Edwards, and Henry Hall, natives of Cheshire, came over to Ireland to avoid the persecution that was raging in England; and they brought with them a Welsh Protestant minister named Thomas Jones. These four gentlemen were received so cordially, were welcomed so hospitably, that they actually founded highly respectable mercantile families in Dublin.

But we have another magnificent proof that the Irish are not a persecuting race. When James II. assembled his Catholic Parliament in Ireland, in 1689,—after they had been for more than one hundred years under the lash of their Protestant fellow-citizens, after they had been robbed and plundered, imprisoned and put to death for their adherence to the Catholic faith,—at last the wheel gave a turn; and, in 1689, the Catholics were up and the Protestants were down. That Parliament assembled to the number of two hundred and twenty-eight members. The Celts—the Irish, the Catholic element—had a sweeping majority. What was the first law that they made? The very first law that that Catholic Parliament passed was as follows:—

"We hereby decree that it is the law of this land of Ireland that, neither now nor ever again, shall any man be persecuted for his religion."

That was the retaliation we took on them. Was it not magnificent? Was it not grand? a magnificent specimen of that spirit of Christianity, that spirit of forgiveness and charity without which, if it be not in a man, all the dogmatic truths that ever were revealed will not save or ennoble him.

Now, coming to "good Queen Bess," as she is called, I must say that Mr. Froude bears very heavily upon her, and speaks of her really in language as terrific in its severity as any that I could use, and far more, for I have not the learning nor the eloquence of Mr. Froude. He says one little thing of her, however, that is worthy of remark. He says:—

"Elizabeth was reluctant to draw the sword; but when she did draw it, she never sheathed it until the star of freedom was fixed upon her banner, never to pale."

Now, that is a very eloquent passage; but the soul of eloquence is truth. Is it true, historically, that Elizabeth was reluctant to draw the sword? Answer it, ye Irish annals! Answer it, oh history of Ireland! Elizabeth came to the throne in 1558. The following year, in 1559, there was a Parliament assembled by her order in Dublin. What do you think were the laws of that Parliament? It was not a Catholic Parliament, nor an Irish Parliament. It consisted of seventy-six members. Generally speaking, Parliaments in Ireland used to have from two hundred and twenty to two hundred and thirty members. This Parliament of Elizabeth consisted of seventy-six picked men. The laws that that Parliament made were, first:—" Any clergyman not using the Book of Common Prayer (the Protestant prayer-book), or using any other form, either in public or in private, the first time that he is discovered, shall be deprived of his benefice for one year, and suffer imprisonment in jail for six months. For the second offence he shall forfeit his income forever, and be put in jail at the Queen's good pleasure;" to be let out whenever she thought proper. For the third offence he was to be put in close confinement for life. This was the lady that was "reluctant to draw the sword!" and, my friends, remember that this was the very year after she was crowned Queen—the very next year. She scarcely waited a year. This was the woman "reluctant to draw the sword!" So much for the priests; now for the laymen. If a layman were discovered using any other prayer-book except Queen Elizabeth's prayer-book, he was to be put in jail for one year; and if he were caught doing it a second time, he was to be put in prison for the rest of his life. Every Sunday the people were obliged to go to the Protestant Church; and if any one refused to go, for every time that he refused he was fined twelve pence—that would be about twelve shillings of our present money; and besides the fine of twelve pence, he was to "incur the censures of the church!" "The star of freedom," says Mr. Froude, "was never to pale." "The Queen drew the sword in the cause of the star of freedom!" But, my friends, freedom meant whatever fitted in Elizabeth's mind. Freedom meant slavery tenfold increased, with the addition of religious persecution, to the unfortunate Irish. If this be Mr. Froude's idea of the star of freedom, all I can say is, the sooner such stars fall from heaven and the firmament of the world's history, the better.

In what state was the Irish Church? Upon that subject

we have the authority of the Protestant historian, Leland. There were two hundred and twenty parish churches in Meath, and in a few years time there were only one hundred and five of them left with the roofs on.

" All over the kingdom" (says Leland) " the people were left without any religious worship, and under the pretence of obeying the orders of the State, they seized all the most valuable furniture of the churches, which was actually exposed for sale without decency or reserve."

A number of hungry adventurers were let loose upon the Irish churches and upon the Irish people by Elizabeth. They not only robbed them and plundered their churches, but they shed the blood of the Bishops and priests and of the people in torrents, as Mr. Froude himself acknowledges. He tells us that, after the second rebellion of the Geraldines, such was the state to which the fair Province of Munster was reduced, that you might go through the land, from the farthermost point of Kerry until you came into the eastern plains of Tipperary, and you would not as much as hear the whistle of a ploughboy, or behold the face of a living man. But the trenches and ditches were filled with the corpses of the people, and the country was reduced to a howling, desolate wilderness. The poet Spenser describes it emphatically, in language the most terrific. Even he, case-hardened as he was,—for he was one of the plunderers and persecutors himself—acknowledges that the state of Munster was such that no man could look upon it with a dry eye. Sir Henry Sidney, one of Elizabeth's own deputies, addressing her, says of the overthrown churches:—

" There are not, I am sure, in any region where the name of Christ is professed, such horrible spectacles, as are here to be beheld; as the burning of villages, the ruin of churches,—yea, the view of the bones and skulls of the dead, who, partly by murder and partly by famine, have died in the fields. It is such that hardly any Christian can with a dry eye behold."

Her own Minister,—her own General!—there is his testimony of the state to which this terrible woman reduced unhappy Ireland. Strafford, another English authority, says:—"I knew it was bad in Ireland; but that it was so stark-wrought I did not believe."

In the midst of all this persecution, what was still the reigning idea in the mind of the English Government? To root out and to extirpate the Irish from their own land, added to which was now the element of religious discord and persecution. It is evident that this was still in the minds of the English people. Elizabeth, who, Mr. Froude says, "never dispossessed an Irishman of an acre of his land," during the terrible war which she waged in the latter days of her reign against the heroic Hugh O'Neill, of Ulster, threw out such hints as these: "The more slaughter there is, the better it will be for my English subjects; the more land they will get." This is the woman, who, Mr. Froude tells us, never confiscated, and would never listen to the idea of confiscation of property! This woman, when the Geraldines were destroyed, took the whole of the vast estates of the Earl of Desmond, and gave them all, quietly and calmly, to certain English planters, that she sent over from Lancashire, Cheshire, Devonshire, and Somersetshire. And in the face of these historic truths, recorded and stamped on history, I cannot understand how any man can come forward and say of this atrocious woman that whatever she did she intended it for the good of Ireland.

In 1602, she died, after reigning forty-one years, leaving Ireland at the hour of her death one vast slaughter-house. Munster was reduced to the state described by Spenser. Connaught was made a wilderness through the rebellion of the Clanricardes, or the Burke family. Ulster, through the agency of Lord Mountjoy, was left the very picture of desolation. The glorious Red Hugh O'Donnell and the magnificent O'Neill were crushed and defeated after fifteen years of war. And the consequence was that, when James the First succeeded Elizabeth, he found Ireland almost a wilderness. What did he do? He acted well at first. He promised the Irish that they should be left their lands. He succeeded to the throne of England in 1603; and for four years—I must give him the credit—for four years he kept his word. But, in 1607, Hugh O'Neill, and O'Donnell, of Tyrconnell, fled from their country to escape imprisonment; and then, Sir Arthur Chichester, an Englishman, the agent of the King, developed one of the most extraordinary systems that ever was heard of in the relation of one country to another. They took the whole of the province of Ulster, and scarcely left to the Irish a foot of land of their finest province. They transferred it from the original population; and handed it over to settlers from England and from Scotland. It was called "The Plantation of Ulster." They gave to the Protestant Archbishop of Armagh 43,000 acres of the finest land in Ireland. They gave to Trinity College, in Dublin, 30,000 acres. They gave to the "Skinners" and "Cordwainers" and "Drysalters," all those corporations of trade in London, 208,000 acres of the finest land in Ireland. They brought over a colony of Scotch Presbyterians, and of English Protestants, and gave them tracts of a thousand and fifteen hundred and two thousand acres of land, making them swear, as they did so, that they would not employ one single Irishman, or single Catholic, nor let them come near them. Thus millions of acres of the finest land in Ireland were taken at one blow from the Irish; and the people were crushed out of their property.

Mr. Froude, in his rapid historical sketch, said that all this, of course, bred revenge; and he tells us that, in 1641, the Irish rose in rebellion. So they did. Now, he makes one statement, and with the refutation of that statement I will close this lecture. Mr. Froude tells us that, in the rising under Sir Phelim O'Neil, in 1642, there were 38,000 Protestants massacred by the Irish. That is a grave charge, a most terrific one, in the case of a people: and if it be true, all I can say is that I blush for my fathers. But if it be not true, why, in the name of God, repeat it? Why not wipe it out from the records for a lie as it is. Is it true? The Irish rose under Sir Phelim O'Neill. At that time there was a Protestant parson in Ireland who called himself a Minister of the Word of God. He gives an account of the whole transaction in a letter to the people of England, begging of them to help their fellow-Protestants of Ireland. Here are his words: "It was the intention of the Irish to massacre all the English. On Saturday they were to disarm them, on Sunday to seize all their cattle and goods, and on Monday they were to cut all the English throats. The former they executed; the latter—that is the massacre—they failed in." Petty, another English authority, tells us, that there were 38,000 Protestants massacred at that time. A man of the name of May foots it up at 200,000. I suppose he thought "in for a penny in for a pound." But there was an honest Protestant clergyman in Ireland who examined minutely into the details of the whole conspiracy, and of all the evils that came from it. What does he tell us?

"I have discovered" (he says—and he gives proof, State papers and authentic records)—"that the Irish Catholics in that rising massacred 2,100 Protestants; that other Protestants said there were 1,600 more; and that some Irish authorities themselves say there were 3,000, making altogether 4,026 persons."

This is the massacre that Mr. Froude speaks of; he tosses

it off, as if it were Gospel,—38,000 Protestants were massacred—that is to say, he multiplies the original number by ten; whereas Mr. Warner, the authority in question, says actually that there were 2,100; and I am unwilling to believe in the additional numbers that have been stated. And this is the way that history is written! This is the way that people are left under a false impression!

And now, first of all, that we have seen the terrible nature of the evils which fell upon Ireland in the days of Henry VIII., Elizabeth, and James I., I ask you, people of America, to set these two thoughts before your minds, contrast them, and give me a fair verdict. Is there anything recorded in history more terrible than the persistent, undying resolution,—so clearly manifested,—of the English Government to root out, extirpate and destroy, the people of Ireland? Is there anything recorded in history more unjust than this systematic, constitutional robbery of the people whom Almighty God created in that island, to whom he gave that island, and who have the aboriginal right to every inch of Irish soil? On the other hand, can history bring forth a more magnificent spectacle than the calm, firm, united resolution with which Ireland stood in defence of her religion, giving up all things rather than sacrifice what she conceived to be the cause of truth? Mr. Froude does not believe it is the cause of truth. I do not blame him. Every man has a right to his religious opinions. But Ireland believed it was the cause of truth; and Ireland stood for it like one man. I speak of all these things only historically. I do not believe in animosity. I am not a believer in bad blood. I do not believe, with Mr. Froude, that the question of Ireland's difficulty must remain without solution. I do not give it up in despair. But this I do say, that he has no right, nor has any other man the right, to come before the audience of America,—of

America, that has never persecuted in the cause of religion,—of America, that respects the rights even of the meanest citizen upon her imperial soil,—and to ask that American people to sanction by their verdict the robberies and persecutions of which England is guilty.

4

THIRD LECTURE.

(*Delivered in the Academy of Music, New York, Nov. 19, 1872.*)

THE CROMWELLIAN ERA.

LADIES AND GENTLEMEN: We now approach, in answering Mr. Froude, to some of the most awful periods of our history. I confess that I approach this terrific ground with sadness, and I extremely regret that Mr. Froude should have opened up questions which oblige an Irishman to undergo the pain of heart and anguish of spirit, which a revision of this portion of our history must occasion.

The learned gentleman began his third lecture by reminding his audience that he had closed the second lecture with a reference to the rise, progress, and collapse of a great rebellion, which took place in Ireland in the year 1641—that is to say, somewhat more than two hundred years ago. He made but a passing allusion to that great event in our history; and in that allusion—if he has been reported correctly—he stated simply that the Irish rebelled in 1641: that was his first statement—that it was a rebellion; secondly, that this rebellion began in massacre and ended in ruin; thirdly, that, for nine years, the Irish leaders had the destinies of their country in their hands; and fourthly, that these nine years were years of anarchy and mutual slaughter. Nothing, therefore, can be imagined more melancholy than the picture drawn by this learned gentleman of those nine sad years, and yet I will venture to say, and hope I shall be able to prove, that each of those four statements is without sufficient historical foundation.

My first position is that the movement of 1641 was not a rebellion; second, that it did not begin with massacre, although it ended in ruin; third, that the Irish leaders had not the destinies of their country in their hands during those nine years; and fourth, that whether they had or not, those years were not a period of anarchy and mutual slaughter. They were but the opening to a far more terrific period. We must discuss these questions, my friends, calmly and historically. We must look upon them rather like antiquarians prying into the past, than with the living, warm feelings of men, whose blood boils up at the remembrance of so much injustice and so much bloodshed.

In order to understand these questions fully and fairly, it is necessary for us to go back to the historical events of the time. We find, then, that James I., the man who "planted" Ulster,—that is to say, who confiscated, utterly and entirely, six of the fairest counties in Ireland,—an entire Province,—rooting out the aboriginal Irish Catholic inhabitants, even to a man, and giving the whole country to Scotch and English settlers of the Protestant religion, under the condition that they were not to employ even as much as an Irish laborer on their grounds—that they were to banish them all;—we find that this man died in 1625, and was succeeded by his unfortunate son, Charles I. When Charles came to the throne, bred up as he was in the traditions of a monarchy which Henry VIII. had rendered almost absolute, as we know;—whose absolute power was still continued under Elizabeth, under a form the most tyrannical;—whose absolute power was continued by his own father, James I.; —Charles came to the throne with the most exaggerated ideas of royal privilege and royal supremacy. But, during the days of his father, a new spirit had grown up in Scotland and in England. The form which Protestantism took in Scotland was the hard and uncompromising, and, I will add, cruel, form of Calvinism, in its most repellent aspect. The men who rose in Scotland in defence of their Presbyterian religion, rose not against Catholicity at all, but against the Episcopal Protestantism of England. They defended what they called the "Kirk," or the "Covenant." They fought bravely, I acknowledge, for it; and they ended in establishing it as the religion of Scotland. Now, Charles I. was an Episcopalian Protestant of the most sincere and devoted kind. The Parliament of England, in the very first years of Charles, admitted members who were strongly tinged with Scotch Calvinism; and they at once showed a refractory spirit to their King. He demanded of them certain subsidies, and they refused him. He asserted certain sovereign rights, and they denied them. But whilst all this was going on in England, from the year 1630, to, let us say, the year 1641, what was taking place in Ireland? One Province of the land had been completely confiscated by James I. Charles I. was in want of money, for his own purposes; his Parliament refused to grant him any; and the poor, oppressed, down-trodden, persecuted Catholics of Ireland imagined, naturally enough, that the King, being in difficulties, would turn to them, and, perhaps, lend them a little countenance and a little favor, if they proclaimed their loyalty and stood by him. Accordingly, the Lord Lieutenant of Ireland, Lord Falkland—sincerely attached, as he was, to his royal master—hinted to the Catholics, and proposed to them, that, as they were under the most terrific penal laws, from the days of Elizabeth and James I.,—that, perhaps, if they should now petition the King, they would get certain "graces" or concessions granted to them. What these "graces" were, simply involved permission to live in their own land, and permission to worship their God according to the dictates of their own conscience. They asked for nothing more, and nothing more was promised to them. When their petition went before the King, his Royal Majesty of England issued a proclamation, in which he declared that it was his intention, and that he had plighted his word, to grant to the Catholics, and to the people of Ireland, certain concessions and indulgences which he named by the name of "graces." No sooner did the newly-founded Puritan element, in England and in the Parliament,—that were fighting against their King,—no sooner did they hear that the slightest relaxation of the penal laws was to be granted to the Catholics of Ireland, than they instantly rose and protested that it should not be. And Charles—to his eternal disgrace—broke his word with the Catholics of Ireland, after they had sent him £120,000 in acknowledgment of his promise. More than this, it was suspected that Lord Falkland was too mild a man, too just a man, to be allowed to remain as Lord Lieutenant of Ireland. He was recalled; and, after a short lapse, Wentworth, who was afterwards Earl Strafford, was sent to Ireland as Lord Lieutenant.

Wentworth, on his arrival, summoned a Parliament, which met in the year 1634. He told them the difficulties the King was in; he told them how the Parliament in England was rebelling against him; and how he looked to his Irish subjects as loyal. He, perhaps, told them that, amongst Catholics, loyalty was not a mere sentiment, but an unshaken principle, resting upon conscience and religion. And then he assured them that Charles, the King of England, still intended to keep his word and grant them the concessions or "graces."

Next came the usual demand for money; and the Irish Parliament granted six subsidies of £50,000 each. Strafford wrote to the King, congratulating him on getting so much money out of Ireland; "For," said he, "your Majesty remembers, that you and I expected only £30,000, and they have granted subsidies of £50,000." More than this, they granted him 8,000 infantry and 1,000 horse, to fight against his Scottish rebellious subjects and enemies.

The Parliament met the following year, in 1635; and what do you think was the fulfilment of the Royal promise to the Catholics of Ireland? Strafford had got the money. He did not wish to compromise his master, the King; and he took upon himself, and fixed upon his own memory the indelible shame and disgrace of breaking his word, which he had plighted, and disappointing the Catholics of Ireland. Then, in 1635, the real character of this man came out; and what do you think was the measure he proposed? He instituted a Commission for the express purpose of confiscating,—in addition to Ulster, that was already gone,—the whole Province of Connaught, so as not to leave an Irishman or a Catholic one square inch of ground in that land. This he called the "Commission of Defective Titles." The commissioners were men that were to inquire into the title that every man had to his property, and to inquire into it with the express and avowed purpose of finding a flaw in it, if they could, and confiscating the land to the Crown of England. Now, remember how much was gone already, my friends. The whole of Ulster was confiscated by James I. The same King had taken the county of Longford from the O'Farrells, who owned it from time immemorial. He had seized upon Wicklow, and taken it from the O'Tooles and O'Byrnes. He had taken the northern part of the county of Wexford from the O'Kavanaghs. He had taken Iracken, in the Queen's County, from the McGeoghegans. He had taken Kilcoursey, in the King's County, from the O'Molloys. And now, with the whole of Ulster, and the better part of Leinster in his hands, this Minister had instituted a Commission by which he was to obtain the whole of the Province of Connaught, root out the native Irish population, expel every man that owned a rood of land in the Province, and reduce them to beggary, starvation, and death. Here is the description of his plan as given by Leland, a historian who was hostile to Ireland's faith and Ireland's nationality. Leland thus describes the business:—

"This project was nothing less than to subvert the title of every estate in every part of Connaught,—a project which, when first proposed in the late reign, was received with horror and amazement, but which suited the undismayed and enterprising genius of Lord Wentworth."

Strafford's Commission, accordingly, began in the County of Roscommon, passed thence into Sligo, thence to Mayo, and thence to Galway. Now, mark how he managed this tribunal. The only way by which a title could be upset, was by having a jury of twelve men, to declare by their verdict whether the title was valid or not. Strafford began by packing the juries,—packing them! It is the old story over again,—the old policy that has been continued down to our time,—the policy of a packed and prejudiced jury. He told the jury, before the trial began, that he expected them to find a verdict for the king; and between bribing them and threatening them, he got juries to find for him, until he came into the county of Galway. And to the honor of old Galway be it said, that as soon as the Commission arrived in that county, they could not find twelve jurors in the county of Galway base enough and wicked enough to confiscate the lands of their fellow-subjects. What was the result? The result was that the county Galway jurors were called to Dublin before the Castle Council Chamber, and every man of them was fined £4,000, and was put into prison until the fine was paid. Every inch of their property was taken from them; and the High Sheriff of the county Galway, not being a wealthy man, died in jail because he was not able to pay his fine. More than this. Not content with threatening the juries, and coercing them, my Lord Strafford went to the Judges, and told them that they were to get four shillings in the pound for the value of every piece of property they confiscated to the Crown of England. Then, he boasted, publicly, that he had made the Chief Baron and the Judges attend to this business as if it were their own private concern. This is the kind of rule the English historian comes to America to ask the honest and upright citizens of this free country to indorse by their verdict, and thereby to make themselves accomplices of English fraud and robbery.

In this same year, Strafford instituted another tribunal in Ireland, which he called the "Court of Wards;" and do you know what this was? It was found that the Irish people, gentle and simple, as they were, were very unwilling to become Protestants. I have not a harsh word to say of Protestants. But this I will say, that every high-minded Protestant in the world must admire the strength and fidelity with which Ireland, because of her conscience, clung to her ancient faith. This tribunal was instituted in order to get the heirs of the Catholic gentry, and to bring them up in the Protestant religion. And it is to this "Court of Wards" that we owe the significant fact that some of the most ancient and the best names in Ireland,—the names of men whose ancestors fought for faith and fatherland,—are now Protestants, and the enemies of their Catholic fellow-subjects. It was by this, and such means as this, that the men of my own name became Protestants. There was no drop of Protestant blood in the veins of the Dun Earl, or Red Earl of Clanricarde. There was no drop of any other than Catholic blood in the veins of the heroic Burkes who fought during the long five hundred years that went before this time. . . . . There was no Protestant blood in the O'Briens of Munster, or in the glorious O'Donnells and O'Neills of Ulster, that are Protestants to-day. Let no Protestant American citizen here imagine that I am speaking in disdain of him or his religion. No; but as a historian, I am pointing out the means,—which every high-minded man must pronounce to be nefarious,—by which the aristocracy of Ireland were obliged to change their religion.

The Irish, meantime, waited, and waited in vain, for the fulfilment of the King's promise, and the concession of the "graces," as they were called. At length, matters grew desperate between Charles and his Parliament; and, in the year 1640, he again renewed his promise to the Irish people; and he called a Parliament which gave him four subsidies, 8,000 men, and 1,000 horse, to fight against the Scotch, who had rebelled against him. Strafford went home rejoicing that he had got those subsidies and this body of men; but no sooner did he arrive in England, than the Parliament, now in rebellion, laid hold of him. In that same year, 1640, Strafford's head was cut off; and he would be a strange Irishman that would regret it.

Meantime, the people of Scotland rose in armed rebellion against their King. They marched into England, and what do you think they made by their movement? They got a full acknowledgment of their religion, which was not the Protestant, but Presbyterian; they got £300,000; and they got, for several months, £850 a day to support their army. Then they retired into their own country, having achieved the purposes for which they had rebelled; and, in the meantime, the Catholics of Ireland were ground into the very dust. What wonder, I ask you, that, seeing the King so afraid of his English people, though personally inclined to grant these "graces"—as he had declared that he wished to grant them; he had declared that it was his intention to grant them; he had plighted his royal word to grant them,—what wonder that the Irish thought they had every evidence that, if the King were free, he would grant them? But he was not free, because his Parliament and the Puritan faction in England were in rebellion against him. So the Irish said: "Our King is not free; if he were, he would be kind to us; let us rise, then, in the name of the King and assert our own rights." They rose in 1641; they rose like one man; every Irishman—and every Catholic in Ireland, rose on the 23d of October, 1641, with the exception of the Catholic Lords of the "Pale." And, now, I give you the reasons of this rising, as recorded in the "Memoirs" of Lord Castlehaven, who was by no means prejudiced in favor of Ireland. He tells us that they rose for six reasons. The first was because they were generally looked down upon as a conquered nation, and seldom or never treated like natural or free-born subjects. The old evil still coming up, my dear friends. The very first reason given by this Englishman, why the Irish people rose, was that the English people treated them contemptuously. Oh! when will England learn to treat her subjects or her friends with common respect? When will that proud, stubborn Anglo-Saxon haughtiness condescend to urbanity and kindliness in dealing with those around them? I said it in my first lecture; I said it in my second lecture; and I now repeat it in this, that it was the contempt as much as the hatred of Englishmen for Irishmen that lay at the root—that lies at the root to-day—of that bitter spirit and terrible antagonism that exists between those two nations.

The second reason given by my Lord Castlehaven is, that the Irish saw that six whole counties in Ulster were escheated to the Crown and little or nothing restored to the natives; but in great part bestowed by King James I., on his own countrymen—the Scotch. The third reason was, that in Strafford's time, the Crown laid claim to the counties of Roscommon, Mayo, Galway, and Cork, and to parts of Tipperary, Wicklow, Limerick, and other counties. The fourth reason was, that great severities were used against the Roman Catholics, which to a people so fond of their religion as the Irish were, was no small inducement to make them, whilst there was an opportunity, stand upon their guard. The fifth reason was, they saw how the Scots, by pretending grievances, and taking up arms to get them redressed, had not only gained divers privileges and immunities, but a grant of £300,000, for their visit to England, besides £850 a day for several months together. The sixth and last reason was that they saw the storm drawing near;—such a misunderstanding arose between the King and the Parliament, that they believed the King would grant them anything that they could in reason demand; at least more now than they could otherwise expect. Now, I ask if these reasons were not sufficient? I appeal to the American people,—I appeal to men who know what civil and religious liberty means to a proud, high-spirited people, whose spirit was never broken, and never will be;—to a people not inferior to the Anglo-Saxon, either in gifts of intellect or in bodily energy; for a people thus persecuted, thus down-trodden,—as our fathers were,—would not any one of these reasons be sufficient justification to rise? And, with this accumulation of causes, would they not have been the meanest of mankind if they had not seized upon that opportunity?

An English Protestant writer of the times, in that very year 1641, writing in Howell's *Hibernicus*, says that the Irish had sundry grievances and grounds of complaint touching both their estates and consciences, which they pretended to be far greater than those of the Scots. "For, still, they think," he says, "that if the Scots were suffered to introduce a new religion, it was a reason that they should not be punished for the exercise of their own, which they gloried never to have altered."

There was another reason for the revolt, my friends, and a very potent one. It was this: Charles had the weakness and the folly—I can call it nothing else—to leave at the head of the Irish Government two Lords Justices, named Sir John Borlaese and Sir William Parsons. These were both ardent Puritans and partisans of the Parliament. They were anxious to see the fall of the English monarch,—for they were his bitterest enemies; and they thought that he would be embarrassed, in his fight with the Parliament in England, by a revolution in Ireland. And so the very men who were the guardians of the State lent themselves to promote the rebellion by every means in their power. For instance, six months before the revolt broke out, Charles gave them notice that he had received intelligence that the Irish were going to rise. They took no note whatever of the King's advertisement. The Lords of the "Pale," who refused to join the Irish in their uprising, applied to the Lords Justices in Dublin for protection; and it was refused them. They asked to be allowed to come into the city, that they might be safe from the incursions of the Irish. That permission was refused them; and they were forced to stay in their castles and houses, out in the country; and the moment that any of the Irish in revolt came near them, their houses and castles were declared forfeited to the State. Thus the English Catholics and Lords of the "Pale,"—the Gormanstowns, the Howths, the Trimblestons, and many others,—were actually forced by the Government to join hands with the Irish, and to draw their swords in the glorious cause that was before them. Moreover, the Irish knew that their friends and fellow-countrymen were earning distinction, honor, and glory, upon all the battle-fields of Europe, in the service of Spain, France, and Austria;—and they hoped, not without reason, that these friends, their countrymen, would help them in the hour of their need. Accordingly, on that 23d of October, 1641, they rose. What was the first thing they did? According to Mr. Froude, the first thing they did was to massacre all the Protestants they could lay their hands on. Well, thank God, that is not the fact. The very first thing their leader, Sir Phelim O'Neill, did, was to issue a proclamation on the very day of the rising, which he spread throughout all Ireland, and in which he declared:—

"We rise in the name of our Lord the King. We rise to assert the power and prerogative of the King. We declare we do not wish to make war on the King or any one of his subjects. We declare, moreover, that we do not intend to shed blood, except in legitimate warfare ; and that any one of our troops, any soldier, who robs, plunders, or sheds blood, shall be severely punished."

Did they keep this declaration of theirs? Most inviolably. I assert in the name of history, that there was no massacre of the Protestants ; and I will prove it from Protestant authority. We find dispatches from the Irish Government to the Government in England, dated the 25th to the 27th of that same month, in which they give an account of the rising of the Irish people. There they complained, telling how the Irish stripped their Protestant fellow-citizens; how they took their cattle, took their houses, took all their property; but not one single word or complaint about the shedding of one drop of blood. And if they took their cattle, houses, and property, you must remember that they were only taking back what was their own. A very short time afterwards the massacre began ; but who began it? The Protestant Ulster settlers fled from the Irish. They brought their lives with them at least ; and they entered the town of Carrickfergus, where they found a garrison of Scotch Puritans. Now, in the confusion that arose, the poor country people, frightened, fled into an obscure part of the country, near Carrickfergus,—a peninsula, called Island Magee. They were there collected for the purposes of safety, to the number of more than three thousand. The very first thing that these English Puritans and the Scotch garrison did, when they came together, was to sally out of Carrickfergus, in the night time, and to go in among those innocent and unarmed people; and they slaughtered every man, woman, and child, until they left three thousand dead behind them. We have the authority of Leland, the English Protestant historian, who expressly says that " this was the first massacre committed in Ireland, *on either side.*" This was the first massacre! How, in the name of Heaven, can any man so learned, and I make no doubt, so truthful as Mr. Froude,—how can he assert that these people began by massacring thirty-eight thousand of his fellow-countrymen and fellow-religionists, when we have, in the month of December, a few months after, a Commission issued by the Lords Justices in Dublin to the Dean of Kilmore and seven other Protestant clergymen, to make diligent inquiry about the English and Scotch Protestants who were *robbed and plundered;* but not one single word—not one single question—of those who were *murdered?*

Here are the words of Castlehaven:

" The Catholics were urged into rebellion; and the Lords Justices were often heard to say that the more that were in rebellion the more lands would be forfeited to the Crown."

It was the old story;—it was the old adage of James the First: " Root out the Catholics—root out the Irish, and give Ireland to English Protestants and Puritans, and you will regenerate the land." Oh! from such regeneration of my own or any other people, good Lord deliver us, I pray! " This rebellion," says Mr. Froude, " began in massacre and ended in ruin." It ended in ruin the most terrible; but, if it began in massacre, Mr. Froude, you must acknowledge, as a historical truth, that the massacre was on the part of your countrymen, and your co-religionists.

Then, the Irish having risen, the war began. It was a war between the Puritan Protestants of Ulster and other parts of Ireland, aided by constant armies that came over to them from England. It was a war that continued for eleven years; and it was a war in which the Irish Chieftains had not the destinies of the nation in their own hands, but were obliged to fight, and fight like men, in order to try to achieve a better destiny and a better future for their people. . . . . Who can say that the Irish Chieftains held the destinies of Ireland in their own hands during these nine years, when they had to meet every successive army that came to them inflamed with religious hatred and enmity, and animated, I must say, by a spirit of bravery of which the world has seldom seen the like. Then, Mr. Froude adds that these were "years of anarchy and mutual slaughter." Now let us consider the history of the events.

No sooner had the English Lords of the "Pale"—who were all Catholics—joined the Irish, than they turned to the Catholic Bishops of the land. They called them together in a Synod; and on the 10th of May, 1642, the Bishops of Ireland, the Lords of Ireland, and the gentry and Commoners and estated gentlemen of Ireland met together and founded what is called the "Confederation of Kilkenny." Amongst their number they selected for the Supreme Council, three Archbishops, two Bishops, four Lords, and fifteen Commoners. These men were to meet and remain in permanent session, watching over the country, making laws, watching over the army; and above all, preventing cruelty, robbery, and murder. A regular government was formed. They actually established a mint, and there coined money for the Irish nation. They established an army under Lord Mountcashel and General Preston; and in a short time after, under the glorious and immortal Owen Roe O'Neill. During the first months they gained some successes. Most of the principal cities of Ireland opened their gates to them. The garrisons were carefully saved from slaughter; and the moment they laid down their arms their lives were as sacred as that of any man in the ranks of the Irish armies. Not a drop of unnecessary blood was shed by the Irish with any sort of countenance on the part of the Government of the country—that is to say, the Supreme Council at Kilkenny. I defy any man to prove that there was a single law, which that Supreme Council enacted, that was not enacted to prevent bloodshed or murder.

Now, after a few months of success, the armies of the Confederation experienced some reverses. The Puritan party was recruited and fortified by English armies coming in; and the command in Dublin was given to a Governor whose name ought to be known to every Irishman;—his name was Sir Charles Coote. Some of his exploits are thus portrayed by Clarendon, who was no friend of Ireland :—

"Sir Charles, besides plundering and burning the town of Clontarf, at that time, did massacre sixteen townspeople, men and women, besides three suckling infants; and in that very same week fifty-six men, women, and children, in the village of Bullock, being frightened at what was done at Clontarf, went to sea to shun the fury of a party of soldiers, who came out from Dublin under command of Col. Clifford. Being pursued by the soldiers in boats, they were overtaken and thrown overboard."

Sir William Borlaese had, by letter, advised the Governor, Sir Charles Coote, to burn all the corn, and to give man, woman, and child to the sword; and Sir Arthur Loftus wrote to the same purpose and effect. An edict of the

Council at that time will tell you in what spirit our Protestant friends waged their war with us:—

"It is resolved that it is fit that his Lordship," (and, mind, this was given to the Marquis of Ormonde,)—"that his Lordship do endeavor to wound, kill, slay, and destroy, by all the ways and means that he may, all the said rebels, their adherents and relatives; and burn, spoil, waste, consume, destroy, and demolish, all the places, towns, and houses where the rebels are or have been relieved or harbored; and all the hay and corn therein, and kill and destroy all the men there inhabiting capable of bearing arms. Given at the Castle of Dublin, on the 23d day of February, 1641," and signed by six precious names.

Listen to this:—

"Sir Arthur Loftus, Governor of Naas, marched out with a party of horse. He was met on the way, and joined by another party sent from Dublin, by the Marquis of Ormonde; and they both together killed such of the Irish as they met, and did not stop to inquire whether they were rebels or not."

But, oh! my friends, listen to this:—

"But the most considerable slaughter was in a great strait of furze, situated on a hill, where the people of several villages, taking alarm, had sheltered themselves. Now, Sir Arthur having invested the hill, set fire to the furze on all sides, where the people being in considerable numbers, were all burned, men, women, and children. I saw," (says Castlehaven,) "the bodies and the furze still burning."

"In the year 1641 or 1642, many thousands of poor innocent people of the county of Dublin, shunning the fury of the English soldiery, fled into the thickets, which the soldiers actually fired, killing as many as attempted to escape, or forcing them back to be burned. And, as to the rest of the inhabitants, for the most part, they died of famine."

Not only by land, where we read, sometimes, of seven thousand of our people, men, women, and children, without discrimination, being destroyed by these demons,—not only were the Irish pursued on the land, but even on the sea. We read that there was a law passed that if any Irishmen were found on board ship, by his Majesty's cruisers, they were to be destroyed. Clarendon gives this account :—

"The Earl of Warwick, as often as he met an Irish frigate, or such freebooters as sailed under commission, all the seamen who became prisoners who belonged to the nation of Ireland; they tied them back to back, and threw them overboard into the sea, without distinction as to their condition, for they were only Irish." "In this cruel manner very many poor men perished daily. Of all of which the King knew nothing, and said nothing, because his Majesty could not complain of it without being concerned in it, in favor of the rebels in Ireland."

Again :—

"The Marquis of Ormonde sent Captain Anthony Willoughby, with 150 men, who had formerly served in the fort at Galway, from thence to Bristol, to look after and follow a party of men who were in the service of the King, and had actually fought for him. The ship in which they sailed was taken by Capt. Swanley, who threw seventy of the soldiers, who were Irish, overboard, although these same soldiers had faithfully served his Majesty against the rebels during all the time of the war."

You will ask me, "Was that Captain punished for the murder?" Here is the punishment he got. In June, 1644, we read in the Journal of the English House of Commons, that Capt. Swanley was called into the House, and had thanks given to him for his good service, and a chain of gold, equal in value to £200; and that Captain Smith also had another of £100 in value given him.

"Sir Richard Grenville was very much esteemed by the Earl of Leicester, who was Lord Lieutenant for Ireland;— and more still by the Parliament, for the signal acts of cruelty he committed on the Irish; hanging old men who were bedridden, because they would not discover where their money was hidden; and old women, some of them of quality, after he had plundered them, and found less than he expected."

In a word, they committed atrocities which I am ashamed and afraid to mention. The soldiers tossed the infants taken from their dead mothers' bosoms on their bayonets Sir Charles Coote saw one of his soldiers playing with a child, throwing it into the air, and then spitting it upon his bayonet as it fell; and he laughed and said "he enjoyed such frolic"! They brought children into the world before their time by the Cæsarean operation of the sword; and the children thus brought forth in misery from out the wombs of their dead mothers, they immolated and sacrificed in the most cruel and terrible manner. I am afraid,—I say, again, I am afraid of your blood and mine, to tell you the one-tenth, aye, the one-hundredth part of the cruelties that those terrible men put upon our people.

Now, I ask you to contrast this with the manner in which the Irish troops and the Irish people behaved. Lord Castlehaven says:

"I took Naas, and I found in it a garrison of English soldiers, seven hundred strong; and I saved the life of every man amongst them, and made them a present to General Oliver Cromwell, with the request that, in like circumstances, he would do the same by me."

But it was only a few days later the town of Gouran capitulated. Cromwell promised quarter; but as soon as he entered, he took the governor of the town, and all the officers of the army, and put them all to death.

"Sir Wm. St. Leger, going down into Munster, slaughtered every man, woman, and child he met on his march; and, among others, was a man named Philip Ryan, who was the principal farmer of the place, whom he put to death without the slightest hesitation. But some of Philip Ryan's friends, brothers, and relatives, retaliated somewhat on the

English; and there was a fear that the Catholic people would massacre all the Protestant inhabitants of the place."

Now, mark what follows:—

"All the rest of the English"—(this is in Carte's "Life of Ormonde")—"all the rest of the English were saved by the inhabitants of that place; their houses and all their goods, which they confided to them, were safely returned. Doctor Samuel Pullen, the Protestant Chancellor of Cashel, and the Dean of Clonfert, with his wife and children, were preserved by Father James Saul, a Jesuit. Several other Romish priests distinguished themselves on this occasion by their endeavors to save the English. One Father Joseph Everard and Father Redmond English, both of them Franciscan Friars, hid some of them in their chapel, and actually under the very altar. The English who were thus preserved were, according to their desires, safely conducted into the county Cork by a guard of the Irish inhabitants of Cashel."

Now, my friends, the war went on, from 1641 to 1649, with varying success. Cardinal Rinuccini was sent over by the Pope to preside over the Supreme Council of the Confederation of Kilkenny, and about the same time news came to Ireland that gladdened the nation's heart, namely, that the illustrious Owen Roe O'Neill had landed on the coast of Ulster. This man was one of the most distinguished officers in the Spanish service at a time when the Spanish infantry were acknowledged to be the finest troops in the world. He landed in Ireland, he organized an army, drilled them, and armed them, however imperfectly. But he was a host in himself; and, in the second year after his arrival, he drew up his army to meet General Monroe, and his English forces, at the ford of Benburb, on the Blackwater. The battle began in the morning, and raged throughout the early hours of the day; and, before the evening sun had set, England's main and best army was flying in confusion, and thousands of her best soldiers were stretched upon the field and choked the ford of Benburb; while the Irish soldier stood triumphant upon the field which his genius and his valor had won.

Partly through the treachery of Ormonde and Preston; partly and mainly through the English lords who were coquetting with the English Government, the Confederation began to experience some of its most disastrous defeats; and Ireland's cause was already broken, and almost lost, when, in the year 1649, Oliver Cromwell arrived in Ireland. Mr. Froude says, and truly, that he "did not come to make war with rose-water," but with the thick warm blood of the Irish people. And Mr. Froude prefaces the introduction of Oliver Cromwell in Ireland by telling us that the Lord-General was a great friend of Ireland, that he was a liberal-minded man, and that he interfered with no man's liberty of conscience. And he adds that,—"If Cromwell's policy were carried out, in all probability I would not be here speaking to you of our difficulties with Ireland to-day." He adds, moreover, that "Cromwell had formed a design for the pacification of Ireland, which would have made future trouble there impossible." What was this design? Lord Macaulay tells us what this design was. Cromwell's avowed purpose was to end all difficulties in Ireland,—whether they arose from the land question or from the religious question,—by putting a total and entire end to the Irish race; by extirpating them off the face of the earth. This was an admirable policy, my friends, in order to pacify Ireland and create peace: for the best way and the simplest way to keep any man quiet is to cut his throat. The dead do not speak; the dead do not move; the dead do not trouble any one. Cromwell came to destroy the Irish race, and the Irish Catholic faith of the people, and so put an end at once to all claims for land, and to all disturbances arising out of religious persecution. But,

I ask this learned gentleman, does he imagine that the people of America are either so ignorant or so wicked as to accept the monstrous proposition that a man who came into Ireland with such an avowed purpose as this can be declared a friend of the real interests of the Irish people? Does he imagine that there is no intelligence in America, that there is no manhood in America, that there is no love of freedom in America, no love of religion and of life in America? And the man must be an enemy of freedom, of religion, and of life itself before such a man can sympathize with the blood-stained Oliver Cromwell. These words of the historian, I regret to say, sound like bitter irony and mockery in the ears of the people whose fathers Cromwell came to destroy. But he says the Lord Protector did not interfere with any man's conscience. The Irish demanded liberty of conscience. " I interfere with no man's conscience," said Cromwell: " but if, by liberty of conscience, you, Catholics, mean having priests and the Mass, I tell you you cannot have this; and you never will have it, as long as the Parliament of England has power to prevent it." I now ask you, my friends, what these words mean? To grant the Catholics liberty of conscience, their conscience telling them that their first and greatest duty is to hear the Mass; to grant them liberty of conscience, and then deny them priests to say the Mass: assuredly it is a contradiction in words: it is an insult to the intelligence, to propound so extravagant a proposition! " Oh! but," Mr. Froude says, " you must go easy. Of course, I acknowledge that the Mass is a beautiful rite, ancient and beautiful; but you must remember that, in Cromwell's mind, the Mass meant the system that was shedding blood all over Europe; the system of the Church that never knew mercy, that slaughtered the Protestants everywhere; and therefore he was resolved to have none of it." Ah! my friends, if the Mass were the symbol of slaughter,

Oliver Cromwell would have had more sympathy with the Mass.

And so the historian seeks to justify cruelty in Ireland against the Catholics, by alleging cruelty on the part of Catholics, against their Protestant fellow-subjects in other lands. Now, these words the historian has repeated, over and over again, in many of his writings, and at other times, and in other places; and I may as well at once put an end to this. Mr. Froude says: "I hold the Catholic Church accountable for all the blood that the Duke of Alva shed in the Netherlands;" and I say to Mr. Froude I deny it. Alva fought in the Netherlands against the subjects that rebelled against Spain. Alva fought in the Netherlands against a people the first principle of whose new religion seemed to be an uprising against the authority of the State. With Alva or his state questions the Catholic Church had nothing to do; and if Alva shed the blood of rebels, and if those who rebelled happened to be Protestants, that is no reason to father the shedding of that blood upon the Catholic Church. Mr. Froude says that the Catholic Church is responsible for the blood that was shed in the massacre of St. Bartholomew's Day, by Mary de Medicis, in France. I deny it. The woman that gave that order had no sympathy with the Catholic Church. It was altogether a State measure. She saw France divided into factions; and she endeavored, by court intrigue and villainy of her own—for a most villainous woman she was—she endeavored to stifle opposition in the blood of the people. Tidings were sent to Rome that the King's life was in danger, and that that life had been preserved by Heaven; and Rome sang a Te Deum for the safety of the King, and not for the blood of the Huguenots. Amongst the Huguenots there were Catholics that were slain, because they were of the opposite faction; and that alone proves that the Catholic Church was not answerable for the shedding of such blood.

But, on the other hand, the blood that was shed in Ireland was shed exclusively on account of religion, at this particular time; for when, in 1643, Charles I. made a treaty for a cessation of hostilities with the Confederation of Kilkenny, the English Parliament, as soon as they heard that the King had ceased hostilities for a time with the Irish Catholics, at once intervened, and said the war must go on. They said: "We will not allow hostilities to cease; we must root out these Irish Papists, or else we shall incur danger to the Protestant religion." I regret to say, my Protestant friends, that the men of 1643, the members of the Puritan Houses of Parliament in England, have fastened upon that form of religion which you profess the formal argument and reason why Irish blood should flow in torrents,—lest the Protestant religion might suffer! In these days of ours, when we are endeavoring to put away all sectarian bigotry, we deplore the faults committed by our fathers on both sides. Mr. Froude deplores the blood that was shed as much as I do; but, my friends, it is a historical question, arising upon historic facts and evidence; and I am bound to appeal to history as well as my learned antagonist, and to discriminate and put back the word which he puts out, namely, that toleration is the genius of Protestantism. He asserts—and it is an astounding assertion—in this, his third lecture, that religious persecution was hostile to the genius of Protestantism. Nay, he goes further. Speaking of the Mass, he says, that "the Catholic Church has learned to borrow one beautiful gem from the crown of her adversary. She has learned to respect the consciences of others." I wish that the learned gentleman's statements could be more approved by history. Oh! much I desire that, in saying those words, he had spoken historic truths! No doubt he believes what he says; but I ask him, and I ask every Protestant here, at what time, in what age, or in what land has Protestantism ever been in the ascendant without persecuting the Catholics who were around them? It is not in bitterness I say it, but it is simply as a historic truth. I cannot find any record of history,—any time during these ages, up to a few years ago,—any time when the Protestants in England, in Ireland, in Sweden, in Germany, or anywhere else gave the slightest toleration, or even permission to live, where they could take it from their Catholic fellow-subjects. Even to-day where is the strongest spirit of religious persecution exhibited? Is it not in Protestant Sweden? Is it not in Protestant Denmark? And who to-day are persecuting? I ask you is it Catholics? No, but Protestant Bismarck, in Germany. All this I say with regret. I am not only a Catholic, but a priest; not only a priest, but a monk; not only a monk, but a Dominican monk; and, from out the depths of my soul, I repel and repudiate the principle of religious persecution in any cause, or in any age, or in any land.

Oliver Cromwell, the apostle of blessings to Ireland! landed in 1649, and went to work. He besieged Drogheda, which was defended by Sir Arthur Aston and a brave garrison. He made a breach in the walls; and when the garrison found that their position was no longer tenable, they asked, in the military language of the day, if they would be spared,—if quarter would be given them. And quarter was promised if all the men would cease fighting and lay down their arms. They did so; and the promise was observed until the town was taken. When the town was in his hands, Oliver Cromwell gave orders to his army for the indiscriminate massacre of the garrison, and every man, woman, and child in that large city. The people, when they saw the soldiers slain around them,—when they saw so many killed on every side,—when they saw the streets of Drogheda flowing with blood for five days,—fled to the number of one thousand aged men, women, and children, and took refuge in the great church of St. Peter, in Drogheda. Oliver Cromwell drew his soldiers around that church, and out of that church he never allowed one of those thousand innocent people to escape alive. He then proceeded to Wexford, where a certain commander named Stafford admitted him into the city; and he massacred the people there again. Three hundred of the women of Wexford, with their little children, gathered round the great market-cross in the public square of the city. They thought in their hearts that all terrible as Cromwell was, he would respect the sign of man's redemption and spare those who were under the arms of the Cross. Oh! how vain the thought! Three hundred poor defenceless women were there, screaming for mercy, under the Cross of Jesus Christ; and Cromwell and his barbarous demons around them, destroying them, so as not to let one of these innocents escape; until they were ankle deep in the blood of the women of Wexford!

Cromwell retired from Ireland after having glutted himself with the blood of the people. He retired from Ireland; but he wound up the war by taking 80,000,—some say 100,000,—of the men of Ireland, and driving them down to the southern ports of Munster, where he shipped them—80,000 at the lowest calculation—he shipped them to the sugar plantations of the Barbadoes, there to work as slaves; and in six years time, such was the treatment they received, that, out of eighty thousand, there were only twenty men left. He collected six thousand Irish boys, fair and beautiful stripling youths; and he put them into ships and sent them off also to the Barbadoes, there to languish and die before ever they came to the fulness of their age and manhood. Oh! great God! is this the man that has an apologist in the learned, the frank, the generous and gentlemanly historian, who comes in oily words to tell the American people that Cromwell was one of the bravest men that ever lived, and one of the best friends that Ireland ever had!

Now, we must pass on. Oliver Cromwell died in 1658. Here is a most singular assertion of Mr. Froude, who tells us that, much as he regrets all the blood that was shed, and all the terrible vengeance that was poured out, still it resulted in great good to Ireland; and the good consisted in this: —The Parliament, after Cromwell's victories, found themselves masters of Ireland, and the Irish people lying in blood and in ruin before them. What was their next move? Their next move was to pass a law driving all the people of Ireland who owned any portion of the land,—all the Irish land-owners,—and all the Catholics,—out of Ulster, Munster, and Leinster; and, on the 1st of May, 1654, all the inhabitants of Ireland were driven across the Shannon into Connaught. The coarse phrase used by the Lord Protector, on this occasion, was that they were to "go to hell, or to Connaught"! The solemnity of the historic occasion which brings us together will not permit me to make any remark upon such a phrase as this. However, the Irish did not choose to go to hell, but they were obliged to go to Connaught. . . . . Lest, however, that any relief might come to them by sea,—lest they might ever enjoy the sight of the fair provinces and fair lands that were once their own,—the English Parliament made a law that no Irishman, banished into Connaught, was to come within four miles of the river Shannon, on one side, or four miles of the sea on the other side. There was a cordon of English soldiery and English forts drawn around them; and there they were to live, in the bogs, in the fastnesses, and in the wild wastes of the most desolate country in Ireland; and there they were doomed to expire by cold, by famine, and by every form of suffering that their Heavenly Father might permit to fall upon them.

Then we read that numbers of Englishmen came over;—and I don't blame them;—for the fair plains of Munster were there waiting for them. The splendid vales of Leinster were there, with their green bosoms waiting for the hand that would put in the ploughshare or the spade into the bountiful earth;—waiting for an owner. So the English came from every direction to get this fair land of Ireland,—the fairest under heaven. Cromwell settled down his troopers there,—those rough, Puritan soldiers, who came to Ireland with the Bible in one hand and the sword in the other. They took possession of the country; and, according to Mr. Froude, here is the benefit that resulted from Cromwell's transplantation,—that, "in fifteen years, they changed Ireland into a garden"! All the bogs were drained!—all the fields were fenced in! and all the meadows were mowed! all the fallow fields were ploughed; and the country was smiling in peace! There never was anything so fine seen in Ireland, as the state of things brought about by Cromwell! More than that; the poor Irish peasantry, that were harassed and plundered by the priests, and bishops, and chieftains, now enjoyed peace and quiet and comfort as the *servants* of the new English owners and possessors of the soil! Well! I wish, for Ireland's sake, that this picture were true. I would have no objection to see one-half of Ireland in the hands, for a time, of the English settlers, if the other half was possessed by the Irish, and they lived there happy and comfortable in their homes. But these fifteen years, of which Mr. Froude speaks, must have begun in 1653; because it was only in September of that year that the English Parliument declared the war over in Ireland. Up to that time there was war and bloodshed. Now there was peace; but what kind of peace? Oh, my friends, they made a solitude, —they made a desert; and Mr. Froude calls it peace! He calls it peace; and it was a peaceful desert!

Oliver Cromwell died in 1658: and now I want to read for you the state of Ireland—the "garden"—Mr. Froude's "garden,"—at that time:—

"Ireland, in the language of Scripture, now lay void as a wilderness. Five-sixths of her people had perished. Men, women, and children were found daily perishing in the ditches—starved. The bodies of many wandering orphans, whose fathers had embarked for Spain, and whose mothers had died of famine, were preyed upon by the wolves."

In the years 1652 and '53, a terrible famine had swept over the whole country; so that a man might travel twenty or thirty miles and not see a living creature. Man, beast, and bird, were all dead, or had quitted those desolate places. The troopers would tell stories of places where they saw a smoke,—it was so rare to see either fire or smoke by day or by night. In two or three cabins where the soldiers went, they found none but aged men, women, and children, who, in the words of the Prophet, had "become like a bottle in the smoke—their skins black like an oven, because of the terrible famine." They were seen to eat the filthy carrion out of the ditches,—black and rotten,—so great was their hunger. It was even said that they took the corpses out of the graves. A party of horsemen, out hunting "Tories," on a dark night, descried a light, and thought it was a fire which the Tories had made. They used to make fires in those waste places, to cook their food and warm themselves. Drawing near, they saw that it was a ruined cabin. Surrounding it on all sides, some of them alighted and peeped in at the window; and there they saw a great fire of wood, and, sitting around it, was a company of miserable old women and children; and there, between them and the fire, a corpse lay broiling, which, as the fire roasted it, they cut and ate!

The year before Cromwell died, in 1657, we find a member of the Irish Parliament, Major Morgan, declaring that the whole land of Ireland was in ruins. "For, besides the cost," he says, "of rebuilding the churches and court-houses, and the market-houses,—they were under very heavy charges for public rewards, paid for the destruction of three beasts." What do you think the three "beasts" were? The wolf, the priest, and the Tory! Now let me explain the state of this "garden" to you. During those fifteen years, of which Mr. Froude speaks so flatteringly, there was actually a grant of land issued, within nine miles of the city of Dublin, on the north side,—that is to say, on the most cultivated side,—to a man—with an abatement of one hundred pounds a year in his rent,—provided he would engage to kill the wolves. The wolves increased in Ireland from the desolate state of the country. They fed upon the carcasses of men and beasts; and they increased in Ireland, so that, actually, they came famished up to the very gates of Dublin, and had to be driven away! Does this look like a "garden"? Is this the kingdom of peace, plenty, and happiness, where the Irish peasant was, at length, getting fat in comfort; where everything was peace and serenity;— where the bogs were all drained, and the fields were so carefully fenced in, by the dear Cromwellians that had got possession of the land? When the relics of the Irish army were embarking for Spain, some of the Irish officers had their dogs,—magnificent Irish wolf-dogs,—which they wanted to take with them; but they were stopped; and the dogs were taken from them, for the purpose of hunting the wolves that infested the country. That is my first answer to Mr. Froude's assertion that Ireland was a "garden."

The second "beast" mentioned by Major Morgan, in the Irish House of Commons, was the priest. He was to be hunted down like the wolf. There were five pounds set upon the head of a dog-wolf, and there were five pounds set upon the head of a priest; and ten pounds upon the head of a Bishop or a Jesuit. Mr. Froude says that these severe laws were not put into execution. He tells us that, while Parliament passed these laws, they privately instructed the magistrates that they were not to execute them. Not they!—so merciful, so tolerant is the genius of Mr. Froude's Protestantism! We have, however, the terrible fact before us, that Parliament after Parliament made law after law, commanding the magistrates, under heavy fines,—under heavy penalties of fine and forfeiture,—to execute these laws. We find the country filled with informers; we find priest-hunting actually reduced to a profession in Ireland; and we find, strange enough, Portuguese Jews, coming all the way from Portugal, in order to hunt priests in Ireland, so profitable was the occupation. In 1698, under William the Third, there were in Ireland 495 regular and 872 secular priests; and in that very year, out of 495 friars, 424 were shipped off from Ireland into banishment, into slavery; and, of the 800 and odd secular priests that remained in the land, not one of them would be allowed to say Mass, in public or private, until he first took the Oath of Abjuration, and renounced the See of Rome; in other words, unless he became a Protestant. It is all very well for my learned friend to tell us that the laws were not put into execution. But what is the meaning of such entries as these?—

"Five pounds on the certificate of Thomas Stanley."— (This was in the year 1657, the year the severe laws were *not* enforced!)—"To Thomas Gregson, Evan Powell, and

Samuel Alley, being three soldiers in Colonel Abbott's horse dragoons,—for arresting a Popish priest by the name of Donough Hagerty, taken and now secured in the county jail at Clonmel; and the money" (it says) "is to be equally divided between them!"

"To Arthur Spollen, Robert Pierce, and John Bruen, five pounds, to be divided equally between them, for their good service performed in apprehending and bringing before the Right Honorable Lord Chief Justice Pepys, on the 21st of January, one Popish priest named Edwin Duhy."

"To Lieutenant Edwin Wood, on the certificate of Wm. St. George, Esq., Justice of the Peace of the county of Cavan, twenty-five pounds, for five priests and friars apprehended by him, namely, Thomas McGeoghegan, Turlough McGowan, Hugh McGowan, Terence Fitzsimmons, and another, who, on examination, confessed themselves to be priests and friars."

"To Sergeant Humphrey Gibbs," (a nice name,) "and to Corporal Thomas Hill, of Colonel Lee's company, ten pounds, for apprehending two Popish priests; namely, Maurice Prendergast and Edward Fahy, who were sentenced to the jail of Wexford, and, afterwards, being adjudged accordingly, were transported to foreign parts."

The third "beast" was the "Tory," which means, that, in these terrible years, several of the Irish gentlemen, and Irish people, who were ordered to transplant themselves into Connaught, not finding there the means of living, remained in the desolate countries of Leinster and Munster; and there, goaded to desperation, formed themselves into wild bands of outlaws, robbing the cattle of the Cromwellian settlers; descending upon them, with fire and sword; achieving, in their own way, "the wild justice of revenge." If Ireland was the "garden" that Mr. Froude describes it to be, how comes it to pass that no Cromwellian settler, throughout the length and breadth of the land, dared to take a piece of land unless there was a garrison of soldiers within his immediate neighborhood? Nay, even under the very eyes of the garrison of Timolin, in Meath, the "Tories" came down, and robbed, plundered, set fire to, and destroyed the homesteads of certain English Cromwellian settlers; for which all the people of the neighborhood, of Irish names and of Irish parentage, were at once taken and banished out of the country. In a word, the outlaws who, thirty years afterward, appeared as "Rapparees,"—who are described to us in such fearful terms, by the English historians,—continued to infest and desolate the country; and we find accounts of them in the State papers, and other papers, down to the latter end of the reign of George III. And this was the "garden"! This was the land of peace, of comfort, and of plenty!

Now, my friends, came the Restoration. In 1659, Charles II. was restored to the throne of England. Well, the Irish had been fighting for his father; they had bled, and suffered, fighting against his enemies; and they were now banished into Connaught. They naturally expected that, when the rightful heir to the throne would come into his rights, they would be recalled and put into their estates. They might have expected more. They might have expected to be rewarded by honors, titles, and wealth. But what is the fact? The fact is that Charles II., at the Restoration, left nearly the whole of Ireland in the hands of the Cromwellian settlers; and, by the "Act of Settlement and Explanation," secured them in these estates, leaving the property and the wealth of the country to the men who had brought his father to the scaffold; and leaving in beggary, destitution, and ruin, the brave and loyal men who had fought for him and his house. At first, indeed, there was a "Court of Claims" opened; for, remember, that, in England, no sooner had Charles come to the throne, than all the Cromwellian settlers who had taken the property of the English Royalists were at once put out, and the English lords and gentlemen got back their properties and estates. But not so in Ireland. The "Court of Claims" was opened in the first year of the reign of Charles. As soon as it was perceived that the Irish Catholics began to claim their property, the Government shut up the Court at once. Three thousand of these claims remained unheard. As Leland says:—

"The people of Ireland were denied the justice which is given to the commonest criminal—the justice of having a fair and impartial hearing."

Nugent, afterwards Lord Riverston, writes at this time:—

"There are in Ireland to-day, five thousand men who never were outlawed, who yet have been put out of their estates; and now by law they never can recover their estates again."

More than this. No sooner was Charles seated on the throne, than the English and Irish Parliaments began to afflict and grind the already down-trodden people of Ireland by legislation the most infamous that can be imagined. In 1673, the English Parliament furiously demanded that the King should expel all the Catholic Bishops and priests from Ireland, and prohibit the Papists from dwelling there without a license. In order to encourage the Protestant "planters," Charles,—against his conscience, and against his royal gratitude,—obeyed them. Law after law was passed in that and the succeeding years, abolishing and destroying, as far as they could, every vestige of the Catholic religion in Ireland. Mr. Froude here again makes the customary assertion, that, "when the Restoration came, the Catholic religion and the Catholic priests came back with it." He tells us that the Catholic Archbishop of Dublin "was received in state at the Castle." What are the facts? The Primate, Edmund O'Reilly, was banished. Peter Talbot, the Archbishop of Dublin,—although, being in a dying state, he had got leave, but a short time before, to return to Ireland, that he might die in the land of his birth,—was arrested in Maynooth, near Dublin, and shut up in a dungeon; and there he died a miserable death of martyrdom. We find, at this very time, a reward of ten pounds offered for any one who should discover an officer of the army attending at Mass; five pounds for a trooper; and four shillings for any private soldier, who was discovered to have heard Mass. Oliver Plunkett, the holy Primate of Armagh, was seized by Lord Ormonde, in 1679. They knew that they could not convict him of any lawlessness or treason in Ireland; and they brought him over to London, packed an English jury to try him; and they murdered him at Tyburn, in this year.

It is true that these penal laws were relaxed for some years before the death of Charles II. That event took place in 1685; and James II. came to the throne. Three years afterwards, William of Orange landed to dispute with him the title to the crown of England. Now, that James II. was the lawful King of England, no man will deny. William was married to Mary, the daughter of James; and William came to England with an army of 15,000 men at his back, pretending that he came only to inquire about the birth of the Prince of Wales, who was the lawful heir to the crown. Well, James, as soon as William arrived with his army, fled to France. Mr. Froude tells us that he abdicated when he fled to France. I deny that James II. abdicated. Mr. Froude has no authority to say it. He only retired, for a time, from the face of his enemy. He called upon his subjects, both in England and Ireland, to stand to their King like loyal men. The English betrayed him; the Irish,—fools as they were,—rose up again for a Stuart King, and declared they were loyal men, and they would stand by their monarch.

James came to Ireland in 1689; and he summoned a Parliament, of which Mr. Froude speaks in his lecture. He speaks of that Parliament as a persecuting Parliament. He says that "they attainted every single Protestant proprietor in Ireland, by name;" and that they did this, "lest any one should escape out of their net." Now, what are the facts of that Parliament of 1689? The very first thing that they declared, although they had suffered more than any other people from religious persecution,—the very first law they made was that there should be no more religious persecution in Ireland, and that no man, from that day forward, should suffer for his conscience or his faith. It is perfectly true that they passed a bill of attainder; but they passed that bill not against Protestants but against every man of the land that was in arms against King James, whom they recognized as their king;—every man who refused to obey him and his government. I ask you, in doing that, did they not do their duty? Did they not do precisely what is always done in times of rebellion? England was in rebellion against James. James was the lawful king. James was in Ireland; and the Irish Parliament, with James at their head, declared that every man who was in arms against him was to be outlawed. Against these outlaws the Bill of Attainder was passed,—this "persecuting measure" of which Mr. Froude speaks when he mentions this Parliament.

William came to Ireland, and opened the campaign in 1690. Mr. Froude says, in his description of him, that William brought with him only a small army, badly equipped, badly drilled; but that the Irish were never so strong, never so well drilled, or so perfectly equipped as they were at the time. Now here are the numbers as given by history:—William's army consisted, at first, of 46,000 veteran soldiers, well clad, well fed, and perfectly drilled and equipped. The Irish army of James numbered 23,000 imperfectly disciplined troops, wanting in nearly everything necessary for a campaign. This we have on the evidence of the Duke of Berwick, who was serving in the army at the time. At the battle of the Boyne, Mr. Froude says that "the Irish did not make even a respectable stand"! And I regret,—I bitterly regret,—that the learned gentleman should, himself, have so far forgotten what was due to himself, as to have ventured, even in the faintest whisper, to impute a want of courage to the soldiers of Ireland. At the battle of the Boyne, James and his army were on the south bank of the river. William with his army advanced down from the north. The muster roll of William's army, on that morning, shows the figure of 51,000 men. The army of James had not increased from the original 23,000. William was a lion-hearted and brave soldier. James, I am sorry to say, had forgotten the tradition of that ancient courage and gallantry which belonged to him as Duke of York, when he was Lord High Admiral of England. On one side was "an army led by a lion;" on the other was "an army led by a stag." The Irish have fixed upon James an opprobrious name, in the Irish language, which on an occasion like this I will not repeat.

On the morning of the battle of the Boyne, William detached 10,000 men, who went up the stream some miles, to ford it near the Hill of Slane. James could scarcely be prevailed upon to send one or two regiments of horse to oppose these 10,000 men, with their artillery, headed by the Duke of Schomberg. The evening before the battle, James sent away six guns towards Dublin. How many do you think remained? Only six pieces of artillery remained with the Irish on that day! How many were opposed to them? We have it on historic record, that William brought into the field on that day at the Boyne, fifty heavy pieces of artillery and four mortars. Then he advanced and crossed the river. These Irish troops, of whom Mr. Froude says that "they did not make even a respectable stand," were outgeneralled that day. They had at their head a timorous king,—a king who had already sent away his artillery and his baggage; who had drawn around his person, two miles away, all the best disciplined of the French soldiers; and these raw levies of young Irishmen were opposed to 51,000 of the bravest men of Europe. Well, William crossed the Boyne, and the Duke of Berwick is my authority for stating this. He says:—

"With admirable courage and gallantry, the Irish troops charged the English ten times after they had crossed the river."

Ten times did these poor young fellows, with no General, and scarcely an officer, charge upon the English with a dash as brave as that with which O'Brien, Lord Clare, swept down upon them at Fontenoy. Ten distinct times did they dash against the terrible lines of William's veterans. And when they retreated, they retreated like an army, in perfect order, at the command of their superior officers.

Now came the siege of Athlone. In that same year, 1690, the English army advanced, on the line of the Shannon, against Athlone. And here, Mr. Froude says, that, "At Athlone the Irish deserted posts which they easily might have made impregnable." Now, what are the facts? The town of Athlone stands on the river Shannon, partly on one bank and partly on the other, connected by a stone bridge. The portion of the town that is on the Leinster side is called the "English town;" that upon the Connaught side is called the "Irish town." When the English army advanced against the town of Athlone, in the first siege, Colonel Richard Grace, who held the town, beat back the English,—many times,—aye, eight times more than his number,—with so much bravery, that the whole army of England was obliged to retire from before Athlone, and give up the siege.

Then, William advanced upon Limerick. He brought with him the whole strength of his army. He had, when he went to Limerick, 26,000 men in regular line of battle. In the town of Limerick there was an army of James's made up partly of Irish, under the immortal Sarsfield, and partly of French, under a General named Lazun. When the great English army, with its King, was approaching the city, the French General, seeing it so defenceless, actually left the town with his troops, swearing that "the town could be taken with roasted apples." Sarsfield, with the Irish, remained. William advanced before the town and battered it with his cannon, until he made a breach thirty-six feet wide; and then he assaulted it with 12,000 of his picked men. They actually entered the town, and were beaten out of the walls of Limerick;—beaten back over the broken interior walls,—beaten so that, whilst even the women of Limerick entered into the contest, fighting side by side with the men,—after three hours and a half of fighting, William, Prince of Orange, withdrew from the assault, leaving 2,000 men and 155 officers in the breach of Limerick. The next day King William sent a message to the city, asking them for leave to bury his dead; and the answer he got was: "Begone! we will give you no leave. Take yourself away; and we will bury your dead!"

In the second siege of Athlone, in the following year, the English town was occupied by Colonel Fitzgerald. General St. Ruth, with the Irish army, lay two miles away, on the other side of the Shannon. The English town was assailed by William's General, Ginckle, with 8,000 men against the 400 who defended it. Fitzgerald and his Irish troops remained, and stopped the whole English army, and fought until, out of the 400 men, not 200 were left, before they crossed the bridge and gave up that portion of the town. Before they crossed the bridge they broke one of the arches; and then crossing over they joined the garrison in the Irish town. The English army with all their artillery battered the Irish town until they did not leave a house standing there, or a stone upon a stone. Before they forced the Irish troops to retire, the English attempted to plank over the broken arch of the bridge. They had their guns ranged to sweep it. Eleven Irish soldiers came out to tear up the planks, and cast them into the river; and such was the sweeping fire of the English artillery, that out of the eleven, only two of the poor fellows survived. Again the English advanced to the attack; and again eleven other Irish sergeants of the various regiments came out in the face of the whole English army, and in the face of all their artillery, and deliberately destroyed the wooden bridge they were making over the Shannon. And when the town was taken, at last, it was a mere heap of ruins. It was taken not through any want of bravery on the part of the Irish soldiers, but through the folly and obstinacy of the French General, St. Ruth, who refused to succor them or stand by them.

Of Aughrim I will not speak; because Mr. Froude himself acknowledges that, at Aughrim, the Irish soldiers fought bravely. And because I have for this English gentleman, really and truly, a sincere regard and esteem, I would ask him to do what I myself would do if I were in his position: I would ask him to reconsider the word by which he seems to imply a taint of cowardice on Irishmen, at home and abroad, and, in the name of God, to take that word back.

In 1691, the second siege of Limerick began; and so gallant was the resistance, so brave the defence, that William of Orange, who was a brave man,—and if left to himself would have been a tolerant and mild man,—offered terms. He bore no ill-will to the Irish, because he was a stranger to them, and only came to Ireland simply as a warrior in the service of war; he saw in the Irish a high-spirited and brave people; and he was obliged to come to terms. In the articles of capitulation signed for the Irish, they received honorable terms from the royalty of England. By those very articles, their rights, as citizens and as Catholics, to every liberty of conscience and of religion were recognized. Scarcely was the treaty of Limerick signed by the Lords Justices, than a French fleet entered the Shannon,—a French fleet of eighteen ships of the line, with twenty transports, bringing 3,000 men, 200 officers, and above all, 10,000 stand of arms, with clothing and provisions. They came; but they came too late for Sarsfield and for Ireland. Sarsfield had surrendered. He might have taken back that word; he might have broken these articles, when he found the French forces and fleet at his back. But Sarsfield, to his glory, was an Irishman;—and he was far too honorable a man to violate the treaty of Limerick which he had signed with his honorable hand. Would to God that the honor of Sarsfield had also been in the hearts of the other men, who, on the part of England, signed that treaty! But, no! The Lords Justices went back to Dublin, with the treaty signed, with the honor of the royalty of England committed to it; and the next Sunday after they arrived in Dublin, they went to Christ Church Cathedral to perform their devotions; and the sermon was preached by a Dr. Dopping, the Lord Bishop of Meath. Now, I am more or less a professional preacher,—not so much a lecturer as a preacher,—and I have a certain feeling of *esprit du corps*—I have the feeling for preachers that every man has for his own profession. I like to see them uphold the honor of their profession.— What do you think was the sermon that Dr. Dopping preached. He preached,—I regret to say and I am ashamed to say (it is true he was a Protestant Bishop)—but still he preached *on the sin and the sinfulness of keeping your oath or faith with a Papist.*

Immediately after the articles of Limerick were signed,— we have the testimony of Harris, the historian of William the Third. He says:

"Justices of the Peace, and Sheriffs, and other Magistrates, presuming on their power in the country, did, in an illegal manner, dispossess several of their Majesties' subjects not only of their very goods and chattels, but of their lands and tenements, to the great disturbance of the peace, the subversion of the law, and the reproach of their Majesties' Government."

We find those Lords Justices themselves, in a letter of the 19th November, six weeks after the treaty was signed,— complaining that their lordships had received complaints from all parts of Ireland of the ill-treatment of the people who had submitted to their Majesties' protection, and were included in the articles of that treaty. And the consequence was that, actually, the men who refused to embark with Sarsfield, to go to Spain and France, came in thousands to beg of the English Lords Justices to give them leave, to let them go and join Sarsfield in exile,—to let them go to fight the battles of France, Spain, and Austria,—because there was no room in Ireland for a Catholic and an Irishman, nor even for an honest man.

Now began a time the most lamentable for Ireland. William himself was anxious to keep his royal word, and would have kept it, if they had allowed him. But the same pressure was put upon him as was brought to bear on Charles I. The Irish Protestant faction would not allow a Catholic to live in the land. The English Parliament would not allow a Catholic to breathe in the land. William was coerced to comply with their requests; and a series of the most terrible laws that can be imagined were passed in the very teeth of the articles that were signed at Limerick. Three years after the siege of Limerick, the two Parliaments were urged by the grievances of the Protestants of Ireland. The poor fellows complained "that the Catholics would not give them leave to live"! They poured in their petitions to the House of Commons. We find a petition from the Protestant Mayor and Aldermen of Limerick, complaining, in their own words, that they were "greatly damaged in their trade by the great number of Papists residing there;" and praying to be relieved of them. We find the "coal-porters" of Dublin sending in a petition to Parliament, and it was as follows:— "Petition of one Edward Spragg" (another nice name) "and others, in behalf of themselves and other Protestant porters, in and about the city of Dublin,"—complaining that one Darby Ryan, a Papist, actually employed porters of his own religion. And the petition was entertained by the Irish House of Commons, and was sent to the "Committee on Grievances." Listen to the words and description by the historian, John Mitchel, of this time :—

"The Parliament met, and they passed an Act for the better securing of the Government against the Papists; and the first act of that Parliament was that no Catholic in Ireland was to be allowed to have a gun, pistol, or sword, or any kind of weapon of offence or defence. The consequence of disobeying this law was fine and imprisonment, at the discretion of the court, or else the pillory or whipping."

Now here are the reflections of Mr. Mitchel:—

"It is impossible to describe the minute and curious tyranny to which this statute gave rise in every parish of the island; especially in districts where there was an armed Yeomanry, exclusively Protestant. It fared ill with any Catholic who, for any reason, fell under the displeasure of his formidable neighbors. Any pretext was sufficient to point him out for suspicion. Any neighboring magistrate might visit him, at any hour of the night, and search his bed for arms. No

Papist was safe from suspicion who had any money to pay in fines; and woe to the Papist who had a handsome daughter!"

The second act that they passed was designed to brutalize the Irish Catholic people, by ignorance. They made a law that no Catholic was to teach; no Catholic was to send his son to a Catholic school, or to a Catholic teacher. No Catholic child was to be sent out of Ireland to receive a Catholic education elsewhere; and if any parent or guardian were found sending money, clothing, or anything else to a Catholic child, in a Catholic school, there was forfeiture, imprisonment, or a fine; and for a second offence he was treated as guilty of high treason and was liable to be put to death for doing it.

The third act they passed was:—

"That all Popish Archbishops, Bishops, Vicars-General, Deans, Jesuits, Monks, Friars, and all other regular Popish clergy, and all Papists exercising any ecclesiastical jurisdiction,—shall depart out of this Kingdom before the 1st day of May, 1698."

If any remained after that day, or returned, the delinquents were to be transported; and if they returned again, they were to be guilty of high treason, and to suffer accordingly;—that is to say—to be hanged, drawn, and quartered.

You would imagine now, at least, that the Papists were down as far as they could be put down. You would imagine, now, at least, that the Protestant religion was safe in Ireland. Ah! no, my friends. William was succeeded by his sister-in-law, Queen Anne. She was a Stuart; she was a daughter of James II., for whom Ireland shed its blood; she was a granddaughter of Charles I., for whom Ireland shed its blood; and one would imagine she would have some heart, some feeling for that people. Here is the way she showed it. A Parliament, under this good Queen, passed a law "to prevent the growth of Popery"! What a strange plant this

Popery must be! They had been chopping it up, and cutting it down, trampling it under foot, blowing it up with gun powder, digging it out by the roots, as if they thought that would extirpate it; and yet, year after year, Parliament said: "We must stop the growth of Popery," and passed laws to stop the growth of Popery. By the first act of this Parliament of good Queen Anne, it was enacted that, if the son of any Papist should ever become Protestant, his father might not sell or mortgage his estate, or dispose of it, or any portion of it, by sale; for the Protestant son became master of his father's estate. Or if any child, no matter how young, conformed to the Protestant religion, he reduced his father at once to be a tenant for life; and the child was to be taken from the father, and placed under the guardianship of some Protestant relative. This clause of this act, according to law, made a Papist incapable of purchasing any landed estates, or collecting rents or profits arising out of the land, or holding any lease for life, or for any term exceeding thirty-one years, unless in such lease the reserve rent were at least one third of the improved rent value. That is to say, that if a Protestant discovered that a Catholic had improved his land, so as to make it one-third more in value, the Protestant could seize the money, could seize the land, could get a reward for betraying his neighbor to the Government.

Finally, they capped the climax by passing a law that no Papist or Catholic was to have a horse worth more than five pounds. If he had one worth five thousand pounds, and a Protestant came up to offer him five pounds for the horse;—whether he took it or not, the Protestant was at liberty to seize the Catholic's property. In a word, every enactment that could degrade, vilify, or annihilate the people, was the order of the day, and the business of Parliament, from the days of Elizabeth down to the days when America burst her chains, and before her terrible presence England grew afraid, and began to relax her penal laws.

I feel, my friends, that I have detained you too long upon a subject which, indeed, was dreary and desolate ground to travel over. For my part, I never would have invited the citizens of America, or my fellow-countrymen, to enter upon such a desolate waste, to renew, in my heart and yours, so deep and terrible a sorrow, if Mr. Froude had not compelled me to lift the veil, and to show you the treatment which our fathers received at the hands of England. I do it not at all to excite national animosity, not at all to stir up bad blood. I am one of the first willing to say, "Let by-gones be by-gones; let the dead past bury its dead." But, if any man,—I care not who he be, how great his reputation, how grand his name, in any walk of learning, or of science, or history;—if any man dare to say that England's treatment of Ireland was just,—was necessary,—was such as can receive the verdict of an honest man or of an honest people;—if any man dare to say that, either at home or abroad, the Irish have ever shown the white feather in the hour of danger,—if I were on my death-bed I would rise up to contradict him.

FOURTH LECTURE.

(Delivered in the Academy of Music, New York, Nov. 21, 1872.)

IRELAND AND AMERICA.

LADIES AND GENTLEMEN: I perceive, from the public papers, that Mr. Froude seems to be somewhat irritated by remarks that have been made as to his accuracy as a historian. Lest any word of mine might hurt, in the least degree, the just susceptibilities of an honorable man, I beg, beforehand, to say that nothing was further from my thoughts than the slightest word either of personality or disrespect for one who has won for himself so high a name as the English historian. And, therefore, I sincerely hope that it is not any word of mine,—which may have fallen from me, even in the heat of our amicable controversy,— that can have given the least offence to that gentleman. Just as I would expect to receive from him, or from any other learned and educated man, the treatment which one gentleman is supposed to show to another, so do I also wish to give him that treatment.

And now, my friends, we come to the matter in hand. On the last occasion, I had to traverse a great portion of my country's history in reviewing the statements of the English historian; and I was obliged to leave almost untouched one portion of that sad story; namely, the period which covers the reign of Queen Anne. This estimable lady, of whom history records the unwomanly vice of an overfondness for eating—came to the English throne, on the demise of

William of Orange, in 1702; and on that throne she sat until 1714. As I before remarked, it was, perhaps, natural that the Irish people,—the Catholics of Ireland,—trodden into the very dust,—should have expected some quarter from the daughter of the man for whom they had shed their blood, and from the granddaughter of the other Stuart King for whom they had fought with so much bravery in 1649. The return that the Irish people got from this good lady was quite of another kind from what they might have expected. Not content with the atrocious laws that had been already enacted against the Catholics of Ireland; not content with the flagrant breach of the Articles of Limerick, of which her royal brother-in-law, William, was guilty;— no sooner does Anne come to the throne, and send the Marquis of Ormonde, as Lord Lieutenant, to Ireland, than the Irish Ascendancy,—that is to say the Protestant faction in Ireland,—got upon their knees to the new Lord Lieutenant to beg of him, for the honor of the Lord, to save them from these desperate Catholics! Great God!—a people, robbed, persecuted, and slain, until only a miserable remnant of them were left;—without a voice in the nation's councils; —without a vote, even at the humblest board that sat to transact the meanest parochial business;—these were the men against whom the strong Protestant Ascendancy of Ireland made their complaints, in 1703. And so well were these complaints heard, my friends, that we find edict after edict coming out, declaring that no Papist should be allowed to inherit or possess land, or to buy land, or have it even under a lease: declaring that if a Catholic child wished to become Protestant, that moment that child became the owner and the master of his father's estate; and his father remained only his pensioner, or a tenant for life upon the bounty of his apostate son; declaring that, if a child, no matter how young,—even an infant,—conformed and became Protestant,—that moment that child was to be removed from the guardianship and custody of the father, and was to be handed over to some Protestant relation. Every enactment that the misguided ingenuity of the tyrannical mind of man could suggest was adopted and put in force. "One might be inclined," says Mr. Mitchel, "to suppose that Popery had been already sufficiently discouraged; seeing that the Bishops and clergy had been banished, that Catholics were excluded, by law, from all honorable or lucrative employments; carefully disarmed, and plundered of almost every acre of their ancient inheritance." But enough had not yet been done to make the Protestant interest feel secure; consequently new laws were enacted, and new clauses were added, under this "good Queen Anne," declaring that no Papist or Catholic could live in a walled town, especially in the towns of Limerick or Galway; that no Catholic could even come into the suburbs of these towns; they were obliged to remain several miles outside the town, as if they were lepers, whose presence would contaminate their sleek and pampered Protestant fellow-citizens of the land.

The persecution went on. In 1711, we find them enacting new laws; and later on, to the very last day of Queen Anne's reign, we find them enacting their laws, hounding on the magistrates and the police of the country, and the informers of the country,—offering them bribes and premiums to execute these atrocious laws, and to hunt the Catholic people and the Catholic priesthood of Ireland as if they were ferocious and untamable wolves. And, my friends, Mr. Froude justifies all this on two grounds. Not a single word has he of compassion for the people who were thus treated. Not a single word has he of manly protest against the shedding of that people's blood by unjust persecutions, as well as their robbery by legal enactment. But, he says, there were two reasons which, in his mind, seemed to justify the atrocious action of the English Government. The first of these was, that, after all, these laws were only retaliation, upon the Catholics of Ireland, for the terrible persecutions that were suffered by the Huguenots, or Protestants of France. And, he says, that the Protestants of Ireland were only following the example of King Louis XIV., who revoked the "Edict of Nantes." Let me explain this somewhat to you. The "Edict of Nantes" was a law that gave religious liberty to the French Protestants as well as the French Catholics. It was a law founded on justice. It was a law founded on the sacred rights that belong to man. And this law was revoked; consequently the Protestants of France were laid open to persecution. But, there is this difference between the French Protestants and the Catholics of Ireland:—The French Protestants had never had their liberty guaranteed to them by treaty; the Irish Catholics had their liberties guaranteed by the Treaty of Limerick,—the treaty they won by their own brave hands and swords. The "Edict of Nantes" was revoked; but that revocation was no breach of any royal word pledged to them. The Treaty of Limerick was broken with the Catholics of Ireland; and, in the breach of it, the King of England, the Parliament of England, the aristocracy of England, and the people of England, as well as the miserable Irish Protestant faction at home, became perjurers before history and the world. Here are the words of the celebrated Edmund Burke on this very subject of the revocation of this edict:—

"This act of injustice" (says the great Irish statesman), "which let loose on that monarch, Louis XIV., such a torrent of invective and reproach, and which threw such a dark cloud over the splendor of such an illustrious reign—falls far short of the case of Ireland."

Remember, he is an English statesman,—though of Irish birth,—and a Protestant who speaks:

"The privileges which the Protestants of France enjoyed antecedent to this revocation, were far greater than the Roman Catholics of Ireland ever aspired to, under the Protestant Establishment. The number of their sufferers, if considered absolutely, is not half of ours; and, if considered relatively to the body of the community, it is perhaps not a twentieth part. Then the penalties and incapacities which grew from that revocation, are not so grievous in their nature, or so certain in their execution, nor so ruinous, by a great deal, to the people's prosperity in that State, as those which were established for a perpetual law in the unhappy country of Ireland."

In fact, what did the revocation of the Edict of Nantes do? It condemned those who relapsed into the Protestant faith, after having renounced it,—it condemned them; not, indeed, to the confiscation of their goods,—there was no confiscation, except in cases of relapsation, and in cases of quitting the country. There was nothing at all of that complicated machinery which we have described in referring to Ireland's persecutions; there was nothing at all beggaring one portion of the population, and giving its spoils to the other part; while, side by side with this, we find the Irish people ruined, beggared, persecuted, and hunted to the death; and Mr. Froude, the English historian, says: "Oh, we were only serving you as your people, and your own fellow-religionists in France, were serving us!"

The other reason that he gives to justify these persecutions, was that "the Irish Catholics were in favor of the Pretender,"—that is to say—of the son of James II.;—"and consequently were hostile to the Government." Now, to that statement I can give, and do give a most emphatic denial. The Irish Catholics had had quite enough of the Stuarts: they had shed quite enough of their blood for that treacherous and shameless race; they had no interest whatever in the succession; nor cared they one iota whether the Elector of Hanover, or the son of James II., succeeded to the throne of England. For well they knew, whether it was Hanoverian or Stuart that ruled in England, the faction at home in Ireland, and the prejudices of the English people, would make him, whoever he was, a tyrant over them and over their nation.

Thus the persecution went on; and law after law was passed, to make perfect the beggary and the ruin of the Irish people; until at length Ireland was reduced to such a state of misery, that the very name of Irishman was a reproach; and a small number of the glorious race had the miserable weakness to change their faith, and to deny the religion of their fathers and their ancient race. The name of Irishman was a reproach! My friends, Dean Swift was born in Ireland: and he is looked upon as a patriotic Irishman; yet Dean Swift said:—"I no more consider myself an Irishman, because I happened to be born in Ireland, than an Englishman, chancing to be born in Calcutta, would consider himself a Hindoo!" Of the degradation of the Irish, and their utter prostration, he went so far as to say, that he would not think of taking them into account, on any matter of importance, "any more than he would of consulting the swine"! Lord Macaulay gloats over the state of the Catholics in Ireland, thus; and Mr. Froude views,—perhaps not without some complacency,— their misery. Lord Macaulay calls them "Pariahs," and says that they had no existence, that they had no liberty even to breathe in the land, and that land their own! And we find this very view emphasized by Lord Chancellor Bowes, in the middle of the century, rising in an Irish court, laying down the law quite coolly and calmly, and saying that,—

"The law did not presume a Papist to exist in the kingdom, nor could they breathe without the connivance of Government!"

Chief Justice Robinson made a similar declaration. Here are the words of his Lordship, the Chief Justice:—

"It appears" (he says) "plain, that the law does not suppose any such person to exist, as an Irish Roman Catholic."

And yet, at that very time, we find Irishmen proclaiming their loyalty, and saying, "Look at the Catholics of Ireland, how loyal they are!" Mr. Froude says that they favored the "Pretender" at the very time when the Government itself was attributing the quietude of the people in Ireland, not to their prostration, not to their ruin,—as was the real state of the case,—but to their devoted loyalty to the Crown of England! Well did that brave Irish gentleman, John Mitchel, reject that idea. "They were," he says, "as degraded as England could make them; but there was another degradation that could only come through themselves, that they were not guilty of;—and that would be the degradation of loyalty."

Now, my friends, we have at this very time an Irishman of the name of Phelim O'Neill,—one of the glorious old line of Tyrone,—one in whose veins flowed the blood of the great and the heroic "Red Hugh," who struck the Saxon at the "Yellow Ford," and purpled the stream of the Blackwater with his blood; one in whose veins flowed the, perhaps, still nobler blood of the immortal Owen Roe O'Neill, the glorious victor of Benburb. This Phelim O'Neill changed his religion and became a Protestant. But it seemed to him a strange and unnatural thing that a man of the name of O'Neill should be a Protestant; so he changed his name from Phelim O'Neill, and called himself "Felix Neale"! There has been a good deal said lately about the pronunciation of proper names, and what they rhyme with. This man made his name rhyme with *eel*,—the slippery eel. Now, on this change of the gentleman's name and religion, an old Irish priest wrote some Latin verses, which were translated by Clarence Mangan. I will read them, just to let you see how things were in Ireland at that time: —

> "All things has Felix changed. He changed his name;
> Yet, in himself, he is no more the same.
> Scorning to spend his days where he was reared,
> To drag out life among the vulgar herd,
> And trudge his way through bogs, in bracks and brogues,
> He changed his creed, and joined the Saxon rogues
> By whom his sires were robbed; and laid aside
> The arms they bore, for centuries, with pride,—
> The 'ship,' the 'salmon,' and the famed 'Red Hand;'
> And blushed when called O'Neill in his own land!
> Poor, paltry skulker from thy noble race!
> *Infelix Felix*, weep for thy disgrace!"

But, my friends, the English Ascendancy,—or the Protestant Ascendancy in Ireland, if you will,—seeing, now, that they had got every penal law that they could ask for; seeing that the only thing that remained for them was to utterly exterminate the Irish race,—and this they had nearly accomplished: for they had driven them into the wilds and wastes of Connaught; and they would have killed them all, only that the work was too much, and that there was a certain something in the old blood, and in the old race, that still terrified them when they approached them; they had so far subdued the Catholics, that they thought, now, at last, their hands were free, and nothing remained for them but to make Ireland, as Mr. Froude says, "a garden." They were to have every indulgence and every privilege. Accordingly, they set to work. They had their own Parliament. No Catholic could come near them, or come into their towns; they were forbidden to present themselves at all. They were greatly surprised to find that, now the Catholics were crushed into the very earth, England began to regard the Cromwellians themselves with fear and hatred. What! They, the sons of the Puritans! They, the brave men that had slaughtered so many of the Irish, and of the Catholic religion? Are they to be treated unjustly? Is their trade, or their commerce, or their Parliament to be interfered with? Ah! now, indeed, Mr. Froude finds tears, and weeps them over the folly of England; because England interfered with the commerce and with the trade of the Protestant Ascendancy in Ireland. But England did it. These Irish Protestant tradesmen were first-class woollen weavers: they made splendid cloth, which took the very best prices in all the markets of Europe, because the wool of the Irish sheep was so fine. The English Parliament made a law that the Irish traders were not to sell any more cloth; they were not to go into any of the foreign markets to rival their English fellow-merchants. They were to stay at home; they had the island, and they might make the most of it; but, any trade, any freedom; anything that would enrich Ireland,—*that* the English Parliament denied. Mr. Froude attributes this, in his lecture, to the accident that England, at that time, happened to be under the dominion of a paltry, pitiful-hearted lot of selfish money-jobbers: "mere accident," according to him: but an accident which he confesses so discontented the Orange faction in Ireland, that many hundreds of them emigrated, and came over to America, to settle in the New England States. There, as he asserts, with some truth, they carried their hatred with them, that was one day to break up the British Empire. *I* have another theory on this great question. I hold that *it was no accident of the hour, at all*, that made England place her restrictive laws on the Irish woollen trade. I hold that it was *the settled policy of England.* These men, who were now in the ascendancy in Ireland, imagined that, because they had ruined and beggared the ancient race, and the men of the ancient faith, therefore they were friends, and they would be regarded as friends by England. I hold that it was at that time,—as in a great measure it is to-day,—the fixed policy of England to keep Ireland poor, to keep Ireland down, to be hostile to Ireland, no matter who lives in it—whether he be Catholic or Protestant, whether he be Norman, Cromwellian, or Celt. "Your ancestors," says Curran, speaking to the men of his time, a hundred years afterwards,—"your ancestors thought themselves the oppressors of their fellow-subjects; but they were only their jailors; and the justice of Providence would have been frustrated if their own slavery had not been the punishment for their vice and their folly." That slavery came, and it fell on commerce. The Protestant inhabitants of Ireland, the Protestant traders of Ireland, the "planters," and the sons of the "planters" were beggared by the hostile legislation of England, simply because they were now in Ireland and had an interest in the Irish soil, and in the welfare of the country.

The inimitable Swift, speaking on this subject, makes use of the following quaint fable of Ovid. He says:

"The fable which Ovid relates of Arachne and Pallas is to this purpose. The goddess had heard of one Arachne, a young virgin, very famous for spinning and weaving. They both met upon a trial of skill, and Pallas, finding herself almost equalled in her own art, stung with rage and envy, knocked her rival down, and turned her into a spider, enjoining her to weave forever out of her own bowels and in a very narrow compass." "I confess," (the Dean goes on,) "that from a boy, I always pitied poor Arachne, and never could heartily love the goddess, on account of so cruel and unjust a sentence, which, however, is fully executed upon us by England, with further additions of rigor and severity; for the greatest part of our bowels and vitals is extracted without allowing us the liberty of spinning and weaving."

He alludes in this to a strange piece of legislation, which Mr. Froude acknowledges. The Irish wool was famous for its superior fineness, and the English were outbid for it by the French manufacturers. The French were willing to give three shillings a pound for the wool; and the English passed a law that the Irish people,—the farmers,—should not sell their wool anywhere but in England; so they fixed their own price on it; and they took the wool, made cloth, and, as the Dean says, poor Ireland,—Arachne,—had to give her vitals without the pleasure of spinning or weaving. Then the Dean goes on to say:—

"The Scripture tells us that oppression makes a wise man mad; therefore the reason that some men in Ireland are not mad is because they are not wise men. However, it were to be wished that oppression would in time teach a little wisdom to fools."

Well, we call Dean Swift a patriot. How little did he ever think,—as great a man as he was,—of that oppression, compared with which the restriction upon the wool trade was nothing,—the oppression that beggared and ruined a whole people; that drove them from their land; that drove them from every pleasure in life; that drove them from their country; that maddened them to desperation; and all because they had Irish names and Irish blood, and because they would not give up the faith which their consciences told them was the true one.

And now, my friends, Mr. Froude, in his lecture, comes at once to consider the consequences of that Protestant emigration from Ireland; and he says: "The manufacturers of Ireland and the workmen were discontented, and they shipped off and came to America." And then he begins to enlist the sympathies of America upon the side of the Protestant men who came over from Ireland. If he stopped here, I would not have a word to say to the learned historian. When an Englishman claims the sympathy of this, or of any other land, for men of his blood and of his religion—if they are deserving of that sympathy, I, an Irishman, am always ready, and the first, to grant it to them, with all my heart. And, therefore, I do not find the slightest fault with this learned Englishman, when he challenges the sympathy of America for the Orangemen of Ireland, and the Protestants who came to this country. If those men were deserving of American sympathy, why not let them have it?

But, Mr. Froude went on to say, that, whilst he claimed sympathy for the Protestant emigrants from Ireland, as stanch Republicans and lovers of American liberty, the Catholics of Ireland, on the other hand, were clamoring at the foot of the throne,—telling King George III. that they would be only too happy to go out at his command, and to shed American blood in his cause. Was that statement true or not? My friends, the learned gentleman quoted a petition that was presented to Sir John Blaquiere, in 1775, the very year that America began to assert her independence. In that petition he states that Lord Fingal and several other Catholic noblemen of Ireland, speaking in the name of the Irish people, pronounced the American Revolution an unnatural rebellion; and expressed their desire to go out, and to devote themselves, for "the best of kings," to the suppression of American liberty. First of all, I ask, when,—at any time in our history,—was Lord Fingal, or Lord Howth, or Lord Kenmare, or any one of these "Catholic Lords of the Pale," as they were called,—when, at any time in our history, has any one of them been authorized to speak in the name of the Irish people. . . . . Their presence in Ireland,—although they have kept the Catholic faith,—their presence in Ireland in every struggle, in every national movement, has been a cross, a hindrance, and stumbling-block to the Irish nation; and the people know it well. But, not doubting Mr. Froude's word at all, and only anxious to satisfy myself by historic research, I have looked for this petition. I have found, indeed, a petition in "Curry's Collection." I have found a petition signed by Lord Fingal and other Irish Catholic noblemen, addressed to his Majesty the King, in which they protest their loyalty in terms of the most slavish and servile adulation. But in that petition I have not been able to discover one single word about the American Revolution, not a single word of address to the King, expressing a desire to destroy the liberties of America; not one word about America at all. I have sought, and my friends have sought, in the records, and in every document that was at our hands, for this petition of which Mr. Froude speaks; and we could not find it at all. There must be a mistake somewhere or other. It is strange that a petition of so much importance should not be published amongst the documents of the time. We know that Sir John Blaquiere was Chief Secretary to the Lord Lieutenant of Ireland. Naturally enough, the petition would go to him, not to rest with him, but to be presented to the King. And, yet, I think I may state with certainty, that the only petition that was presented to the King, in 1775, was the one of which I speak, and in which there was not a single word about America, or about the American Revolution. But the learned historian's resources are far more ample than mine; his resources of time of preparation and of talent; his resources in the varied sources of information amongst which he has lived and passed his years;—and no doubt he will be able to explain this. In any case, the petition of which he spoke must have passed through Sir John Blaquiere's hands, for he was the Secretary of the Lord

Lieutenant; then it must have passed from him to the Lord Lieutenant, to be inspected by him; then, from him to the Prime Minister of England; and then to his Majesty, the King. We have an old proverb in Ireland, which indicates the way they manage these things at home:—"Speak to the maid, to speak to the mistress, to speak to the master."

And now I come to the question. In that glorious year of 1775, the Catholics of Ireland were down in the dust; the Catholics of Ireland had no voice; they had not as much as a vote for a parish beadle, much less for a Member of Parliament. Does Mr. Froude mean to tell the American people that these unfortunate people would not have welcomed the cry that came across the Atlantic,—the cry of a people who rose like a giant—yet only an infant in age,— proclaiming the eternal liberty of men and of nations,— proclaiming that no people upon the earth should be taxed without representation; and gave the first blow, right across the face of English tyranny, that that old tyrant had received for many a year; a blow before which England reeled, and which brought her to her knees? Does he mean to tell you or me, citizens of America, that such an event as this would be distasteful to the poor, oppressed Catholics of Ireland? It is true that England had crushed them as far as she could, but she had not taken the manhood out of them. Now, here are the proofs of this:—

Howe, the English General, in that very year of 1775, writes to his Government, expressing his preference for German troops. You know England was in the habit of employing Hessians. I do not say this with the slightest feeling of disrespect; I have the deepest respect for the great German element in this country; but in these times, certain it is, and it is an historic fact, that the troops of Hesse Cassel, Hesse Darmstadt, and other of the smaller German States, were hired out by their princes to whoever took them, and engaged them to fight their battles. General Howe proceeds to compliment the old race of Ireland, by giving emphasis to his "great dislike for Irish Catholic soldiers; as they are not at all to be depended upon."

They sent out four thousand troops from Ireland; but listen to this:—Arthur Lee, a diplomatic agent of America in Europe, writes home to his Government in June, 1777, and he says:

"The resources of our enemy" (that is to say, of England) "are almost annihilated in Germany, and their last resort is to the Roman Catholics of Ireland. They have already experienced their unwillingness to go, every man of a regiment raised there" (in Ireland) "last year, *having obliged them to ship him off tied and bound.*"

When the Irish Catholic soldiers heard that they were to go to America to cut the throats of the American people, and to scalp them, they swore they never would do it; and they had to take them and carry them on board the ships. But Arthur Lee goes on to say, "and most certainly they will desert more than any other troops whatsoever"!

Francis Plowden, a historian of the time, tells us, that the war against America was not very popular, even in England. "But, in Ireland," he says, "the people assumed the cause of America from sympathy."

Let us leave Ireland and come to America. Let us see how the great men, who were building up the magnificent edifice of their country's freedom,—laying the foundation in their own best blood, in those days,—how they regarded the Irish. In 1790, the immortal George Washington received an address from the Catholics of America, signed by Bishop Carroll, of Maryland, Dominick Lynch, of New York, and many others. In reply to that address, the calm, magnificent man makes use of these words:—

"I hope" (he says) "ever to see America among the foremost nations in examples of justice and liberality; and I presume that your fellow-citizens will not forget the patriotic part which you took in the accomplishment of their revolution, and the establishment of their government; or the important assistance they received from a nation in which the Roman Catholic religion is professed."

In the month of December, 1781, the Friendly Sons of Saint Patrick, in Philadelphia, (of which the first as well as the last President was General Stephen Moylan, brother of the Catholic Bishop, Francis Moylan, of Cork,) made George Washington an adopted member of their society. These friendly Sons of Saint Patrick were great friends of the great American Father of his country. When his army lay at Valley Forge, twenty-seven members of this society of the Friendly Sons subscribed between them, in July, 1780, one hundred and three thousand five hundred pounds, Pennsylvania currency,—principally gold or silver coin,—for the American troops, who were in dire want of provisions. George Washington accepts the fellowship of their society, and he says:—" I accept with singular pleasure the ensign of so worthy a fraternity as that of the Sons of St. Patrick in this city—a society distinguished for the firm adherence of its members to the glorious cause in which we are embarked."

During that time, what greater honor could have been bestowed by Washington, than that which he bestowed upon the Irish? When Arnold betrayed the cause at West Point —the traitor Arnold—a name handed down to eternal execration in the history of America,—Washington was obliged to choose the very best and most reliable soldiers in his army, and send them to West Point—to guard the place that was so well-nigh being betrayed by the traitor. From his whole army he selected the celebrated " Pennsylvania Line," as they were called; and those men were mainly made up of Irishmen. Nay, more; not merely of Protestant Irishmen, or North of Ireland men, or of those who were in that day called "Scotch Irish,"—for that was the name which, in the era of the Revolution, designated Mr. Froude's friends, who emigrated from Ulster. But looking over the muster-roll of the "Pennsylvania Line," we find such names as Duffey, Maguire, and O'Brien;—these were the names—these and such as these are the names—not of "Palatines," nor of Scotch "Planters," in Ireland, but they are the names of thorough-bred Irish Celts. . . . . And now I wish to give you a little incident in the history of that celebrated corps, to let you see how their hearts were in relation to America :—

"During the American Revolution," (says Mr. Carey,) " a band of Irishmen were embodied to avenge in the country of their adoption, the injuries of the country of their birth. They formed the major part of the celebrated Pennsylvania Line. They bravely fought and bled for the United States. Many of them sealed their attachment with their lives. Their adopted country was shamefully ungrateful. The wealthy, the independent, and the luxurious, for whom they fought, were rioting in the superfluities of life, while their defenders were literally half starved and half naked. Their shoeless feet marked with blood their tracks upon the highway. They long bore their grievances, patiently. They at length murmured. They remonstrated; they implored a supply of the necessaries of life, but in vain; a deaf ear was turned to their complaints. They felt indignant at the cold neglect and ingratitude of that country, for which so many of their companions in arms had expired on the crimson field of battle. They held arms in their hands. They had reached the boundary line, beyond which forbearance and submission become meanness and pusillanimity. As all appeals to the gratitude, justice, and generosity of their country had proved unavailing, they determined to try another course. They appealed to her fears; and they mutinied."

Well, as soon as the English commanders heard that the Irish soldiers had mutinied, what did they do?

"The intelligence was carried to the British camp, and there it spread joy and gladness. Lord Howe hoped that a period had arrived to the rebellion, as it would have been termed, and that there was a glorious opportunity of crushing the half-formed embryo of the Republic. He counted largely on the indignation and on the resentment of the natives of the Emerald Isle; he knew the irascibility of their tempers; he calculated on the diminution of the strength of the rebels, and accessions to the number of the royal army. Messengers were dispatched to the mutineers. They had *carte blanche*. They were to allure the poor Hibernians to return, like Prodigal Children, from feeding upon husks, to the plentiful fold of their royal master. Liberality herself presided over Howe's offers. Abundant supplies of provisions, comfortable clothing, to their heart's desire; all arrears of bounty; and pardon for past offences were offered. There was, however, no hesitation among these poor, neglected warriors. They refused to renounce poverty, nakedness, suffering, and ingratitude. Splendid temptations were held out in vain; there was no Judas, no Arnold there. They seized upon the tempters. They trampled upon their shining ore. They sent them to their General's tent. The miserable wretches paid with their forfeited lives for attempting to seduce a band of ragged, forlorn, and deserted, but illustrious heroes. We prate" (he says) "about the old Roman and Grecian patriotism. One-half of it is false. In the other half there is nothing that excels this noble trait, which is worthy of the pencil of a West or a Trumbull."

Mark! how it is that America regarded them—mark the testimony of some of America's greatest men. Mr. Froude seems to think that the American people look upon the Irish nation and the Irish people pretty much with the eyes with which the men of the last century would look upon them in Ireland, where the Irish nation meant the Protestant people of Ireland, and the Catholics did not exist at all. Was this the view that America and her statesmen took of them? No! Here is the testimony of George

Washington Parke Custis, the adopted son of Washington. The Irish, in 1829, won 'Catholic Emancipation; and before that time, when they were struggling for emancipation, they appealed for sympathy and moral support to America. And now this is how this great American gentleman, who had been one of the foremost of American advocates for the emancipation of the Irish Catholics, speaks of them:

"And why is this imposing appeal made to our sympathies? It is an appeal from the Catholics of Ireland, whose generous sons, alike in the days of our gloom and of our glory, shared in our misfortunes and joyed in our successes; who, with undaunted courage breasted the storms which once, threatening to overwhelm us, howled with fearful and desolating fury through this now happy land; who, with aspirations, deep and fervent, for our cause, whether under the walls of the Castle of Dublin, in the shock of our liberty's battles, or in the feeble and expiring accents of famine and misery, amid the horrors of the prison ship, cried from their hearts, 'God save America!' Tell me not" (he goes on to say)—"tell me not of the aid we received from another European nation, in the struggle for Independence. That aid was most, nay, all-essential to our ultimate success; but remember the years of the conflict that had rolled away; and many a hard field had been fought ere the fleets and the armies of France gave us their powerful assistance. We gladly and gratefully admit that the chivalry of France, led by the young, the great, the good and gallant Lafayette, was most early and opportunely at our side. But the capture of Burgoyne had ratified the Declaration of Independence. The renowned combats of the Heights of Charleston and Fort Moultrie; the disastrous and bloody days of Long Island, of Brandywine, and of Germantown; the glories of Trenton, of Princeton, and of Monmouth, all had occurred; and the rank grass had grown over the grave of many a poor Irishman who had died for America, ere the Flag of the Lilies floated in the field by the Star-spangled Banner. .... Of the chiefs of the army and the navy of the Revolution, we have to thank Caledonia for the honored names of Mercer, McDougal, Stirling, St. Clair, and the chivalric Jones; England for a Davie. But of the operatives in war—the soldiers I mean—up to the coming of the French, Ireland furnished in the ratio of a hundred for one of any foreign nation whatever."

Then this generous American gentleman, to whom Ireland appealed for sympathy—for Mr. Froude's is not the first appeal that has been made to the people of America;—this high-minded gentleman goes on to say:

"Then honored be the good old service of the sons of Erin, in the War of Independence. Let the shamrock be intertwined with the laurels of the Revolution; and truth and justice, guiding the pen of history, inscribe on the tablets of America's remembrance—eternal gratitude to Irishmen!"

Remember that this was Washington's adopted son; remember that he tells us, that the old, gray-headed, crippled veterans, who had fought under his father's banner in that War of Independence, were accustomed to come to his house; and there he would receive them at his door, and bring them in; and he tells us most affectionately of one old Irishman who had fought in the wars; who, after drinking the health of the gentlemen who had entertained him, lifted up his aged eyes, and, with tears, said: "Here's to the memory of General Washington, who is in heaven!" He says on the same occasion:

"Americans, recall to your minds the recollections of the heroic time when Irishmen were our friends, when in the whole world we had not a friend beside. Look to the period that tried men's souls, and you will find that the sons of Erin rushed to our ranks; and amid the clash of steel, on many a memorable day, many a John Byrne was not idle."

Remember, he does not say "many a *Spragg*," or "many a *Gibbs*," or the men that came over with Cromwell; but, honest John Byrne! Who was this honest John Byrne of whom he speaks? He was an Irish soldier of Washington's, who was taken prisoner by the English, and put on board a prison-ship, in the harbor of Charleston; and we have it on the authority of Mr. Custis, that he there was left in chains in the hold of the ship, pestilence being on board. He was more than half-starved; he was scarcely able, when he was summoned on deck, to crawl like a poor, stricken creature to the commander's feet, to hear what sentence was to be pronounced upon him. And then the English commander offered him liberty, life, clothing, food, and money, if he would give up the cause in which he was taken prisoner, and join the ranks of the British army. In a voice scarcely able to speak, with a hand scarcely able to lift itself, the Irishman looked to Heaven, and, throwing up his hands, cried out, "Hurrah for America!"

In the face of such facts, in the face of such testimony, in the presence of the honored name and record of George Washington, testifying to what Irish Catholic men have done for America, Mr. Froude speaks as vainly as if he were addressing the hurricane that sweeps over his head, when he tries to impress the American mind and the American people with any prejudice against the Catholics of Ireland.

What does MacNevin tell us? In the year 1807, when America was preparing for her second war with England, MacNevin records, that, "One of the offences charged upon the Irish—and one among the many pretexts for refusing redress to the Catholics of Ireland, was that sixteen thousand of them fought on the side of America." But he adds that, "many more thousands are ready to maintain the Declaration of Independence; and that will be their second offence."

Now, my friends, there are other testimonies as well as these of the men of the time. We have the testimony of American literary gentlemen, such, for instance, as that of Mr. James K. Paulding. Here are the words of this distinguished gentleman:—

"The history of Ireland's unhappy connection with England exhibits, from first to last, a detail of the most persevering, galling, grinding, insulting, and systematic oppression to be found anywhere, except among the *helots* of Sparta. There is not a national feeling that has not been insulted and trodden under foot; a national right that has not been withheld, until fear forced it from the grasp of England; or a dear or ancient prejudice that has not been violated in that abused country. As Christians, the people of Ireland have been denied, under penalties and disqualifications, the exercise of the rites of the Catholic religion, venerable for its antiquity, admirable for its unity, and consecrated by the belief of some of the best men that ever breathed. As men they have been deprived of the common rights of British subjects, under the pretext that they were incapable of enjoying them, which pretext they had no other foundation for than resistance of oppression, only the more severe by being sanctioned by the laws. England first denied them the means of improvement, and then insulted them with the imputation of barbarism."

Dr. Johnson had anticipated Mr. Paulding when he said:—
"There is no instance, even in the Ten Persecutions, of such severity as that which has been exercised over the Catholics of Ireland."

Thus thought and thus spoke the men whose names are bright in the records of literary America, and of the world. Take again the address agreed to by the members of the Legislature of Maryland. Speaking of Ireland, these American Senators and Legislators say:—

"A dependency of Great Britain, Ireland has long languished under oppression reprobated by humanity, and discountenanced by just policy. It would argue penury of human feelings, and ignorance of human rights, to submit patiently to those oppressions. The lapse of centuries has witnessed the struggles of Ireland but with only partial success. Rebellions and insurrections have continued with but short intervals of tranquillity. Many of the Irish, like the French, are the hereditary foes of Great Britain. America has opened her arms to the oppressed of all nations. No people have availed themselves of the asylum with more alacrity or in greater numbers than the Irish. High is the meed of praise, rich is the reward which Irishmen have merited from the gratitude of America. As heroes and statesmen they honor their adopted country."

Bravo America! When such glorious words as these are wiped out of the records of American history; when the generous sentiments which inspired them have ceased to be a portion of the American nature;—then, and not before then, will Mr. Froude get the verdict which he asks from America to-day.

I have looked through the "American Archives" and I have found that the foundation of this sympathy lies in the simple fact that the Catholics of Ireland were heart and soul with you—with you, American gentlemen—with you and your fathers in their glorious struggle. I find in the third volume of the "American Archives" a letter from Ireland, dated September 1st, 1775, to a friend in New York, in which the writer says:—

"Most of the people here wish well to the cause in which you are engaged, and would rejoice to find you continue firm and steadfast. . . . They" (the Government) "are raising recruits throughout the kingdom. The men are told they are only going to Edinburgh to learn military discipline, and are then to return."

Before they got a single Irishman to enlist they had to tell him a lie, well knowing that, if they told him that they were going to arm him and send him to America to fight against the American people, he would never think of entering the ranks of the British Army. A certain Major Roache went down to Cork to recruit men for America, and he made a great speech to them. I read his speech; it was very laughable. He called upon them as Irishmen, by all that they held sacred, and the glorious nationality to which they belonged, the splendid monarch that governed them,—and in fact the very words almost which Mr. Froude alleges to have been used by Lord Fingal, were used by Major Roache to these poor men. And then he held up the golden guineas and pound notes before them: and here is the result, as given in the third volume of the "American Archives:"

"An account of the success of Major Roache in raising recruits to fight against the Americans. The service is so distasteful to the people of Ireland in general, that few of the recruiting officers can prevail upon the men to enlist and fight against their American brethren."

The same year, in the British House of Commons, Governor Johnstone said:—

"I maintain that some of the best and the wisest men in this country are on the side of the Americans; and that, in Ireland, three to one are on the side of the Americans."

In the House of Lords, in the same year of '75, the Duke of Richmond makes this statement:—

"Attempts have been made to enlist the Irish Roman Catholics, but the Ministry know well that these attempts have proved unsuccessful."

We find again the Congress of America addressing the people of Ireland, in that memorable year of 1775; and here are the words that America's first Congress sends over the Atlantic waves to the afflicted, down-trodden, Catholic Irish :—

"Accept our most grateful acknowledgments for the friendly disposition you have always shown towards us. We know that you are not without your grievances; we sympathize with you in your distress, and are pleased to find that the design of subjugating us has persuaded the administration to dispense to Ireland some vagrant rays of ministerial sunshine. Even the tender mercies of government have long been cruel towards you. In the rich pastures of Ireland many hungry parricides have fed and grown strong laboring in her destruction."

We find such words as these addressed not to the "Palatines" and "Planters;" for if the Congress of America was addressing the Planters and Cromwellians in Ireland, they would not have had the bad taste to use such language as this: "In the rich pastures of Ireland many hungry parricides have fed and have grown strong laboring in her destruction."

Benjamin Franklin, of glorious and immortal name, was in Versailles, as Minister from the American Government; and he writes to the people of Ireland, in October, 1778. Here are his words:—

"The misery and distress which your ill-fated country has been so frequently exposed to, and has so often experienced by such a combination of rapine, treachery, and violence as would have disgraced the name of government in the most arbitrary country in the world, have most sincerely affected your friends in America, and have engaged the most serious attention of Congress."

Now I come to another honored name; and I find the testimony of Gulian C. Verplanck. When the Catholic Emancipation Act was passed, there was a banquet in the city of New York to celebrate the event; and this distinguished American gentleman proposed a health, or a toast, and it was a Catholic toast—"The memory of the Penal Laws—*requiescant in pace*. May they rest in peace." "And now that they are gone," continues Mr. Verplanck, "I have a good word to say for them." What was that good word? Here it is:—

"Both in the glorious struggle for independence, and in our more recent contest for national rights, those laws gave to the American flag the support of hundreds of thousands of brave hearts and strong arms; and have they not, too, contributed at the same time an equal proportion of intellectual and moral power?"

Coming down to our time, passing over the testimony of Henry Clay and his sympathies with the Irish nation (which he speaks of as so "identified with our own as to be almost part and parcel of ours—bone of our bone and flesh of our flesh")—passing over this magnificent testimony, America, even at this hour, is mourning over the grave of a great man. But a few days ago a nation accompanied to his last resting-place William H. Seward. And this illustrious statesman said in 1847:—

"Ireland not only sympathized profoundly with the trans-Atlantic colonies in their complaints of usurpation, but with inherent benevolence and ardor she yielded at once to the sway of the great American idea of universal emancipation. The bitter memory of a stream of ages lifted up her thoughts; and she was ready to follow to the war, for the rights of human nature, the propitious God that seemed to lead the way."

Finally, one extract and I have done with this portion of my lecture. I find that such were the relations between Ireland and America in this struggle, that a certain Captain Weel's, of the ship *Reprisal*, in the summer of 1776, captured three prizes near the West Indies, which were English property. He detailed some of his own men on board of them, and sent them to the nearest port to be adjudged as prizes. Shortly after, he came across another vessel, and he let her go, finding she was Irish property.

The Marquis de Chasteloux, a distinguished Frenchman, who was in America in 1782, published an account of his travels in America. An English gentleman in his translation of this work, in a note to a friendly allusion to an Irish soldier of the Revolution, writes thus:—

"An Irishman, the instant he sets foot on American ground, becomes, *ipso facto*, an American. This was uniformly the case during the whole of the late war. Whilst Englishmen and Scotsmen were regarded with jealousy and distrust, even with the best recommendation of zeal and attachment to the cause, a native of Ireland stood in need of no other certificate than his *dialect*."

Which shows that the Irishman that our friend is speaking of was not a Palatine nor a Planter, but a genuine *Paddy*, and no mistake.

"*His* sincerity was never called in question; he was supposed to have a sympathy of suffering: and every voice decided, as it were, intuitively in his favor. Indeed," (he adds,) "their conduct in the late revolution amply justified this favorable opinion; for whilst the Irish emigrant was fighting the battles of America, by sea and land, the Irish merchants, particularly at Charleston, Baltimore, and Philadelphia, labored with indefatigable zeal, and at all hazards, to promote the spirit of enterprise, and increase the wealth and maintain the credit of the country. Their purses were always opened, and their persons devoted to the common cause. On more than one imminent occasion Congress owed their existence, and America possibly her preservation, to the fidelity and firmness of the Irish. I had the honor" (he says) "of dining with an Irish Society, composed of the steadiest Whigs on the Continent, at the City Tavern, in Philadelphia, on St. Patrick's Day."

Mr. Froude must not run away with the assertion that the Irish merchants of Charleston, and Baltimore, and Philadelphia were the Puritan settlers. If they had been, they would have gone home and eaten a *cold* dinner on St. Patrick's Day.

So much for America, and Ireland's relations with her.

When the four thousand men were asked for by the English Government, to go out and fight Americans, they offered to send to Ireland four thousand Protestant Hessians; and the Irish Parliament of that day must have had a ray of grace, for they refused the Hessians. They said "No! If the country is in danger, we can arm some of our Protestant people, and they can keep the peace." Out of this sprang the "Volunteers of '82." Mr. Froude has little or nothing to say of them; consequently, as I am answering, or trying to answer him, I must restrict myself also in their regard. All I can say is this: Ireland, in 1776, began to arm. At first the movement was altogether a Protestant one, and confined to the North. The Catholics of Ireland, ground, as they were, into the very dust,—no sooner did the Catholics of Ireland hear that their Protestant oppressors were anxious to do something for the old land, than they came and said to them: "We will forgive everything that ever you did to us; we will leave you the land; we will leave you our country; we will leave you the wealth and the commerce; all we ask of you is to put a gun into our hands, for one hour, for Ireland." At first they were refused, and, my friends, when they found they would not be allowed to enter the ranks of the "Volunteers," they had the generosity, out of their poverty, to collect money and to hand it over to clothe the army of their Protestant fellow-citizens. Anything for Ireland! Anything for the man that would lift his hand for Ireland, no matter what his religion was! The old generous spirit was there; the love that never could be extinguished was there, self-sacrificing as of old; aye, the humble love for any man, no matter who he was, that was a friend of their native land—was there, in such generous acts as this of the blood of the O'Conors, the O'Briens, the O'Neills, and the O'Donnells.

But, after a time, our Protestant friends in the "Volunteers" began to think that these Catholics, after all, were fine, strapping fellows. Somehow, centuries of persecution could not knock the manhood out of them. "They be strong men," says an old writer, "and can bear more of hard living, hunger, and thirst than any other people that we know of." God knows, our capability of enduring nakedness, hunger, and thirst, and every other form of misery, was well tested!

Accordingly, we find that, 1780, there were fifty thousand Catholics amongst the Volunteers—every man of them with arms in his hands. Mr. Froude says that Grattan—the immortal Grattan—whilst he wished well for Ireland—whilst he was irreproachable in every way, public or private,—that at this time he was guilty of a great mistake. For, says the historian, "England had long ruled Ireland badly; but she had been taught a lesson by America, and she was now anxious to govern Ireland properly and well; and no sooner was an abuse pointed out than it was immediately remedied; and no sooner was a just law demanded than it was immediately granted; and the mistake Grattan made was that, instead of insisting on just legislation from England, he stood up and insisted on the legislative independence of the Irish nation, and that the Irish should have the making of their own laws. Thus," according to Mr. Froude, "the energies of the nation, which were wasted in political contention, could have been husbanded to influence England to grant just and fair laws." But he goes on the assumption, my dear American friends, and others,—the gentleman assumes to say that England was willing to redress grievances, to repeal the bad laws and make good ones; and he proves this assertion by saying that "she struck off the wrists of the Irish merchants the chains of their commercial slavery," and that she "restored to Ireland her trade." You remember that this trade was taken away from them: the woollen trade, like nearly every other form of trade, was discountenanced or ruined.

Now, I wish, for the sake of the honor of England, that she was as generous, or even as just, as Mr. Froude represents her, and, no doubt, would wish her to be. But we have the fact before us, that, in 1779, when a movement was made to repeal the law restricting the commerce of Ireland, the English Parliament, the English King, the Lord Lieutenant of Ireland and the English Government opposed it to the very death. They would not have it: not one fetter would they strike off from the chain that encumbered even the Protestant "planters" of Ireland. And it was only when Grattan rose up in the Irish Parliament, and insisted that Ireland should get back her trade—it was only then, that England consented to listen—because there were fifty thousand "Volunteers" armed outside.

The state of Ireland at this time is thus described:—

"Such is the Constitution that three millions of good, faithful subjects, in their native land, are excluded from every trust, power, and emolument in the State, civil and military; excluded from all corporate rights and immunities; expelled from grand juries, and restrained in petit juries; excluded in every direction from every trust, from every incorporated society, and from every establishment, occasional or fixed, that was instituted for public defence; from the bank, from the bench, from the exchange, from the university, from the college of physicians, and from what are they not excluded?" (demands the writer.) "There is no institution which the wit of man has invented, or the progress of society has produced, which private charity or public munificence has founded for the advancement of education around us, for the permanent relief of age, infirmity, and misfortune, the superintendence of which, in all cases where common charity would be promoted, from the enjoyment of which the Legislature has not excluded, and does exclude the Catholics of Ireland."

Grattan rose up in the Senate, and, lifting up his heroic hand and voice to Heaven, he swore before the God of Justice that that should come to an end. . . . . . . The English Government met him with a determination as great as that of the Irish patriot, and swore equally that that should remain the law. Was it not time to assert for Ireland her independence? Mr. Froude claims that England willingly consented to give up the restrictions on Irish commerce. When Grattan proposed it in the House, an official of the Government, named Hussey Burgh, rose up, to the astonishment of the Government, and seconded Grattan's resolution, to the rage and consternation of the Government faction, and the unequivocal dissatisfaction of the Executive and the Ministerial bench. "Hussey Burgh, the Prime Sergeant, was one of the most eloquent and fascinating men of the day; he was an official of the Government, and its stanch supporter,—one to whom, from the spirit of his office, patriotism should have been impossible." He moved "that we beg to represent to his Majesty that it is not by any temporary expedients, but by free trade alone, that this nation is now to be saved from impending ruin."

While they were fighting the Government from within, Grattan took good care to have the Volunteers drawn out in the streets of Dublin—there they were in their thousands,—armed men, drilled men; and they had their cannon with them, and about the mouths of the guns they had tied a label or card, inscribed with these words: "Free Trade for Ireland, or else—" So it happened that Lord North was obliged, greatly against his will, to introduce measures to restore to Ireland her trade. Now, I ask, was not Henry Grattan justified, seeing that it was only by pointing the cannon's mouth at "the best of Governments" they threw off the restraints on Irish trade;—was he not justified when he said, "The English Parliament will never do us justice;

and, in the name of God, now that we have our men armed around us, let us demand for Ireland perfect independence of the people and the Parliament of England, and the right to make whatever laws are most conducive to the welfare of our own people."

It is perfectly true that Grattan failed; it is perfectly true that although that declaration of independence was proclaimed by law, and, as Mr. Froude observes, "Home Rule was tried in Ireland from '82 to '99, and it was a failure." All this is true; but why was it so, my friends? Reflect upon this; the Irish Parliament did not represent the nation. The Irish Parliament consisted of three hundred members; and of these three hundred there were only seventy-two that were elected by the people. All the others were "nomination boroughs," as they were called. Certain great lords, peers, and noblemen had three or four little towns on their estates, which towns returned a member of Parliament; and the poor people who had the votes were completely at the mercy of the landlord,—the rack-renting landlord,—and whomsoever he nominated was elected as member. Just as, in the Protestant Church, whenever a bishop dies, the Queen writes to the clergy and says: "You will name such a one for bishop;" and, then, they *elect* him, after the Queen has nominated him.

Even of the seventy-two, who were, in some sense, representatives of the people, whom did they represent? There were nearly three millions of Catholics in Ireland, men of intellect and of education, in spite of all the laws that were made against schools and colleges for Catholics; there were nearly three millions of Irish Catholics in the land, and not a man of them had a vote even for a Member of Parliament. And, therefore, this wretched Parliament, that only represented one-tenth of the nation, if it was venal and corrupt, it is no disgrace to the Irish people, and it is no argument to prove that they did not know how to govern themselves.

Meantime, the "Volunteers" made the most tremendous mistake, and that was by letting Catholics in amongst their ranks. This is what my Lord Sheffield says;—and it will give you clearly to understand, ladies and gentlemen of America, how the English people looked upon us Irish one hundred years ago; indeed, according to Cobbett, one of their most distinguished writers, this was how they looked upon you, until you taught them with the sword to look upon you with more respect: "It is now necessary," says Lord Sheffield, "to go back to the year 1778, to take notice of a phenomenon which began to appear at that time; it is a wonderful thing." What was it?

"The like has never been seen in any country, at least where there was an established government. To describe it: it is an army unauthorized by the law, and unnatural; and generally known by the name of the Volunteers of Ireland. The arms issued from the public stores were insufficient to supply the rapid increase of the Volunteers; the rest were procured by themselves, and the necessary accoutrements, with a considerable number of field-pieces. The Opposition in England speak highly of them; and the supporters of the Government in both countries mention them with civility."

It is not easy to be uncivil to an army of 95,000 men.

"The wonderful efforts of England in America were, somehow or other, wasted to no purpose."

The wonderful efforts of England in America were wasted to no purpose! There happened to be a man in the way, and that man was George Washington.

He goes on to speak of the Volunteers. The "many-headed monster," as he calls it, "now began to think it would be proper to reform the State and to purge the Parliament of Ireland." Henry Grattan said,

"I will never claim freedom for 600,000 of my countrymen while I leave 2,000,000 or more of them in chains. Give the Catholics of Ireland their civil rights and their franchise; give them the power to return members to the Irish Parliament, and let the nation be represented; put an end to the rotten nomination boroughs: let the members represent the people truly, and you will have reformed your Parliament, and you will have established forever the liberties which the Volunteers have won."

This was what the Volunteers wanted; and for this they got, from my Lord Sheffield, the very genteel name of "the many-headed monster." But they did something still more strange than this. "So far," he says, "everything went on as might have been expected. But there is another part of their conduct neither natural nor rational. Some of the corps, for the purpose of increasing their numbers, perhaps, or possibly without consideration, admitted Roman Catholics." [They must have been mad. They did it "without consideration."] "And others, perhaps, enrolled them latterly for the sake of acquiring numbers and strength to force a reform of the government from England"—[to force a reform, which England would never permit; because she wanted to have a rotten Parliament to her hand, and through that Parliament to destroy the country]:—

"Well, but that Protestants should allow and encourage this also, and form a whole corps of Roman Catholics, when all Europe was at peace, is scarcely to be believed,—above all, in view of their number. It has become the system of the Roman Catholics to enroll as many as possible, particularly since the peace of last summer; and there is nothing unequivocal in this. Already, perhaps, five thousand of these are in arms, and in a year or less, they may be ten thousand. All the Protestants are gradually quitting the service; and the only Protestants are those who continue since the peace, in order to prevent the Volunteer arms from falling into more dangerous hands, and to counterbalance the Catholics."

Then he goes on to say:

"They are many. If they were only one-fifth, instead of four-fifths, of the people, the writer of this observation would be the last man to suggest a difficulty about their being admitted into power or every right or advantage given to them. But they do not forget the situation in which their ancestors have been. They are not blind to what they might acquire. Persevering for upwards of two centuries under every discouragement, under every severity, subjected to every disadvantage, does not prove an indifference to the principles of their religion. Thinking as they do, feeling as they do, believing as they do, they would not be men if they did not wish for a change. Nor would Protestants be worthy of the designation of reasonable creatures if they did not take precautions to prevent it."

Thus, it is to this fact, that the English Government steadily opposed Reform,—that they would not hear of Reform, because they wanted to have a venal, corrupt, miserable seventy-two in their hands,—it is to this fact, and not to any mistake of Grattan, that we owe the collapse of that magnificent revolutionary movement of the "Irish Volunteers."

Well, England now adopted another policy. We have evidence of it. As soon as William Pitt came into office as Premier, his first thought was—"I will put an end to this Irish difficulty. I will have no more laws made in Ireland, for Irishmen. I will unite the two Parliaments into one, and I will not leave Ireland a single shadow of Legislative Independence." This being the programme, how was it to be worked out? Mr. Froude says, or seems to say, that "the Rebellion of '98 was one of those outbursts of Irish ungovernable passion and of Irish inconstancy,

7*

accompanied by cowardice and by treachery, with which" (according to him) "we are all so familiar in the history of Ireland." Now, I have a different account of '98. Mr. Froude says that "the Rebellion arose out of the disturbance of men's minds created by the French Revolution;" and, indeed, there is a great deal of truth in this. The French Revolution set all the world in a blaze, and the flame spread, no doubt, to Ireland.

Mr. Froude goes on to say that "the Irish Government were so hampered by this free Parliament, this Parliament of Grattan's, that although they saw the danger approaching, they could not avert it;—their hands were bound; nay, more," he adds, "the Government, bound by constitutional law, and by Parliament, could not touch one of the United Irishmen until they had first committed themselves by some overt act of treason;—in other words, until they had first risen."

Now, according to this historian, there was nothing done to molest, slay, or persecute the people of Ireland until they rose in arms in '98. My friends, the rising of 1798 took place on the 23d of May. On that day the "United Irishmen" rose. I ask you now to consider whether the Government had any share in that rising, or in creating that rebellion?

As early as 1797, the country was beginning to be disturbed, according to Mr. Froude; and, during the first three months of January, February, and March, in '98, we find Lord Moira giving his testimony as to the action of the English Government.

"My Lords," (he says in the House of Lords,) "I have seen in Ireland the most absurd, as well as the most disgusting tyranny, that any nation ever groaned under. I have been myself a witness of it in many instances; I have seen it practised unchecked, and the effects that have resulted from it have been such as I have stated to your lordships. I have seen in that country a marked distinction between the English and the Irish. I have seen troops that have been sent there full of this prejudice—that every inhabitant of that kingdom is a rebel to the British Government."

Troops were sent there before the Rebellion, and told—"every man you meet is a rebel."—"I have seen most wanton insults practised upon men of all ranks and conditions."

They sent their thousands into Ireland in preparation for the Rebellion; they had, between Welsh and Scotch and Hessian regiments, and between English and Irish militia, an army of one hundred and thirty thousand men prepared for the work; and, in this way, they goaded the people on to rebellion. The rack, indeed, was not at hand, but the punishment of "picketing" was in practice, which had been for some years abolished as too inhuman even for the treatment of savages.

Lord Moira goes on to say that he had known of a man who, in order to extort confession of a crime from him, was "picketed" until he actually fainted;—["picketing" meant putting them on the point of a stake upon one foot,] —"and picketed a second time until he fainted again; and, again, as soon as he came to himself, picketed the third time until he fainted once more; and all this on mere suspicion."

Not only was this punishment used, but every species of torture. Men were taken and hung up until they were half dead, and then threatened with a repetition of the cruel torture unless they made confession of imputed guilt. They sent their soldiers into the country, and quartered them at what was called "free quarters." The English Yeomanry and the Orange Yeomanry of Ireland lived upon the people; they violated the women, they killed the aged, they plundered the houses, they set fire to the villages, they exercised every form of torture the most terrible,—this terrible soldiery. All this took place before a single rising in Ireland, before the rebellion of '98 sprung up at all. We had a brave and gallant man sent to Ireland at that time—Sir Ralph Abercrombie;—and he declared he was so frightened and disgusted at the conduct of the soldiers, that he threw up his commission, and refused to take the command of the forces in Ireland. He issued a general order in February, '98—the rebellion did not begin until May. He began his general order with these words:—"The very disgraceful frequency of great cruelties and crimes, and the many complaints of the conduct of the troops in this kingdom, has too unfortunately proved the army to be in a state of licentiousness that renders it formidable to every one, except the enemy." Then he threw up his commission in disgust; and General Lake was sent to command in Ireland. He says:—

"The state of the country and its occupation previous to the insurrection, is not to be imagined, except by those who witnessed the atrocities of every description committed by the military and the Orangemen, that were let loose upon the unfortunate and defenceless population."

Then he gives a long list of terrible hangings, burnings, and murderings. We read that "at Dunlavin, in the county of Wicklow, previous to the rising, thirty-four men were shot without any trial." But it is useless to enumerate or continue the list of cruelties perpetrated. It will suffice to say that where the military were placed on free quarters all kinds of crimes were committed; but the people were no worse off than those living where no soldiers were quartered; for in the latter places the inhabitants were called to their doors and shot without ceremony, and every house was plundered or burned. Nay, more! We have Mr. Emmet, in his examination, giving his evidence and declaring that it was the fault of the Government, this rebellion of '98. The Lord Chancellor put the following question to Mr. Emmet: " Pray, Mr. Emmet "—this was in August, '98— " what caused the late insurrection ? " to which Mr. Emmet replied, " Free quarters, house-burnings, tortures, and the military executions in the counties of Kildare, Carlow, and Wicklow." Before the insurrection broke out, numbers of houses, with their furniture, in which concealed arms had been found, were burned. Numbers of people were daily scourged, picketed, and otherwise put to death to force confession of concealed crime or plots. Outrageous acts of severity were often committed even by persons not in the regular troops. But we have the evidence of the brave Sir John Moore, the hero of Corunna. He was in Ireland at the time, in military command, and he bears this testimony. Speaking of Wicklow, the very hot-bed of the insurrection, he says, that " moderate treatment by the Generals and the preventing of the troops from pillaging and molesting the people, would soon restore tranquillity; the latter would certainly be quiet if the Yeomanry would behave with tolerable decency, and not seek to gratify their ill-humor and revenge upon the poor."

We have the testimony of Sir William Napier, not an Irishman, but a brave English soldier, saying:

" What manner of soldiers were these fellows who were let loose upon the wretched districts in which the Ascendancy were placed, killing, burning, and confiscating every man's property; and, to use the venerable Abercrombie's words, ' they were formidable to everybody but the enemy'? We ourselves were young at the time ; yet, being connected with the army, we were continually among the soldiers listening with boyish eagerness to their experiences; and well we remember, with horror, to this day, the tales of lust, of bloodshed and pillage, and the recital of their foul actions against the miserable peasantry, which they used to relate."

I ask you, in all this goading of the people into rebellion, who was accountable if not the infamous government which, at the time, ruled the destinies of Ireland? I ask you are the Irish people accountable, if, from time to time, the myrmidons of England have been let loose upon them, ravaging them like tigers, violating every instinct of Irish love of land, of Irish purity, of Irish faith? Is it not a natural though a terrible thing, that, after all these provocations, which they deliberately put before the people, they goaded them into the rebellion of '98, and so prepared the way for that union of 1800 which followed. Mr. Froude says: "Several hot-headed priests put themselves at the head of their people." There was a Father John Murphy in the county of Wexford. He came home from his duties, one day, to find the houses of the poor people around sacked and burned; to find his unfortunate parishioners huddled about the blackened walls of the chapel, crying: "Soggarth dear, what are we to do? what are we to do? where are we to fly from this terrible persecution that has come upon us?" And Father John Murphy got the pikes, put them in their hands, and put himself at their head! So you see, my friends, there are two sides to every story.

My friends, I have endeavored to give you some portions of the Irish side of the story, resting and basing my testimony upon the records of Protestant and English writers, and upon the testimony, which I have been so proud to put before you, of noble, generous American people. I have to apologize for the dryness of the subject, and the imperfect manner in which I have treated it, and also for the unconscionable length of time in which I have tried your patience. In the next lecture we shall be approaching ticklish ground: —"Ireland since the Union;" Ireland as she is to-day; and Ireland as, my heart and brain tell me, she shall be in some future day.

FIFTH LECTURE.

(Delivered in the Academy of Music, New York, Nov. 26, 1872.)

THE FUTURE OF IRELAND.

LADIES AND GENTLEMEN: On this day, a paragraph in a newspaper, the *New York Tribune*, was brought under my notice; and the reading of it caused me very great pain and anguish of mind; for it recorded an act of discourtesy offered to my learned antagonist, Mr. Froude, and supposed to be offered by Irishmen in Boston. In the name of the Irishmen of America, I tender to the learned gentleman my best apologies. I beg to assure him, for my Irish fellow-countrymen in this land, that we are only too happy to offer to him the courtesy and the hospitality that Ireland has never refused, even to her enemies. Mr. Froude does not come among us as an enemy of Ireland; but he professes that he loves the Irish people; and I am willing to believe him. And when I read in the report of his last lecture, which I am about to answer to-night, that he said that he "would yield to no man in his love for the Irish people," I was reminded of what O'Connell said to Lord Derby on a similar occasion. When the noble lord stated in the English House of Lords that he would yield to no man in his love for Ireland, the great Tribune rose and said: "Any man that loves Ireland cannot be my enemy. Let our hearts shake hands." I am sure, therefore, that I speak the sentiments of every true Irishman in America, when I assure this learned English gentleman that, as long as he is in this country, he will receive at the hands of the Irish citizens of America nothing but the same courtesy, the same polite hospitality and attention, which he boasts that he has received from the Irish people in their native land. I beg to assure him that we, Irishmen, in America, know well that it is not with discourtesy, or anything approaching to rudeness or violence, that the Irish citizens of America ever expect to make their appeal to this great nation. If ever the reign of intellect and of mind was practically established in this world, it is in glorious America. Every man who seeks the truth, every man who preaches the truth,—whether it be religious truth or historical truth,—will find an audience in America. And I hope he never will find an Irishman to stand up and offer him discourtesy and violence, because he speaks what he imagines to be the truth.

So much being said in reference to this paragraph to which I have alluded, I now come to the last of Mr. Froude's lectures, and to the last of my own. The learned gentleman, in his fourth lecture, told the American people his view of the movement of 1782, and of the subsequent Irish rebellion of 1798. According to Mr. Froude, the Irish made a great mistake in 1782 by asserting the independence of the Irish Parliament. "They abandoned," says this learned gentleman, "the paths of political reform; and they clamored for political agitation." Now, political agitation is one thing, and political reform is another thing. Political reform, my friends, means the correcting of great abuses, the repealing of bad laws and the passing of good measures, salutary and useful, for the welfare and well-being of the people. According to this learned gentleman, England,—taught, by her bitter American experience, that coercion would not answer with the people, and that it is impossible to thrust unjust laws down the throats of a people or a nation, even at the sword's point—according to him, England was only too willing, too happy, in the year 1780, to repeal all the bad laws that had been passed in the blind and bigoted ages that had gone by, and to grant to Ireland a real redress of all her grievances. But, says Mr. Froude, "The Irish people were foolish. Instead of demanding from England the redress of these grievances, they insisted upon their National and Parliamentary independence; and," he adds, "they were foolish in this; for that very independence led to interior contention, contention to conspiracy, conspiracy to rebellion, rebellion to tyranny." Now, I am as great an enemy of political agitation as Mr. Froude, or any other man. I hold, and I hold it by experience, that political agitation distracts men's minds from the more serious and the more necessary occupations of life; that political agitation draws men's minds away from their business, and from the sober pursuits of industry; that it creates animosities and bad blood between citizens; that it affords an easy and profitable employment for worthless demagogues; and very often brings to the surface the vilest and meanest elements of society. All that I grant. But, at the same time, I hold that political agitation is the only resource left to a people who endeavor to extract good laws from an unwilling and tyrannical government. May I ask the learned historian what were the wars of the seventeenth century, in France, in Germany, and in the Netherlands?— the wars that Mr. Froude himself admires so much, and for which he expresses so much sympathy;—what were they but political agitation taking the form of armed revolt, in order to extort from the governments of that time what the people considered to be just measures of toleration and liberty of conscience? With these wars, that were waged by the people in armed revolt, against France, against Spain, in the Netherlands; against the Emperor Charles the Fifth, of Austria;—with these Mr. Froude has the deepest sympathy; because they were wars made by Protestants against Catholic governments. The men who made these wars were innovators, or revolutionists in every sense of the word. They wanted to overturn not only the altar, but also the established forms of government. But with the Irish, who only stood in defence of their ancient religion and of their time-honored altars, of their lives and property;—not of their freedom—for that was long gone;—for the Irish—this learned gentleman has not a word, except expressions of disdain and disapprobation.

And now we come to consider whether Mr. Froude is right, when he says that the Irish foolishly clamored for political agitation in 1780, when they might have obtained political reform. Now, mark:—In 1780, the Irish people —and mainly the Protestant portion of the Irish people,— demanded of the English Government the repeal of certain laws that restricted and almost annihilated the trade and commerce of Ireland. These laws had been passed under William III. They were levelled at the Irish woollen trade; they forbade the exportation of manufactured cloth from Ireland, except under a duty that was a prohibitive tariff. They went so far as to prohibit the Irish people from even selling their fleeces—their wool—to any foreign power except England. England fixed her own prices; and Mr. Froude himself acknowledges that although the French might be offering three shillings a pound for the wool, Ireland was obliged to sell it to the English merchant at his own price. When the Irish people demanded the repeal of this unjust measure, I ask you, was England willing to grant it? Was England, as Mr. Froude says, only anxious to discover the unjust law in order to repeal it, and to discover grievances in order to redress them? I answer, no. England nailed her colors to the mast, and said, "I never will grant the repeal of the restrictive duties upon Irish trade. Ireland is down, and I will keep her down." The proof lies here: The English Government resisted Grattan's demand for the emancipation of Irish industry, until Henry Grattan brought 50,000 "Volunteers;" and the very day that he rose in the Irish Parliament, to proclaim that Ireland demanded her commercial rights once more, the Volunteers, in College Green and Stephen's Green, in Dublin, had their artillery out, and had them planted before the door of the House of Commons; and around the mouths of the guns they had put a label—a significant label—" Free Trade for Ireland; or——!" If England was so willing to redress every Irish grievance—if the Irish people had only to say, "Look here, there is this law in existence; take it away, for it is strangling and destroying the commerce of the country"—if England was so willing to take away that law,—and Mr. Froude says she was; if she was only anxious to hear where the defect was in order to remedy it, why, in the name of God—why, in that day of 1780, did she hold out until, at the very cannon's mouth, she was obliged to yield the commercial independence of Ireland? Is it any wonder that the Irish people thought, with Henry Grattan, that, if every measure of reform was to be fought for, that the kingdom would be kept in a perpetual state of revolution? Is it any wonder that men said:—"If we have got to fight for every act of justice, we must always be ready, with our torches lighted and our cannons loaded"? Is it any wonder that the Irish people should have said, in that day, with their immortal leader: "It is far better for us to have our own Parliament, free and independent, to take up the making of our own laws, and consult for our interests, and in peace, quietness, and harmony, to take thought for the wants of Ireland and legislate for them"? And this is what Mr. Froude calls "clamoring for political agitation." Thus we see, my friends,—(and, remember, this evening, fellow-countrymen, that I am emphatically and especially appealing to America; that I expect my verdict this evening, as Mr. Froude got his; but it is not from Dr. Hitchcock; it is not the puny crow of a barndoor fowl, but it is the scream of America's Eagle that I expect to hear this evening;)—thus we see that the action of 1782, by which Grattan obtained and achieved the independence of the Irish Parliament, did not originate in any innate love of the Irish for political agitation, but in the action of the British Government, that forced it upon them, and gave them only two alternatives—"Remain subject to me, to my Parliament; but I never will grant you anything except at the cannon's mouth; or take your own liberty and legislate for yourselves." Oh! Henry Grattan! you were not a Catholic; and yet I, a Catholic priest, here, to-night, call down ten thousand blessings on thy name and memory!

It is true that that emancipated Parliament of 1782 failed to realize the hopes of the Irish nation;—perfectly true! The Parliament of 1782 was a failure. I grant it. Mr. Froude says that that Parliament was a failure because the Irish were incapable of self-legislation. It is a serious charge to make against any people, my friends; yet I, who am not supposed to be a philosopher—and, because of the habit that I wear, I am not supposed to be a man of very large mind,—I stand up here to-night and assert my conviction that there is not a nation nor a race under the sun that is not capable of self-legislation, and that has not a right to the inheritance of freedom. But, if the learned gentleman wishes to know what was the real cause of that failure, I will tell him. The emancipated Parliament of 1782, although it inclosed within its walls such honored names as Grattan and Flood, yet it did not represent the Irish nation. There were nearly three millions and a half of Irishmen in Ireland at that day;—three millions of Catholics, and half a million of Protestants; and the Parliament of 1782 only represented the half million. Nay, more: examine the Constitution of that Parliament, and see who they were; see how they were elected, and you will find that not even the half million of Protestants were fairly represented by that Parliament. The House of Commons held 300 members. Of these 300 there were only 72 elected by the people; the rest were the nominees of certain great lords—certain large landed proprietors. A man happened to have an estate,—a side of the country, which contained three or four towns or villages,—and each town returned its member. The landlord went in and said: "You will elect such a man; he is my nominee;" and he was elected at once. They were called "rotten boroughs;" they were called "nomination boroughs;" and they were also called "pocket boroughs," because my lord had them in his pocket. Have any of you, Irishmen, who are here present to-night, ever travelled from Dublin to Drogheda? There is a miserable village;—half a dozen wretched huts;—it is the dirtiest, filthiest place I ever saw; and that miserable village returned a member to the Irish Parliament! Had that Parliament of 1782 represented the Irish people—[the three millions of Catholics had not as much as a vote;—the best and most intellectual Catholic in Ireland had not even a vote for a member of Parliament;]—had that Parliament represented the Irish nation, it would have solved the problem of "Home Rule" in a sense favorable to Ireland, and very unfavorable to the theories of Mr. Froude.

The Irish people knew this well; and the moment that the Parliament of 1782 was declared independent of the Parliament of England,—was declared to have the power of originating its own acts, of legislating, and being responsible to no one except the King,—that moment the Irish people clamored for reform. They said: "Reform yourselves now,

O Parliament. Let the people in, and represent them fairly; and you will make a grand success of your independence."

The "Volunteers," to their honor, cried out for reform. In their first meeting at Dungannon, when they were 95,000 strong, the one thing they demanded was reform of the Parliament. The "United Irishmen" who, in the beginning, were not a secret society, nor a treasonable society, but open, free, loyal men, embracing the first names and first characters in Ireland,—the "United Irishmen" actually originated as a society, embracing the best intellect in Ireland, for the purpose of forcing reform on the Parliament. It may be interesting to the citizens of America who have honored me with their presence this evening; it may be interesting to my Irish fellow-countrymen to know what were the three principles upon which the society of United Irishmen was formed. Here they are: First of all, the first resolution of that society was that "the weight of English influence, in this Government, and this country, is so great as to require cordial union among all the people of Ireland to maintain that balance which is essential to the preservation of our liberties and to the extension of our commerce." Resolution No. 2, "That the only constitutional means by which this influence of England can be opposed is by complete, cordial, and radical reform of the representation of the people in Parliament." Resolution No. 3, "That no reform is just which does not include every Irishman of every religious persuasion." There you have the whole programme of this formidable society of the "United Irishmen;" and I ask you, citizens of America, is there anything treasonable, is there anything reprehensible, is there anything deserving of imprisonment, of banishment, or death in such a resolution as this? Who opposed and hindered that reform? who stood between the Irish people and their Parliament and said—"No; there shall be no reform; you must remain the representatives of a faction, and not of the nation; you must remain the corrupt and venal representatives of only a small portion even of the Protestant faction." Who said this? The Government of England. Here is my proof. On the 29th of November, 1783, Mr. Flood introduced into the Irish Parliament a bill of reform. The moment that bill was read, an honorable member rose up to oppose it. That member was Barry Yelverton, who was afterwards Lord Avonmore. He was the Attorney-General of the Government for Ireland; and he gave to the bill an official and Governmental opposition. The bill was thrown out by a majority of 159 to 77; the 159, every one of them, having a bribe in his pocket. Then, the Attorney-General, Mr. Yelverton, rose up; and he made this motion, "that it has now become necessary to declare that this House will maintain its just rights and privileges against all encroachments whatsoever;"—the "just rights and privileges" being the right to represent a faction, and exclude from all representation five-sixths of the people of Ireland.

"From agitation," says Mr. Froude, "grew conspiracy; from conspiracy, rebellion." By conspiracy, he means the society of "United Irishmen." By rebellion, he means the uprising of '98. Now, in my last lecture, I have shown you, on the evidence of such illustrious men as Sir Ralph Abercrombie, and Sir John Moore, the hero of Corunna, that the rebellion of '98 was, primarily and originally, the work of the British Government, which goaded the Irish people into revolt. We have also seen, a moment ago, that the society of "United Irishmen" was not a conspiracy, but a public society,—a magnificent union of the best intellects and best men in Ireland for a splendid and patriotic purpose, to be accomplished by fair, loyal, and legitimate means. But the principle upon which the "United Irishmen" were formed was the principle of effecting a union among all Irishmen; and this was enough to alarm the Government, which, from time immemorial, for many centuries, had ruled Ireland through division. The motto—the word—that Mr. Froude so eloquently used, when he said, that "on the day that Ireland will be united she will be invincible,"—that was present in the mind of England's Prime Minister, the celebrated William Pitt, when he resolved on three things: He resolved first, to disarm the "Volunteers;" secondly, to force the "United Irishmen" to become a secret society or conspiracy; and thirdly, he resolved to force Ireland into a rebellion, that he might have her at his feet. How did he bring these three things about? Remember that I am reviewing all these things historically. I have no prejudices in the matter. I declare to you, that, with the exception of the momentary ebullition or boiling up of the blood that I feel in my chamber, when preparing these lectures, I feel nothing but that. I am not like others. I believe, for instance, that Mr. Froude has no business to write history, because he is a good philosopher. A philosopher is a man who endeavors to trace effects to their causes; who sets up a theory and tries to work it out; and that is the last man in the world that ought to write history. And why? Because a historian is supposed to be a narrator of dry facts; and I hold, ought not to deal in theories or fancies at all. I believe my learned antagonist to be too much of a philosopher to be a good historian. I also believe that he is too much of a historian to be a good philosopher.

The first of these three designs of William Pitt was accomplished in 1785. He increased the standing army in Ireland to 15,000 men. He obtained, from the Irish Parliament, a grant of £20,000, to clothe and arm the militia. Between the army on the one side, and the militia on the other, he took the "Volunteers" in the centre, and disarmed them. On the day when the last of the "Volunteers" laid down their muskets, Ireland's hopes were laid down with them.

The second of these designs,—namely, the forcing of the "United Irishmen" to become a secret conspiracy, he effected in this manner:—In February, 1793, he passed two bills through Parliament, called the "Gunpowder Bill," and the "Convention Bill." A public meeting of the "United Irishmen" was held in Dublin;—a public meeting,—there was nothing secret about it,—to protest against the inquisitorial measures of certain agents of a secret committee of the House of Lords, in going into people's houses at any hour of the day or night, without any authority,—under pretence that there was gunpowder concealed in the house. For this meeting, held legally and constitutionally, the Hon. Simon Butler, who was president of the meeting, and Mr. Oliver Bond, who was the secretary, were both imprisoned six months, and fined £500 each. When this illustrious society found that they were thus persecuted, they were obliged to take refuge in secresy; and thus it was that the "United Irishmen" were forced to become a conspiracy.

The first really treasonable project that was ever put before the "United Irishmen," was put before them in April, 1794, by the Rev. William Jackson, a Protestant clergyman, who came over commissioned by the French Convention; and the Rev. William Jackson, who was a true man, was accompanied on that mission by a certain John Cockayne, an English lawyer, from London; and *he* was the agent of William Pitt, the Prime Minister of England. Thus did the society of the "United Irishmen" become a secret conspiracy; and this was the action of the English Government. Before that, it was perfectly legitimate and constitutional. Ah! but it had an object, which was far more formidable to the English Government than any commission of Irish treason. The English Government is not afraid of Irish treason; but the English Government trembles with fear at the idea of Irish union. The "United Irishmen" were founded to promote union among all Irishmen, of every religion; and the English Minister had said in his own mind: "Treason is better than union. I will force them to become a treasonable conspiracy; and their project of union will be broken up." It is worth your while, my American friends, to hear what was the oath that was administered by the "United Irishmen." Here it is. Let us suppose that I was going to be sworn in:—

"I, Thomas Burke, in the presence of God, do pledge myself to my country, that I will use all my abilities and influence in the attainment of an impartial and adequate representation of the Irish nation in Parliament, and, as a most absolute and immediate necessity for the attainment of this chief good of Ireland, I will endeavor, as much as lies in my ability, to forward and perpetuate the identity of interests, the union of rights, and the union of power among Irishmen of all religious persuasions, without which every reform in Parliament must be partial, not national; inadequate to the wants, and wholly and entirely insufficient for the freedom and happiness of this country."

This was the United Irishman's oath. I protest before high Heaven to-night, that, priest as I am, if I were asked, in 1779, to take that oath, I would have taken it and kept it. Remember, my friends, that it was no secret oath; remember that it was no treasonable oath; remember that it was an oath that no man could refuse to take, unless he was a dishonorable man and a traitor to his country.

The founder of this society was Theobald Wolfe Tone. I admit that Mr. Tone was imbued with French revolutionary ideas; but he certainly never attempted to impress these views upon the society until Mr. William Pitt, the Prime

Minister of England, forced that society to become a secret organization.

The third object of the Premier and the Government, namely, to create an Irish rebellion, was accomplished by the cruelties and abominations of the soldiers, who were quartered at "free quarters" upon the people, destroying them, —violating that most sacred and inviolable sanctuary of Irish maidenhood and womanhood,—burning the people's villages, plundering their farms, demolishing and gutting their houses; until, at length, they made life more intolerable than death itself; goading the people, at the very bayonet's point, to rise in that fatal Rebellion of '98.

Thus I answer Mr. Froude's assertion that "the Irish people left the paths of political reform, and clamored for political agitation; from agitation grew conspiracy, and from conspiracy grew rebellion." Now, you may ask me, what motive had William Pitt, the Premier of England, to do all this. What advantage was it to him to have conspiracy and rebellion in Ireland? Oh! my friends, I answer you, that William Pitt was a great English statesman, and a great English statesman, in those days, meant a great enemy to Ireland. The object of great statesmanship, from time to time, is the effort and object of concentration;—a fatal principle,—a fatal principle, whenever it interferes with the just liberty, the time-honored traditions, or the genius of a free people. Pitt saw Ireland with a Parliament, free and independent, making her own laws and consulting her own interests. He said to himself: "This will never do; this country will grow happy and prosperous—this country will be powerful: and that will not subserve my purposes, my imperial designs. What do I care for Ireland or the Irish? My only care is for the British Empire; I may have to cross their purposes, and interfere with their interests in a thousand ways; I may have to injure them, in this way or that;

but I cannot do it, so long as they have a free Parliament."
And he made up his mind to destroy the Irish Parliament,
and to carry the "Act of Union." He knew well that, as
long as Ireland was happy, peaceful, and prosperous, he never
could effect that. He knew well that it was only through
humiliation and blood—through the ruin and destruction of
Ireland, that he could do it; and, cruel man as he was, he
resolved to plunge the kingdom into rebellion and bloodshed
in order to carry out his own infernal English State policy.
And yet, dear friends, especially my dear American friends,
my grand jury,—for I feel as if I were a lawyer—pleading
the case of a poor defendant, that has been defendant in
many a court, for many a long century: the plaintiff is a
great, rich, powerful woman; the poor defendant has nothing
to commend her but a heart that has never yet despaired—a
spirit that never yet was broken; and a loyalty to God and
to man that never yet was violated by one act of treason:—
I ask you, O grand jury of America, to consider how easy it
was to conciliate this poor mother Ireland of mine, and to
make her peaceful and happy. Pitt himself had a proof of
it in that very year, 1794. Suddenly the imperious and
magnificent Premier of England seemed to have changed his
mind, and to have adopted a policy of conciliation and kindness towards Ireland. He recalled the Irish Lord Lieutenant, Lord Westmoreland, and he sent to Ireland Earl Fitzwilliam, who arrived on the 4th of January, 1795. Lord
Fitzwilliam was a gentleman of liberal mind and a most estimable character. He felt kindly towards the Irish people;
and before he left England, he made an express compact with
William Pitt that, if he was made Lord Lieutenant of Ireland, he would govern the country on principles of conciliation and kindness. He came. He found in Dublin Castle
a certain Secretary Cooke, a petty tyrant; and he found the
great family of the Beresfords, who, for years and years, had

monopolized all the public offices and emoluments of the State, and held uncontrolled sway over the destinies of Ireland. He dismissed them all,—sent them all " to the right about;"—and he surrounded himself with men of liberal minds and large, statesmanlike views. He began by telling the Catholics of Ireland that he would labor for their emancipation. A sudden peace and joy spread throughout the nation. Every vestige of insubordination and rebellion seemed to vanish out of the Irish mind. The people were content to wait. Every law was observed. Peace, happiness, and joy were, for the time being, the portion of the Irish people. How long did it last? In an evil hour, Pitt returned to his old designs. Earl Fitzwilliam was recalled on the 25th of March; and Ireland enjoyed her hopes only for two short months.

When it was ascertained that Lord Fitzwilliam was about to be recalled, there was scarcely a parish in Ireland that did not send in petitions, resolutions, and prayers to the English Government to leave them their Lord Lieutenant. All to no purpose. The policy was changed. Pitt had made up his mind to carry the Union. On the day that Lord Fitzwilliam left Dublin, the principal citizens took the horses from his carriage; and they drew the carriage themselves down to the water's side. All Ireland was in tears. "The scene," says an historian of the time, "was heart-rending; the whole nation was in mourning." How easy it was, my American friends, to conciliate these people, whom two short months of kindness could have thus changed! Oh! if only the English Government, the English Parliament, the English people,—if they could only realize to themselves, for ever so short a time, the mine of affection, that glorious heart, that splendid gratitude that lies there in Ireland, but to which they have never appealed and never touched;—but instead, they have turned the very honey of human nature into the gall and bitterness of hatred!

The rebellion broke out. It was defeated; and as Mr. Froude truly says, the victors took away the old privileges, and made the yoke heavier. By the " old privileges," people of America, Mr. Froude means the Irish Parliament that was taken away. I hope, citizens of America, that this English gentleman, who has come here to get " a verdict " from you, will be taught by that verdict that the right to home legislation is not a privilege, but the *right* of every nation on the face of the earth. Then, in the course of his lecture, going back to strengthen his argument, he says:—" You must not blame England for being so hard upon you, Irishmen. She took away your Parliament; she afflicted you with a heavier yoke than you bore before. She couldn't help it; it was your own fault; what made you rebel?" This is the argument which the learned gentleman uses. He says that the penal laws would never have been established, never would have been carried out, only for the revolution of 1600 in Ireland. Now, the revolution of 1600 means the war that Hugh O'Neill made, in Ulster, against Queen Elizabeth. And, according to this learned historian, the penal laws were the result, the effect, the consequence of that revolution. Remember, he fixes the date himself:—he says 1600. Now, my friends, here is the record of history: The penal laws began to operate in Ireland in 1534. In 1537 the Archbishop of Armagh and Primate of Ireland, who was an Englishman—his name was Cromer—was put into jail and left there for denying the supremacy of Henry the Eighth over the Church of God. Passing over the succeeding years of Henry the Eighth's reign; passing over the enactments of Somerset, under Edward the Sixth, we come to Elizabeth's reign; and we find that she assembled a Parliament in 1560,—forty years before Mr. Froude's revolution.

Here is one of the laws passed by that Parliament: All officers and ministers, lay or ecclesiastical,—that took us in, you see,—were bound to take the oath of supremacy, and were bound to swear that Queen Elizabeth was the Popess —that she was the head of the Church; that she was the successor of the Apostles—that she was the representative of St. Peter, and, through him, of the Eternal Son of God! Queen Elizabeth! All were obliged to take this oath under pain of forfeiture and total incapacity. Any one who maintained the spiritual supremacy,—mind, the spiritual supremacy,—of the Pope was to forfeit, for the first offence, all his estates, real and personal; and if he had no estate, and if he was not worth £20, he was to be put in jail for one year. For the second offence he was liable to the penalty of "præmunire." And, for the third offence, he was guilty of high treason, and put to death. These laws were made, and commissioners were appointed to enforce them. Mr. Froude says they were not enforced in Ireland. But we actually have the acts of Elizabeth's Parliament, appointing magistrates and officers to go out and enforce these laws. And these laws were made forty years before the revolution which Mr. Froude alludes to as the revolution of 1600. How, then, can that gentleman ask us to regard the penal laws as the effect of that revolution? In my philosophy, and, I believe, in that of the citizens of America, the effect generally follows the cause; but the English philosophical historian puts the effect forty years ahead of the cause. That is, as we say in Ireland, "putting the cart before the horse."

But, Mr. Froude told us, if you remember,—in his second lecture, if you have read it,—that the penal laws of Elizabeth were occasioned by the political necessity of her situation. Here is his argument as he himself puts it. He says:—"Elizabeth could not afford to let Ireland be Catholic; because if Ireland were Catholic, Ireland would be hostile to Elizabeth." I may tell you now (I hope the ladies who are here will excuse me for mentioning such a thing), that Queen Elizabeth was not a legitimate child. Her name, in common parlance, is too vile for me to utter, or for the ladies here to hear. Suffice it to say that Elizabeth's mother was not Elizabeth's father's wife. The Queen of England knew the ancient abhorrence that Ireland had for a base-born child. She knew that abhorrence grew out of Ireland's Catholicity; and therefore she could not allow Ireland to remain Catholic (says Mr. Froude), because Ireland would be hostile to her if Ireland remained Catholic. The only way in which this amiable Queen could root out the Catholics of Ireland was by penal laws; making it a felony for any Irishman to remain in Ireland a Catholic. Therefore, the English historian says: that "she passed these laws because she could not help herself;" and that she was "coerced to do so by the necessity of her situation." Now, I argue from this very argument of Mr. Froude himself, that if Elizabeth, as he states in his second lecture, was obliged to pass these penal laws, whether she would or not, why does he turn round and say that those penal laws were the effect of Hugh O'Neill's revolution? If they were the result of Elizabeth's necessity, then they were not the result of the immortal Hugh O'Neill's brave efforts.

His next assertion, my friends, is that, after the American war, England was only too well disposed to do justice to Ireland; and the proof lies here: He says that the laws against Catholics were almost repealed before 1798. Very well. I ask you, dear friends, to reflect upon what these large measures of indulgence to the Catholics were of which Mr. Froude speaks. Here they are: In the year 1771, Parliament passed an act, to enable Catholics to take a long lease of fifty acres of bog. My American friends, you may not understand the word bog. We Irish understand it. It means a marsh which is almost irreclaimable; which you may drain and drain until doomsday, and it will still remain the original marsh. You may sink a fortune in it, in arterial drainage, in "top-dressing," as we call it in Ireland; and, if you let it alone for a couple of years, and then come back and look at it, it has asserted itself, and is a bog once more. However, my friends, the Parliament was kinder than you imagine, for, while they granted to the Catholic power to take a long lease of fifty acres of bog, they also stipulated, that if the bog was too deep for a foundation, he might take half an acre of arable land upon which to build a house. Half an acre! For the life of him, not more than half an acre. However, this holding, such as it was, should not be within a mile of any city or town. Oh, no! And mark this! If half the bog were not reclaimed, that is five-and-twenty acres, within twenty-one years, the lease was forfeited. Well, my friends, the Scriptures tell us that King Pharaoh, of Egypt, was very cruel to the Hebrews, because he ordered them to make bricks without straw; but here is an order to the unfortunate Irishman to reclaim twenty-five acres of bog, or else give up the lease. Now, beggarly as that concession was, you will be astonished to hear that the very Parliament that passed it was so much afraid of the Protestant Ascendancy in Ireland, that in order to conciliate them for the slight concession, they passed another bill granting £10 a year, in addition to £30 already offered, for every "Popish" Priest duly converted to the Protestant religion!

In October, 1777, the news reached England that General Burgoyne had surrendered to the American General Gates. The moment that news reached home, Lord North, who was then Prime Minister of England, immediately cried out and expressed an ardent desire to relax the penal laws on Catholics. In January, 1778, the following year, the independence of America was acknowledged by glorious France

The moment that piece of news reached England, the English Parliament at once passed a bill for the relaxation of the laws on the Catholics. In May of the same year the Irish Parliament passed a bill,—now mark,—to enable Catholics to lease land—to take a lease for 999 years. So it seems we were to get out of the bog at last. They also, in that year, repealed the unnatural penal laws which altered the succession in favor of the child that became Protestant, and gave him his father's property; also repealing the law for the prosecution of priests, and for the imprisonment of "Popish" schoolmasters. In the year 1793, they gave back to the Catholics the power of electing Members of Parliament—the power of voting; and they also gave them the right to certain commissions in the army. That is, positively, all that we got. And that is what Mr. Froude calls almost a total repeal of the laws against Catholics. We could not go into Parliament; we could not go on the bench; we could not be magistrates; we were still the "hewers of wood and drawers of water;" and this mild and benign Englishman comes and says: "Why, you fools, you were almost free!" O people of America! if this be Mr. Froude's notion of civil and religious freedom, I appeal to you, for Ireland, not to give him the verdict.

"The insurrection of '98," continues the learned gentleman, "threw Ireland back into a condition of confusion and misery, from which she was partially delivered by the Act of Union." The first part of that proposition I admit; the second I emphatically deny. I admit that the unsuccessful rebellion of '98 threw Ireland back into a state of misery. Unsuccessful rebellion is one of the greatest calamities that can befall a nation; and the sooner Irishmen and Irish patriots understand this, the better it will be for them and their country. But I emphatically deny that the Act of Union was any remedy for these miseries; that it was any healing whatever for the wounds of Ireland; that it was anything in the shape of a benefit or a blessing. I assert that the Union of 1800, by which Ireland lost her Parliament, was a pure curse for Ireland, from that day to this, and nothing else; and that it is an evil which must be remedied if the grievances of Ireland are ever to be redressed.

I need not dwell upon the wholesale bribery and corruption by which the infernal Castlereagh, the political apostate, carried that detestable Act of Union. Mr. Froude has had the good taste to pass by the dirty subject without touching it, and I think I can do nothing better.

He says:—"It was expected that whatever grievances Ireland complained of would be removed by legislation after the Act of Union." It was expected, it is quite true. Even the Catholics expected something. They were promised, in writing, by Lord Cornwallis, that Catholic Emancipation should be given them if they would consent to the Union. Pitt himself pledged himself, through his Lord Lieutenant, that he would never take office and that he would never administer or serve in the Government unless Catholic Emancipation was made a Cabinet measure. The honor of Pitt was engaged; the honor of England was engaged; the honor of the brave, though, in America, unfortunate soldier, Cornwallis, was engaged. But the wicked act was accomplished; and, then, the Catholics of Ireland were left to sing Tom Moore's song—"I'd mourn the hopes that leave me." They were left to meditate in bitterness of spirit upon the nature of English faith.

Now, let me introduce an honored name that I shall return to by and by. At that time the Parliament of Ireland was bribed with money and with titles, and the Catholic people of Ireland were bribed by promised emancipation, if they would sanction the Union. Then it was that a young man appeared in Dublin, speaking for the first time against the Union, in the name of the Catholics of Ireland; and that young man was the glorious Daniel O'Connell. Two or three of the Bishops gave a kind of tacit, negative assent to the measure, in the hope of getting Catholic Emancipation. I need hardly tell you, my friends, that the Catholic lords of the Pale were only too willing to pass any measure that the English Government would require. O'Connell appeared before the Catholic Committee in Dublin, and here are his words,—remember that they are the words of the Catholics, of the people, of Ireland:—"Sir," he said, "it is my sentiment, and I am satisfied it is the sentiment not only of every gentleman that hears me, but of the Catholic people of Ireland, that they are opposed to this injurious, insulting, and hated measure of union. And if its rejection has to bring upon us the renewal of the penal laws, we would boldly meet the proscription and oppression, which have been the testimony of our virtue, and throw ourselves once more on the mercy of our Protestant brethren, sooner than give our assent to the political murder of our country." "I know," he says, "I do know that, although exclusive advantages may be ambiguously held forth to the Irish Catholic, to seduce him from the sacred duty which he owes to his country, yet I know that the Catholics of Ireland will still remember that they have a country; and they will never accept of any advantage as a sect which would debase and destroy them as a people." Shade of the great departed, you never uttered truer words. Shade of the great O'Connell, every true Irishman, priest and layman, subscribes to these glorious sentiments, wherever that Irishman is to be found.

Now Mr. Froude goes on, in an innocent sort of way. He says: "It is a strange thing that, after the Union was passed, the people of Ireland were still grumbling and complaining; yet they had no foundation for their complaints; they were not treated unjustly." These are his words. Good God! people of America, what idea can this gentleman have in this? What did this Union, which he admires so much, and which he declares that England will maintain, —what did it bring to Ireland? What gain did it bring to Ireland, and what loss did it inflict on her? I answer, from history. The gain of the Union to Ireland was simply nothing,—absolutely nothing;—and I ask you to consider two or three of the losses.

First of all, then, remember, my friends, that Ireland, before the Union, had her own National Debt, as she had her own military establishment. She was a nation. The National Debt of Ireland, in the year 1793, did not amount to three millions of money. In the year 1800, the year of the Union, the National Debt of Ireland amounted to twenty-eight millions of money. They increased it ninefold in six years. How? I will tell you. England had, in Ireland, for her own purposes, at the time of the Union, 126,500 soldiers. Pretty tough business, that, of keeping Ireland down in these days! She made Ireland pay for every man of them. She did not pay a penny of her own money for them. In order to carry the Union, England spent enormous sums of money for bribes to spies and informers and to Members of Parliament. She took every penny of this money out of the Irish treasury. There were eighty-four rotten boroughs disfranchised at the time of the Union; and England paid to those who owned those boroughs, or who had the nomination of them,—she actually paid them one million two hundred thousand pounds sterling for their loss; the loss being in losing the nomination boroughs, the loss by the proprietor of the corrupt influence in returning these members to Parliament. Ireland was made to pay this money. O'Connell, speaking on this subject, some years later, says:—" Really, it was strange that Ireland was not asked to pay for the knife with which, twenty-two years later, Castlereagh cut his throat!"

But if the debt of Ireland was swollen from three millions before the Union, to twenty-eight millions, I ask you to consider what followed. We now come to the period after the Union. Mark, my friends! In January, 1801,—you may say the year of the Union,—the debt of England was four hundred and fifty millions and a half pounds sterling; and to pay that debt they required £17,708,800; consequently they had to raise by taxation, eighteen millions, to pay the interest on the debt of four hundred and fifty millions in that year. Such was the condition of England. In the year 1817, sixteen years after, the same debt of England had risen from four hundred and fifty millions to seven hundred and thirty-five millions,—nearly double; and they had an annual charge of twenty-eight millions odd to pay. So, you see, they doubled their national debt in the sixteen years during which Pitt had waged war with Napoleon. They were obliged to subsidize and to pay Germans, Russians, and all sorts of people to fight against France. At one time William Pitt was supporting the whole Austrian army. The Austrians had the men, but no money. Now, mark this! In Ireland, the debt, in 1801, was twenty-eight and one-half millions; and, consequently, the annual taxation was one million two hundred and fifty thousand pounds. In the year 1817, the same Irish debt, which, sixteen years before, was only twenty-eight millions, was now £112,704,000 sterling, and the taxes amounted to four millions one hundred and four thousand pounds sterling. In other words, in sixteen years the debt of England was doubled; but the debt of Ireland was made four times as much as it was in the year in which the Act of Union was passed. You may ask me how did that happen? It happened from the very fact that, being united to England, having lost our Parliament, the English Chancellor of the Exchequer took and kept the money and the Irish accounts,—kept the books. Ireland lost the privilege of keeping her own accounts. And this is the account he brought against Ireland in 1817.

Ireland was so lightly burdened with debt, at the time of the Union, as compared with England, that the English did not ask us, when they united our Parliament to their own, —they did not presume to ask us, they had not the presumption to ask us,—to take share and share alike in the taxes. Why should they? We only owed twenty millions and they owed four hundred and fifty millions. Why should we be asked to pay the interest on their debt? They were rich and could bear that taxation; Ireland was poor, and she could not bear it. Ireland was, consequently, much more lightly taxed than England. It was very much easier to pay interest on twenty millions of pounds than on four hundred and fifty millions. But there was an agreement made by Castlereagh with the Irish Parliament. It was this. He said:—"That if the Irish national debt ever comes up to one-seventh of the national debt of England, then we will throw it all in together and tax the people share and share alike." The object of running up the Irish debt was to bring it up within one-seventh of the English debt. This they accomplished in 1817. Then the Irish and the English were taxed indiscriminately, and they all alike were obliged to pay the taxes for the interest on the four hundred and fifty millions of debt that the Crown of England had incurred, before the Union at all. And the Irish, he says, were not unjustly treated! "Ah, but," says Mr. Froude, "consider the advantages of the Union! You have the same commercial privileges that the English had." To this, I answer, in the words of the illustrious, the honest, the high-minded John Mitchel:—

"It is true," (says Mr. Mitchel,) "that the laws regulating trade are the same in the two islands. Ireland may export flax and woollen cloths to England; she may import her own tea from China and sugar from Barbadoes; the laws which made these acts penal offences no longer exist; and why? Because they are no longer needed. By the operation of these old laws Ireland was utterly ruined. England has the commercial marine; Ireland has it to create. England has the manufacturing machinery and skill of which Ireland was deprived by express laws made for that purpose. England has the current of trade setting strongly in her own channels, while Ireland is left dry. To create or recover, at this day, the great industrial and commercial resources, and that in the face of wealthy rivals that are already in full possession,—is manifestly impossible without one or the other of these two conditions, namely—an immense command of capital, or effectual protective duties. But, by the Union, our capital was drawn away to England; and by the Union we were deprived of the power of imposing protective duties."

It was to this very end that the Union was forced upon Ireland through intolerance of Irish prosperity. "Don't unite with us, sir," says the honest old man, Dr. Samuel Johnson, when addressed on the subject of union in his day. "Don't unite with us, sir; we shall rob you!" In the very first year after the Union was passed, Mr. Foster stated in the English House of Parliament, that there was a falling off in the linen trade of Ireland of five millions less of yards exported. The same gentleman, three years later, stated that in 1800,—the year of the Union,—the net produce of the Irish revenue was £2,800,000, while the debt was only £25,000,000. Three years later, after three years' experience of the Union, the debt had increased to £53,000,000, and the revenue had diminished by £11,000.

Ireland was deserted. That absenteeism, which was the curse of Ireland in the days of Swift, had so increased by the Union, that Dublin became almost a deserted city, and all the cities in Ireland were as places in the wilderness. At this very day, in Dublin, the Duke of Leinster's city palace is turned into a museum of Irish industry. Powerscourt House, in Dame Street, has become a draper's shop; Tyrone House is a school-house; the house of the Earl of Bective was pulled down a few years ago, to build up a Scotch Presbyterian Meeting-House in its place. Charlemont House,—Lord Charlemont's residence,—was sold about six months before I came to America; and it is now the head office of the Board of Works; Aldborough House is a barrack; Belvidere House is a convent. So, fashion, trade, commercial activity, intellectual enterprise, political interest, everything has gone to London; and Ireland may fold her hands, and sigh over the ruin that is left her now. And that is the result of the Union. The crumbling Liberties of Dublin attest the decay and ruin of the trade of Ireland; the forsaken harbors of Limerick and Galway tell of the destruction of her commerce; the palaces of Dublin, abandoned to decay, announce that she is no longer the residence of her nobility; the forlorn custom-houses tell of her income transferred elsewhere. What do we get in return for all this? Absolutely nothing. Every Irish question goes now to London to be debated; and the moment an Irish member stands up in the House, the first thing he may expect is to be coughed down, sneered down, or crowed down—unless, indeed, he has the lungs of an O'Connell to turn upon them, like an African lion, and, with a roar, put down their beastly bellowing.

Pitt promised Emancipation. Six months after the Union was passed, he retired from office, on the pretence, indeed, that the King would not grant Emancipation, and would not keep his word. But it is well known that the true reason why Pitt retired was that his Continental policy had failed. The people of England were tired of his wars, and were clamoring for peace. Pitt was too proud a man to sign even a temporary peace with France; and he retired in sullen pride and disgust. He retired under the pretext that he would not be allowed to carry Catholic Emancipation. Some time later, after the Addington Administration was broken up, Mr. Pitt returned again, the second time, to be the Premier of England. Not one word escaped his lips about Catholic Emancipation; and he resisted it until his death. He was as great an enemy to the Catholics of Ireland as ever poor, old, foolish, mad George the Third was. And it was only after twenty-nine years of heroic effort, that the great O'Connell rallied the Irish nation, and succeeded for a time in uniting all the Catholics of Ireland as one man, as well as a great number of our noble-hearted Protestant fellow-Irishmen. And when O'Connell came, and knocked at the doors of the British Parliament, with the hand of an united Irish people,—when he spoke with the voice of eight millions,—then, and only then—even as the walls of Jericho crumbled at the sound of Joshua's trumpet, —so did the old, bigoted threshold of the British House of Commons tremble, while its doors burst open and let in the gigantic Irishman that represented eight millions of the people of Ireland. The English historian cannot say that England granted Catholic Emancipation willingly. She granted it as a man would yield up a bad tooth to a dentist. O'Connell put the forceps into that false old mouth. The old tyrant wriggled and groaned. The bigoted profligate who then disgraced England's crown, shed his crocodile tears over the bill. The eyes that were never known to weep over the ruin of female virtue,—the face that never was known to change color in the presence of any vile deed or

accusation of vice,—that face grew pale; and George the
Fourth wept for sorrow when he had to sign the bill. The
man who had conquered Napoleon upon the field of Waterloo; the man who was declared to be the invincible victor,
and the greatest of warriors,—stood there with that bill in
his hand, and said to the King of England: "I would not
grant it, your Majesty, any more than you: but it is forced
from you and me. You must either sign that paper, or prepare for civil war and revolution in Ireland." I regret to
be obliged to say it, but really, my friends, the history of my
native land proves to me that England never granted any
thing from love or through a sense of justice, or from any
other motive than from a craven fear of civil war, or of
some serious inconvenience to herself.

Now, having arrived at this point, Mr. Froude glances,
I must say in a magnificently masterly manner, over the
great questions that have affected Ireland since the day
Emancipation was passed. He speaks words of most eloquent compassion over the terrible visitation of '46 and '47,
—words the reading of which brought tears to my eyes;
and for the words of compassion that he gave to the people
whose sufferings I witnessed, I prayed to God to bless him
and reward him. He speaks words of generous, enlightened,
and statesmanlike sympathy with the tenant-farmers and the
peasants of Ireland: and for these words, Mr. Froude, if you
were an Englishman ten thousand times over, I love you.
He does not attempt to speak of the future of Ireland.
Perhaps it is a dangerous thing for me to attempt; yet I
suppose that all that we have been discussing in the past
must have some reference to the future; for surely the verdict that Mr. Froude looks for is not a mere verdict of absolution for past iniquities. He has come here,—though he is
not a Catholic—he has come to America like a man going to
confession. He has cried out loudly and generously, "We

have sinned, we have sinned, we have grievously sinned;"—and the verdict which he calls for must surely regard the future more than the past. For how, in the name of common sense, can this great historian, or any man, ask for a verdict justifying the rule of iniquity, the heart-rending record of cruelty, injustice, fraud, robbery, bloodshed, and wrong which we have been contemplating in company with Mr. Froude? It must be for the future. What is that future? Well, my friends,—first of all my American grand jury,—you must remember that I am only a monk and not a man of the world; I do not understand much about these things. There are wiser heads than mine; and I will give you their opinions. There is one class of men who love Ireland—and I will only speak of those who love Ireland—who love her sincerely;—there is one class of men who love Ireland, and who think, in their love for Ireland, that the future of Ireland is to be wrought out by insurrection, rising in arms against the power which holds Ireland enslaved, if you will. Well, if the history which Mr. Froude has been just telling us, and which I have endeavored to review for you—if it teaches us anything as Irishmen, it teaches us that there is no use in appealing to the sword or to armed insurrection for Ireland. Mr. Froude says that we will only succeed when the Irish people have two things they do not seem to have now, namely,—union as one man, and a determination not to sheath that sword until the work is done. I know that I would earn louder plaudits, citizens of America, and speak more popular language to the ears of my auditors, if I declared my adhesion to this class of Irishmen. But there is not living a man that loves Ireland more dearly than I do. There are those who may love her more effectively and serve her with greater distinction—but no man loves Ireland more tenderly and more sincerely than I do. I prize, citizens of America, the good-will of my fellow-Irishmen; I prize it next to the grace of God. I also prize the popularity which, however unworthily, I possess with them; but I tell you American citizens, that for all that popularity, for all that good-will, I would not compromise one iota of my convictions, nor would I state what I do not believe to be true. I do not believe in insurrectionary movements in a country so divided as Ireland.

There is another class of Irishmen who hold that Ireland has a future—a glorious future,—and that that future is to be wrought out in this way. They say,—and I think with justice and right—that wealth acquired by industry brings with it power and political influence. They say, therefore, to the Irish at home, "Try to accumulate wealth; lay hold of the industries, and develop the resources of your country. Try, in the meantime, and labor to effect that blessed union without which there never can be a future for Ireland. That union can only be effected by largeness of mind, by generosity, and urbanity amongst fellow-citizens; by rising above the miserable bigotry that carries religious differences and religious hatreds into the relations of life that do not belong to religion." Meantime, they say to the men of Ireland, "Try and acquire property and wealth. This can only be done by developing assiduous industry; and that industry can only be exercised as long as the country is at peace, and as long as there is a truce to violent political agitation." . Then these men—I am giving the opinions of others, not my own—these men say to the Irishmen in America,—"Men of Ireland in America—men of Irish birth—men of American birth but of Irish blood—we believe that God has largely intrusted the destinies of Ireland to you. America demands of her citizens only energy, industry, temperance, truthfulness, obedience to the laws; and any man that has these, with the brains that God has given to every Irishman, is sure in this land to realize fortune and a grand future. If you are faithful to America in these respects, America will be faithful to you. And in proportion as the great Irish element in America rises in wealth, it will rise in political influence and power—the political influence and power which in a few years is destined to overshadow the whole world, and to bring about, through peace and justice, far greater revolutions in the cause of honor and humanity than have ever been effected by the sword." This is the programme of the second class of Irishmen; and I tell you candidly, that to this programme I give my heart and soul.

You will ask me about separation from the crown of England. Well, that is a ticklish question, ladies and gentlemen. I dare say you remember that, when Charles Edward was Pretender to the Crown of England, during the first years of the House of Hanover, there was a toast which the Jacobite gentlemen used to give. It was this:—

> "God bless the King, our noble faith's defender;
> Long may he live; and down with the Pretender.
> But which be the Pretender—which be King,—
> God bless us all, that's quite another thing."

And yet, with the courage of an old monk, I will tell you my mind on this very question. History tells us that empires, like men, run the cycle of years of their life, and then die; no matter how extended their power, no matter how mighty their influence, no matter how great their sway, how invincible their armies; the day comes, the inevitable day, that brings with it decay and disruption. Thus it was with the empire of the Medes and Persians; thus it was with the mighty empire of the Assyrians; thus with the Egyptians of old; thus with the Greeks; thus with Rome. Who would ever have imagined, for instance, 1,500 years ago—before the Goths first came to the walls of Rome—who would have imagined that the power that was to rule with undisputed sway over a territory greater than the whole Roman Empire, would be the little unknown island flung out in the Western Ocean, known only by having been conquered by the Romans, the *ultima thule*, the tin island in the far ocean? And this was England. Who would have imagined that in the cycle of time this would come to pass? Now, my friends, England has been a long time at the top of the wheel; do you imagine she will always remain there? I do not want to be one bit more loyal than Lord Macaulay: and Lord Macaulay describes the day " when the traveller from New Zealand shall take his stand upon the broken arch of London Bridge to sketch the ruins of St. Paul's." Is that wheel of England rising or falling? Is England to-day what she was twenty years ago? England, twenty years ago, in her first alliance with Napoleon, had a finger in every pie in Europe—and Lord John Russell and Lord Palmerston were busy-bodies of the first order. England to-day has no more to say in the affairs of Europe, than the Emperor of China has. You see I am only talking philosophy. A few months ago, the three great Emperors,—of Germany, Austria, and Russia,—came together in Berlin to fix the map of Europe; and they did not even pay the courtesy of asking England to come in, to know what she had to say about it. The army of England to-day is nothing, a mere cipher. The German Emperor can bring his 1,200,000 men into the field; and England, for the very life of her, cannot put 200,000 men against him. An English citizen— a loyal Englishman—wrote a book called " The Battle of Dorking," in which he describes a German army marching on London. The Englishman was loyal; and why should I be more loyal than he? Of England's navy, Mr. Reade, Chief Constructor of the British navy, has written an article in a London paper, in which he declares and proves that, at this moment, the British fleet would be afraid to go into

Russian waters. They are not able to meet Russia. And why should I be more loyal than Mr. Reade? An empire begins to totter and crumble to decay, when it withdraws its forces from its outlying provinces; as, in the decay of Rome, the Roman legions were withdrawn from Britain. England, to-day, says to Canada and Australia, "Oh, take your government into your own hands; we don't want to be bothered with you any more!" England, that, eighty years ago, fought for the United Colonies of America, as long as she could put a man into the field, has changed her policy. An empire is crumbling to decay when she begins to buy off her enemies, as in the case of the Roman Empire, when she began to buy off the Scythians, the Dacians, and other barbaric races, that were coming down upon her before her Empire fell. England, a few days ago, was presented with a little bill by America. She said, "Why, Jonathan, I owe you nothing;" and John Bull buttoned up his pocket and swore he would not pay a cent. And then America said, "Look here, John, if you don't,—look at this!"—and she took the sword and held it by both hands:—"whichever end you like." John Bull paid the bill.

My friends, it looks very like as if the day of Lord Macaulay's New Zealander was rapidly approaching. On that day, my opinion is, that Ireland will be mistress of her own destinies, with the liberty that will come to her, not from earth, but from that God whom she has never forsaken. And the whole question is, will Ireland, on that day, be worthy of the glorious destiny that is in the womb of time and the hand of God? I say that Ireland will be worthy of it, if that day dawn upon a united people, upon a faithful people, upon a people that will keep, every man, his faith in God and in his holy religion, as his fathers before him kept it in the dark hour and in the terrible day of persecution. I say that Ireland will be worthy of her destiny, if on that day, when it dawns upon her, she will be found as distinctive, as individual a people and race, as she is to-day in her affliction and in her misery; if she foster her traditions, if she keep up her high hopes, if she keep the tender, strong love that her people always have had for the Green Isle that bore them—then will Ireland be worthy of her destiny. What shall that destiny be? My friends, if Mr. Froude has proved anything, I think he has proved this general proposition, that, although Almighty God lavished upon the English people many gifts, there is one gift he never gave them; and that is the gift of knowing how to govern other people. To govern a people requires, first of all, strict justice; and, secondly, to have the interests of the people at heart—their real interests; and, thirdly, it requires tact and urbanity. The French have this, but the English have not. Look at Alsace and Lorraine;—look at the suffering people, the brave people, emigrating like one man, attaching themselves to France, though she is down in the dust, rather than enter into rich and triumphant Germany. And why? Because France won their hearts by her justice, by her consulting their true interests, and by her French urbanity and tact. The history of the English Government's connection with Ireland is a history of injustice; it is a history of heartlessness; and it is, above all, a history of blundering want of tact: not knowing what to do with the people; never understanding them; knowing nothing at all of their genius, their prejudices, and the shape and form of their national character.

But there is another nation that understands Ireland, and has proved that she understands Ireland; whose statesmen have always spoken words of bright encouragement, of tender sympathy, and of manly hope to Ireland in her darkest days; and that nation is the United States of America; the mighty land, placed by the Omnipotent hand between the far East on the one side, to which she stretches out her glorious arms, over the broad Pacific; whilst, on the other, she sweeps with her left hand over the Atlantic, and touches Europe; the mighty land, enclosing in her splendid bosom untold resources of every form of commercial and other wealth; the mighty land, with room for three hundred millions of men; with millions of the oppressed ones, all the world over, flying to her more than imperial bosom, there to find liberty and the sacred rights of civil and religious freedom. Is there not every reason to suppose that, in that future which we cannot see to-day, but which lies before us,—America will be to the whole world what Rome was in the ancient days, what England was but a few years ago,—the great storehouse of the world, the great ruler,—the pacific ruler,—of the destinies of the whole world: the great manufacturing power, dispensing from out her mighty bosom all the necessaries and all the luxuries of life to the whole world around her?—that she may be destined,—as I believe she is destined,—to rise rapidly into that gigantic form that will overshadow all other nations. When that glorious day comes to pass, what is more natural than that Ireland, now, as I suppose, mistress of her own destinies, should turn and stretch out the arms of her sympathy and love across the intervening waves of the Atlantic, and be received, an independent State, into the mighty confederation of America. America,—mark, I am not speaking treason—remember, I say distinctly, all this is to come to pass after Macaulay's New Zealander has arrived;— America will require an emporium for her European trade. Ireland lies there right between her and Europe, with her splendid coast line, and vast harbors and bays, able to shelter all her commercial and other fleets. America may require a great European storehouse, a great European hive for her manufactures; and Ireland has enormous waterpower, now flowing idly to the sea, but which yet, in the future day, may be busy in turning the wheels set upon these streams by American-Irish capital and Irish industry. If ever that day comes, if ever that union comes, it will be no degradation to Ireland to join hands with America, because America does not enslave her States; she accepts them on terms of glorious equality: she respects their rights, and blesses all who cast their lot with her.

Now, I have done with this subject and with Mr. Froude. I have one word to say before I retire, and that is, if during the course of these five lectures one single word personally offensive to this distinguished gentleman has escaped my lips, I take that word back now; I apologize to him before he asks me; and I beg to assure him that such a word never came wilfully from my mind or from my heart. He says he loves Ireland; and I believe according to his lights he does love Ireland; but our lights are very different from his. Still the Almighty God will judge every man according to his lights.

CONCLUDING LECTURE.

(*Delivered in the Academy of Music, Brooklyn, December* 19, 1872.)

REPLY TO MR. FROUDE'S "LAST WORDS."

LADIES AND GENTLEMEN: I need not tell you that this world in which we live is a very changeable world. We have seen so many changes ourselves, in our own day, that we have learned to be astonished at nothing. We have seen, but a few years ago—only four years ago—France, reputed the bravest and most powerful nation in Europe. To-day, France is down in the dust; and there is no one found so poor as to do glorious France honor. So, in like manner, a few years ago, when Lord Palmerston was at the head of the English Ministry, England was considered one of the most influential and one of the most powerful nations of the earth: and to-day we see how things are changed. In our own time, we remember, whenever England had any argument to state, any theory of a national kind to propound, any cause to defend, she sent her fleets and her armies. Even as late as 1858, she had an argument with the Emperor of Russia; and she sent her fleets and armies to discuss the question at the point of the sword. Later still,—but a few months ago, I may say—she had an argument with the Emperor, as he was called, of Abyssinia; and she sent her army there to try conclusions and to reason with him. To-day, my friends, she has an argument with Ireland; and instead of adopting the old policy of sending some Cromwell or other over there at the head of an army, to argue with the Irish,—with the Bible in one hand and the sword in the other,—she sends over to America a talking man, to talk over it.

England has tried issues with my native land for many a long century; for seven hundred years on the National question ; for three hundred years on the still more important religious question. On the religious question England is fairly beaten ; and on the National question, although we have not yet triumphed, she has never been able to knock the nationality out of Ireland. So what does she do ? The days are past and gone when she could send her Cromwell or her William of Orange to Ireland : and to-day she has nothing better to fall back upon than to send an Englishman over to America to abuse us,—to try and make out that we are the most ungovernable and the most God-abandoned race on the face of the earth. So he comes, and delivers his message. When first he came he told the people of America, if you remember—you all remember it as well as I do,—that he intended, as far as he could, to justify England's treatment of Ireland ; and consequently, that this was his intention is clearly manifested by the simple fact that he has gone into the whole history of the relations between England and Ireland. He has gone through them all. He began with the Norman invasion ; and he came down to the present year, for the sole and avowed purpose of white-washing England as far as he could, and making out that, after all, she was not so bad as people were inclined to believe she was. And when he was followed on this great issue, my friends, Mr. Froude turns around and says : " You are all greatly mistaken. I don't want a verdict from the American people, to justify England. I don't want to put America in the confessional, and make my country kneel down and get a plenary absolution for all that she ever did to Ireland. That is not my intention at all. My intention is, and the verdict I seek is simply this : There is a movement going on in Ireland now called the 'Home Rule' agitation. Irishmen," he says, " are beginning at home to say that they have the right to make their own laws, and to be governed by their own laws. They say that it is not right, nor fair, nor just, that the things that could be so well done at home, should be so badly done in London, by men who know very little about Ireland, and who care less. Now," he says, " I come to America simply to obtain the verdict of American public opinion to this effect: that the Irish don't know how to govern themselves ; that whatever other virtues or talents they have, they have not the talent nor the virtue of self-government; they are not wise enough, they are not prudent enough, they are not temperate enough, they are not sufficiently civilized nor sufficiently tolerant to govern themselves; and I will prove it from their history; and I ask the American people to send over this word to the Irish, 'Now, boys, have sense. You don't know what is for your own good;—you never did, and Mr. Froude has brought it home to us. You may have a great many virtues,—he acknowledges that you have some;—but you have no sense at all. We have sense; and the English people have—and always had—twice as much sense as you have. They know how to govern you beautifully—oh! how sweetly! Leave yourselves entirely in their hands, and they will make the finest laws that ever were heard of for your special use and benefit. They love you like the apple of their eye. They are very anxious to see Ireland prosperous, wealthy, rich, and powerful; they are very anxious to give you all that they have themselves; and a great deal more. So, Mr. Froude says, all you have to do, now, is to keep yourselves quiet; leave the Parliament where it is, and send your Members of Parliament over there. Let the English members and the Scotch members,—who have a sweeping majority,—let them make laws for you; and these will be salutary and beautiful laws for Ireland. You don't know how to make such laws yourselves. You don't know anything about your own interests, or the principles of government. You don't understand your own country.'" And he expects America, like an old woman, to send over this advice to Ireland.

It is not with Mr. Froude's facts in detail, so much, that I have to deal, as with the spirit of the man. In his reply to my lectures, he distinctly states that he does not seek justification for England's past conduct; but that he came here to arouse public American opinion against the principle, so dear to Irishmen, that they have the right, and that God has given them the power, and the intelligence, and the capability to make their own laws and to be governed by them. He has traced England's dealings with Ireland: he has traced them, no doubt, in a masterly manner. I wish I could do it half so well. But, my friends, throughout, the leading idea in the mind of this historian, clearly manifested and avowed by him, is to bring home to every thinking man in this land the conviction that we Irish did not know how to govern ourselves. He says,—they have had the country in their own hands for centuries, and how did they govern it? The Chieftains were harrying the very life out of the people. Ireland was divided into little factions; and, indeed, he went on to say, in a manner that does not reflect credit upon him,—that every family in the land had its own independence, and governed itself. Ireland was divided into small factions; each faction had its own chief; and every chieftain was engaged, from Monday morning till Saturday night, and including Sunday, in cutting somebody else's throat, and getting his own cut in return. According to Mr. Froude, it was a miracle that there were a hundred people left in Ireland at the time when there were three, four, or five millions. What would you say, my friends, if I went back to Ireland or England, after my year's residence in New York; and if I said in a public lecture, "Do you know what life is in New York, or Brooklyn, or Jersey City? Every family is independent; and every father of a family, with his sons, is engaged every day in cutting their neighbors' throats; and I will give you proof of it—their own newspapers. They tell us that at this moment there are eighteen or twenty men in jail in New York for murder; how in the saloons and drinking-places they stab one another, and they shoot one another. They tell us how men are knocked down in the street; how a gentleman from Kentucky, the other day, walked out of the hotel, and sight nor light of him was never seen again. This is the way they live in New York,—worse than a parcel of savages,— worse than the red Indians." Now I ask you, if I went back to Dublin or London, and said these words, how would you feel about it? Would you feel quite pleased in your minds? Would you say I was telling the truth? or would you not say, "Surely, I never thought that Father Tom Burke was such an infernal liar?"

I assert that there is not a people living more capable of self-government and of making their own laws and living under them than the Irish people to whom I belong: and I will prove it from Mr. Froude himself. I will not go outside of him. Mr. Froude admits, as every thinking man must, that the great elements of self-government among a people are, first of all, respect for justice and for law; secondly, fidelity to principle; thirdly, affection for their own laws, and love of the law; and fourthly, a capability of being formed by those who govern them and direct them. These are the four great attributes that belong to a people, and that entitle them, if they have them, to the right of self-government. I grant you, that if a race or a people had no respect for the law;—if they despised the law, and were anxious to violate the law precisely because it was the law, that that people do not deserve to have the power of making their own laws; and it would be a mercy from God if somebody governed them and made laws for them. But are the Irish that people? Listen, my friends: Mr. Froude, in the course of his lectures, has quoted frequently a great authority in Irish history, viz.: Sir John Davis, who was Attorney-General in the reign of James the First. This was an Englishman—or I believe, indeed, a Welshman—that came over from England for the express purpose of plundering the Irish of their property; and he, accordingly, accumulated vast wealth, and had great estates in Ireland. Yet this man writes these words: "There is no people under Heaven that love equal and fair justice like the Irish." "There is no people," he adds, "who are more willing to submit to fair, impartial justice, even though it go against themselves, than the Irish." Elsewhere he writes, "When things are peaceful, and there is no war going on, the Irish are far more fearful of offending against the law than the English." If I quoted from some Donough O'Brien, or some Terence O'Neill, or if I quoted the "Four Masters," for this, Mr. Froude would turn round on me and say: "Oh, ho! Do you hear the Friar quoting the old Franciscans,—the old Irish Monks! Oh!" he would say, (if he knew Irish)—"ᴣo ɲ-ouaɪɪc a Oɱ aɪɲɪaᴆ!" but he hasn't the grace to know it.

But I have been reviewing the lectures in which I answered Mr. Froude; and although a New York newspaper has charged me with quoting Catholic authorities, I protest to you, my friends, I can say with truth, from the first words of those lectures down to the last, every single authority that was quoted by me was a Protestant or an Englishman. And does not the history of Ireland bear out the truth of what Sir John Davis says? There were two parties in Ireland for 700 years, my friends; these were the old native Irish, the Mac's and the O's,—the O'Connors, the O'Briens, the McMurroughs, the O'Byrnes, the O'Tooles, the O'Neills, and the O'Donnells. These were the genuine Irish: it was to these men that God Almighty had given Ireland; and the soil was theirs, for they held it by the right by which every people hold their own land, viz.: the right of a gift from God. Then came the Normans, the Fitzgeralds, the De Courceys, the Butlers, the Burkes; and when they entered Ireland, they became, in a hundred years, "more Irish than the Irish themselves." That is the old phrase. Mr. Froude quotes it, and says: "Perhaps Father Burke never heard of that phrase!" The Lord be praised! as if we didn't all know that phrase since we were weaned. But I may remark, in all Mr. Froude's reply to me, that he takes it for granted—I suppose because I am an Irishman—that I know nothing about my native land. "Perhaps Father Burke doesn't know this," and "perhaps Father Burke didn't read that;" but I will tell him about this and that. "Perhaps Father Burke never heard that the Normans were more Irish than the Irish themselves." They were. But of all the traits of the Irish character that they took up, the most prominent amongst those, in which they became truly "more Irish than the Irish themselves," was their love of fighting and of devilment in general. They became the most unruly lot in the land; and we have the proof of it in this: that we have the Earl of Surrey writing home to Henry the Eighth, who had sent him to Ireland, telling him about the Irish Chieftains—the Mac's and the O's; he says, "they are wise men, your Majesty, and good and quiet men; a great deal better than the English."

If then the first element and the first attribute of a people to entitle them to self-government, be their respect for justice and for law, I hold, upon the evidence of English authorities, that no man can deny to the Irish nation the right given by God to every people to govern themselves according to their own laws. But there is another trait in the character of the Irish people that Mr. Froude brings out, both in his lectures and in former essays; and it is well worthy of remark. He says: "They are a people that are singularly adapted to good government." And do you know the instance he gives? He says, in one of his essays:

"Take a wild, ragged peasant boy—one that is willing to fling up his caubeen into the air, and hurrah for Smith O'Brien, and hurrah for every Fenian, and hurrah for every Irish patriot. Catch that boy"—

"Catch" him! as if he were talking of some young beast or wild savage!—

"Catch him, drill him, and teach him, and in a few years you will have one of the finest policemen of any people on the face of the earth."

And this he gives as a very good instance that the Irish people, as he asserts, beyond all other people, are capable of a perfect discipline, under good, wise government. Now, I take him on that point; and I say, if, according to you, my learned friend, a year or two of discipline and of justice and of good government will make such a perfect subject out of an Irishman, tell us, if you please, Mr. Froude, how is it that for seven hundred years you have never been able to make good subjects out of them? The reason is that, for seven hundred years, Ireland has never known, for twenty-four consecutive hours, what good government or sensible government meant. The Scripture says that one of the greatest curses that can fall upon a people is to give them a child for their king: that is to say, a child without reason, without wisdom. And the curse of Ireland has been that she has been governed for seven hundred years, not by one child, nor by one booby, but by a nation of boobies that never knew how to govern. Any other people under the same government would have been driven mad. The Irish have only been made national—every man of them—to the heart's core.

The third great element that asserts a people's right to

govern themselves is their fidelity to principle. A man without principle cannot govern himself; and a nation without principle loses the sacred right to self-government by the judgment of God. What do I mean by principle? I mean certain ideas of right and wrong, fixing themselves in the mind and in the heart and in the conscience of the people, and taking such hold of that mind and heart and conscience that no power on earth or in hell can tear those principles out of the national life. Show me a single principle in the history of the English people to which they have clung with this fervor. There is not one, except, indeed, if you will, the principle of extending their empire by robbery and by the confiscation of their neighbors' goods. Was the principle of religion so fixed in their minds? No; for at the bidding of Henry VIII. they changed their religion. Was the principle of devotion to the throne so fixed in their minds? No; for at the wave of Cromwell's sword all England bowed before him; and England cheered him in the day when he cut off the head of England's king. What principle is there revealed in the philosophy of their history, for which that people were ever prepared to suffer, much less to die? Now, the whole history of the Irish race, from the day that their history dawns upon us, down to this hour, is the assertion of an eternal principle, no matter at what sacrifice or what cost. The first and strongest principle that can govern the mind, the heart, and the conscience of any man, and, consequently, of any people, is their fidelity to what they know to be the truth and their duty to God. Unless you admit this religious principle in the mind and in the conscience of the man with whom you have to deal, the less you have to say to him, the less you trust him, the better. Tell me, my friends, is there a man amongst you who would place, say $10,000, in trust, depending upon the honor of a man who told you he had no religious principle whatever; that he had no rules governing his conscience; that he did not care a snap of his fingers for religion? You would take good care to keep your money out of his hands, I tell you. Ireland, for fifteen hundred years, has held the Catholic faith among the nations. The Catholic faith has three effects operating upon the man, and, consequently, upon the people who profess it. First of all, it acts upon the intellect as an intellectual conviction of the strongest kind, assenting and consenting to the truth. Secondly, it acts upon the heart, purifying the affections and strengthening all the emotions of the spirit in man. Thirdly, it acts upon the conscience, in the form of a strict, immutable, unchanging law, to which every man who professes it,—be he great or small, gentle or simple,—must bow down and conform himself alike. I assert that the Catholic religion alone possesses this triple influence over the intelligence, heart, and conscience of man ; and I will prove it in three words, although it does not enter into the subject of my lecture. First of all, among all religions, it alone acts upon the intellect. The Catholic religion alone tells a man what to believe, and tells him that with so much certainty that he is not at liberty to change it. The best Protestant in the United States can become a Methodist, or a Presbyterian, or a Quaker, or a Mormon, or anything you like. He will go to hear the Rev. Mr. So-and-so this Sunday ; and he will go to hear the Rev. Mr. Somebody-else on the next Sunday. On one day he will hear the Rev. Mr. So-and-so say that black is white ; and the next Sunday Rev. Mr. Such-a-one will tell him that white is black. He has no fixed principle of belief; he has no real, unchanging, intellectual faith at all. His mind is like the open highway, where every traveller can pass along. The Catholic religion alone influences the heart ; and I assert this for her on the simple ground that she alone takes hold of the heart of man, and fixes it forever in one form of affection or love. If she calls that man to the priesthood, she consecrates him forever to the love of the Church, the altar, and the souls of his brethren. Not a single thought, nor affection, nor emotion of any other love must ever enter that consecrated mind, or must ever be let into his heart. She seals, with her sacramental blessing, the matrimonial bonds, and they are fixed forever,—that man and that woman. Heaven and earth may be moved ; every other engagement may be broken ; every other oath may be violated ; but the Catholic Church says that the oath which binds the husband to the wife, and the wife to the husband, is an oath as immutable, in mutual fidelity and love, and as unchanging as the oath which binds Christ to His Church.

Finally, she alone lays hold of the conscience of a man, shakes him, brings him face to face with himself, teaches him to look at himself with fearless eye, teaches him, in her sacraments and in her confessional, to bring up all that was basest, vilest, meanest and most shameful of his sins, to lay them out there under his own eyes, and confess them with his lips. And I say that this is the first principle of fidelity in a nation,—fidelity to the principles of their religion. For fifteen hundred years, Ireland, intellectually, heartily, and conscientiously, has held that Catholic faith. For three hundred years the Danes endeavored to change that faith into paganism; for the Danish war was a religious war. Ireland fought; fought with heroic strength, fought with unwearying arm, fought with undying though bleeding heart; and for three hundred years she struggled; until at length she cast the Dane to the earth, and the Christ put his foot upon the neck of the Pagan Thor of the Scandinavian. Another cycle of three hundred years came, and it was no longer the Dane, but it was the Saxon that held his sword at the throat of Ireland, and said, even as the Dane of old said to her, "Oh, Erin, Paganism or death;" so he said to her, "Protestantism or death." And Ireland answered, as she had answered the Dane of old: "I will fight, I will suffer, I will die. All this I know how to do; and well. But my faith I never will change from God, from His Christ, and from His Holy Church." And just as, after three hundred years of war, on that Good Friday morning, the sun, as it rose in the heavens, beheld an Irish King, with his Irish army, triumphant, pealing forth their notes of gladness over the stricken and conquered Danes; so, after three hundred years of the second cycle, the sun arose, on that fair May morning, in 1829, and beamed upon the face of the great O'Connell and the Irish nation, waving, over the ruined battlements of the tyrant old blood-stained Established Protestant Church of Ireland, the glorious banner of civil and religious equality and freedom which was to be ours forever.

Does Mr. Froude tell me, or tell America, that,—our people having thus stood in the gap, for six hundred years, faithful to the first principle—the religious principle—the principle which includes every other form of virtue and principle, and which, if a man is faithful to it, will make him honest, pure, and faithful in all his commercial, domestic, civil, and national relations;—does this man mean to tell me that a people that have never shown that fidelity to principle, either to God or to king, are fitted by the Almighty God to govern and make laws for such a people as the Irish?

It is worthy of remark, my friends, that the loyalty to God, which distinguished Irish Catholics, was carried into their other relations of life; and none were so loyal, even to kings that were unjust to them. I scarcely mention this in their favor;—I scarcely look upon it as praiseworthy; yet I must say, whenever England rebelled against her king, Ireland stood up and said: "I will not change from him; if he was my king yesterday, he has not forfeited his right; and I will be faithful to him to-day." Charles the First was King of England and Ireland: England rebelled against him; the people and Parliament rose against him; the Scotch sent down their army to fight against him. Ireland came out like one man, and said: "This man has done nothing to forfeit my allegiance. I will not give up my legitimate monarch." James the Second fled from England, and the English people at once said: "Oh, let him go." (And, dear knows, they were right!) Poor, foolish Ireland, strong in the principle of loyalty,—strong in principle,—said: "I will fight for him; for he was my king. If he was my king yesterday, and I was obliged to obey him, why should I not obey him to-day?" They took the field, and bled profusely. I mention this only to show you that, if Mr. Froude's argument against Irish self-government is based upon Irish want of principle, I gather up the refutation of his assertions from out the history of England; and I fling them into his face, and tell him to go home again.

The Irish people have shown the four great attributes which entitle a people to self-government: namely, that they not only love justice and obey the law, but that they love the law, provided it be a just and natural law; and allow that law to sink into their lives: that they are willing to conform all their actions to it; and that their love of good law is only second to the love which they bear for their religion. This I will prove. For four hundred years, England strove, with might and main, to change the laws of Ireland: and she failed. From the year that Strongbow landed, in 1169, until that year, in the sixteenth century, when Henry the Eighth was proclaimed "King of Ireland,"—nay, for many years after,—the Irish people, in spite of all the efforts of England, clung to their old Brehon laws, lived under them, and obeyed them. And I tell you they were right. I tell you, my friends, that there is one portion of Irish history that is not sufficiently known,—not sufficiently considered by the people, either in Ireland or America,—nor by historians, like my friend, Mr. Froude. We are all accustomed to speak, to-day, of the Constitution of America as one of the most glorious,—perhaps the most glorious,—on the face of the earth. And why? Because that Constitution gives the most liberty of any other,—the most liberty to every citizen of the State, no matter how humble he may be; because that Constitution will not recognize the right of any one man in the State to injure or tyrannize over another:—because that Constitution admits the State governments on terms of equality,—every State having its own laws, having its own government, having its own Executive, for its own affairs;—because that Constitution has known how to reconcile the individual liberty,—the State liberty,—with the strong central government which is represented in the President of the United States, who is elected every four years. If we look back at the ancient nations of Europe, there never was anything like the great American Republic. We do not find it. We do not find the State governments in any of the old nations, or in any of the modern nations of Europe. But this very day we find England,—having robbed Ireland of her State government, —having robbed Scotland of her State government. We find Bismarck plotting to rob the German States of their State governments, and concentrate all in the hands of three or four men that they may have absolute power over the lives, and, certainly, over the liberties of their fellow-subjects. We find nothing like the American Constitution, for individual liberty, elsewhere. We find nothing like the American Constitution in that grand principle, that the wisdom of the whole nation is appealed to; every man is asked his opinion: "Who is the best statesman?—who is the wisest, the bravest, and the most virtuous man?—tell us who he is; and we will put him in the Presidency, and make him, for the time being, supreme magistrate and ruler of the land." If you go back to the most ancient nations, you will find nothing of this, until you come upon the ancient Celtic Constitution of Ireland. There, my friends, will you find the very model and type of that glorious government which Washington, and Jefferson, and the other heroes of your revolutionary era established for the happiness of this land. They found the model of the American Constitution in the ancient Celtic Constitution of Ireland. The land was divided into five great portions; and each portion was recognized as an independent State. Munster, Connaught, Ulster, Leinster, and Meath, were perfectly independent, one from another. They were governed by great chiefs, who were elected by every man in the land. Every man had his voice and his vote. The tribe elected their chief. The tribe elected a man who was to succeed the chieftain. And these five great nations, or "Five Bloods," as they were called, enjoyed, on the Democratic principle, their State Rights and State independence. Then, at certain times, they had the election of their President. They came together and elected the bravest and best, wisest and most prudent and most virtuous man, and placed him upon the throne in Tara, as universal King, or Ard-ríg, of all Ireland. He governed the various States; but they were careful, and he was careful, to respect their independence. There was no centralization. The King of Munster, the Prince of Ulster, the King of Connaught, the Kings of Meath and Leinster, rode down from the slopes of Tara,—after having elected their supreme monarch,—they rode down as free, as independent in State rights, as if they had never elected a chief to govern them all. No matter what were the faults, —and they were many,—of that old Irish Constitution, I claim for it this glory, in this century of ours,—that the American Constitution is nothing more or less than a faithful copy of the old Irish laws, under which our fathers lived, in peace and in happiness, until in a moment of the anger of God,—even as fire was let down upon the cities of old,—the Saxon was let in, as a curse, upon Ireland.

If the time permitted, I could contrast the freedom and equality of these grand Republican principles of the Irish Constitution,—I could contrast its workings with the grinding, absolute tyranny of that feudal system under which England was governed,—and which they endeavored to establish in Ireland. The King was absolute,—lord and master of every inch of land: it was his,—his personal property; and any man who held land, held it by virtue of a grant from the King, on condition of doing whatever service the King commanded him to do. In other words, he held it under a condition of slavery. Then, the owner of the land held the tenants upon the land as mere serfs or slaves. If he injured them in person or property, there was no redress. Their domestic affairs were left under his control. If a son or daughter of a family died, he could seize upon their portion; he could seize upon their property and squander it; and no one could call him to account. The King of England could, and often did, beggar the first families in the land; and no one could call him to account; because by the feudal law, the King was not accountable for whatever he did.

Well, my friends, there was a great laugh, the other night (in "Association Hall," I believe they call it;—I was thinking it was "Conciliation Hall,"—remembering the old places); there was a great laugh raised by the English historian at the expense of the poor Irish Friar. "Oh," said he, "whatever else Father Burke is, he is a wonderful man at totting up numbers." Then he was kind enough to make a tot for me that I never made for myself. I asserted (and not upon my own authority; but I expressly said that I heard men say), that there were, probably, *fourteen millions* of human beings, of Irish descent and Irish blood, in this land of America. Making up the account, briefly, with the millions that fled from Ireland, I asserted that, perhaps, there were eight millions of our people who came to this land.

Mr. Froude totted the eight millions up to fourteen, and he made a tot of twenty-two millions. That had not entered into my head; but he was kind enough to lend me the use of his brains and his figures. Then Mr. Froude comes out with *his* account. According to him, of all the millions in America, there are only four millions, altogether, with a drop of Irish blood in their veins! Well, perhaps I overshot the mark a little. I protest to you, I do not think I did. I think that, if the men, women, and children of Irish descent,—in some way or other of Irish blood,—were put on one side, in these United States of America,—that men would be greatly surprised at the millions they would foot up. We were, in Ireland, nearly nine millions and a quarter, in 1846–7. There are not much more than half that number in Ireland to-day; and there have not been, for some years. It is acknowledged that a million and a half or two millions may have been swept away by the visitation of God,—by the terrible famine and by the pestilence that ensued. But, still, you have to account for three or four millions. They must have emigrated,—have gone somewhere: they did not fly up to the moon. Then, since that year of '47, every year has sent out to America its hundreds of thousands of Irishmen. They must be found somewhere. Then, Irishmen have families, like other people; and, generally speaking, good long families too, God bless them! But I need not enter upon this subject; it has already been settled by statistics. In a popular Irish journal of New York, this very week, it is stated that there must be at least more than twelve millions of Irish descent in America; and I hold that twelve millions is not so far from fourteen as four millions is from twelve. If I made a mistake, I only overshot the mark by two millions: Mr. Froude undershot it by eight millions. And I thank God that there are, in America, eight millions more Irish people, and people of Irish blood, than Mr. Froude thought. It is a portentous state of affairs for the learned gentleman. Perhaps, if he knew that his four millions meant something more like fourteen, he would have been more careful, and have taken thought, before he came to America to blackguard us.

The next great point that Mr. Froude makes against me

is where he states that I said, that when the Irish rose in the "rebellion," as he calls it, of 1641,—I denied that they massacred thirty-eight thousand Protestants. My friends, you know there are two ways of looking at everything, and there are two names for almost everything, even the name of a man. A man's friends call him the finest fellow in the world,—a fine, hearty fellow,—and his enemies say he is a dirty blackguard. There was a rising in Ireland, in 1641; —Mr. Froude calls it a "rebellion." The circumstances of that rising were these: The Parliament of England rebelled against their King; the people of England rebelled against their King; the Scotch rebelled against their King, though he was one of their own countrymen, and had their Scotch blood in his veins. The Irish people arose, in the name of the King; and they demanded of him, as a reward (literally and truly, I can call it nothing else,)—they rose in the name of the King, and demanded leave to live in their own land, and the free exercise of their own religion. The King promised he would give this to them; and this promise was called the "graces" of the King. A certain Irish noble,—Sir Phelim O'Neill,—headed that rising; and he produced a document, with the Royal Seal of the Majesty of England to it; and he told the Irish people that he had authority from the King to call upon them to rise. That document, my friends, was a forgery, like many another document. It was as great a forgery as the "Bull" of Pope Adrian, that pretended to give Ireland to England,—as confounded a forgery as ever came out of hell. Sir Phelim O'Neill, when he was dying, acknowledged that that document was a forgery. But the Irish people believed him when he said it was a genuine document; and they rose in the name of the King, believing in the commission that Sir Phelim O'Neill produced. And Mr. Froude calls this "rebellion," because this was a forged document. Now, suppose a man came into your house, produced a bank check and said, "Will you cash that for me?" You look at it and say, "Is it all right?" He tells you that it is all right; and, believing it to be all right, you cash it. Then you go to the bank, present it for payment, and discover that it is a forgery: and the banker takes you by the collar and says: "You thundering robber!

do you want to rob me?" Why, you would say: "I am very sorry for it. I have lost my money. But do not call me a thief; because I did not know that it was a forgery." Now, Mr. Froude calls this rising in the King's name, in 1641, a "rebellion," under a document to which was attached, fraudulently, a seal (but still the real Seal of England); and though the Irish people knew nothing about it, he turns on us and calls us rebels for this! And this is the first thing that he asserts,—that the rising in '41 was a "rebellion." But he adds, a moment after, that the Catholics arose, and that the very first thing they did was to slaughter thirty-eight thousand Protestants. And he gives, as authority, Sir John Temple. Well, my friends, Mr. Froude knew very well, when he was quoting that authority, that there was another authority that said there were *two hundred thousand* Protestants killed! Two hundred thousand! Sir William Petty (whom this learned gentleman quotes as an authority several times, " Sir William says this," and " Sir William says that;") Sir William Petty says that there was great cruelty. Mr. Froude does not quote him; he pares the "massacre" down to thirty-eight thousand. And do you know the reason? The secret is, Sir William Petty overshot the mark, and made out that there were more Protestants killed, that year, than there were in all Ireland! All the Protestants in Ireland did not come up to two hundred thousand, at the time. Sir William forgot this; and he said two hundred thousand were massacred; but Mr. Froude remembered it well, and would not quote him. He thought, " I will not quote him; but I will quote the other liar, that says there were thirty-eight thousand." Is it not a strange thing, my friends, that at that very time,—in that very year,—a Presbyterian minister went through Ireland, for the express purpose of finding out how many people were killed; and he declares that there were only four thousand one hundred at the very outside; but he does not believe that there were so many. And, yet, this man comes to America, and repeats again, and emphatically, the *old lie*, that has been exploded years and years ago; and he asks the American people to believe that we Irish cannot govern ourselves; for he says,—"This is what they did before; and this is what they will do again, if you give them the curse of 'Home Rule,' and the power of making their own laws!"

But, on the other hand, we have the account of another massacre, in which three thousand Catholics were killed by the garrison of Carrickfergus. Mr. Froude says: "Oh! Father Burke knows how to tot up well; he multiplies his numbers by a hundred. *There were only thirty persons killed*, and he says, 'three thousand;' that is a hundred times thirty!" Well, my friends, according to Mr. Froude, there were only *thirty persons* killed; but according to a Protestant author, who wrote shortly after, there were *thirty families;* and there is a great deal of difference between *thirty persons* and *thirty Irish families*, of ten or twelve persons each. But I meet him thus:—within ten years after the event took place, there was an official account, printed and published in London, by an Englishman, asserting that there were three thousand men, women, and children murdered; —that the man who published that account publicly defied any one to contradict it; and the very men who were there in Ireland at the time,—who had an interest in contradicting it,—were afraid to contradict this man: and none ever gainsaid it. Can it be true that there were only thirty people slain, as Mr. Froude says there were,—when a man came out, within ten years after the event, in London, and published his account, and said there were three thousand people killed, and defied anybody to contradict him. And each of the interested parties knew well that this man had made such a statement; yet not a man of them ever contradicted him.

Mr. Froude attaches great importance to this pretended massacre of '41; and he makes his usual appeal. He says: "Let a Commission be sent over to Dublin to search the State papers; let the Lord Chancellor be on it; let this lord and that lord be on it; and they will find that I am right, and that Father Burke is wrong." I will answer the whole thing at once. I will not go rummaging among State papers; for the majority of these State papers are infernal lies, written by courtiers, interested men,—men who at the time were engaged in plundering the Irish, and were anxious to find some excuse for plundering them,—accusing them of every crime,—just as Mr. Froude himself is doing,—in order to justify the asking of a verdict against them;—so these men that wrote the bulk of these State papers were acknowledged interested parties, whose interest it was to abuse and vilify the Irish. I will not go to these State papers, and take their bigoted statements. But, there is the historical fact, that, when the accusation was made, at the very time it was published, it was refuted, and the refutation of it was never so much as questioned or denied by the very men who had a hand in the concoction of that pretended "massacre."

Mr. Froude, I am sorry to say, repeats and reiterates the charge of cowardice against the Irish. In answering my lectures, Mr. Froude said that he never doubted Irish courage,—he never denied it. But, last night, in Philadelphia, he repeated his statement, that the Irish did not know how to fight. It is strange, too, for he acknowledges, and says in another part of his lecture, that all the evils of Ireland,—all the miseries of Ireland,—arose out of the irrepressible love the people had for fighting; and, in another place, he comes out and says they did not know how to fight: and he asserts again that the Irish troops did not behave well at the battle of the Boyne. But what then? What have I to say? What I have to say is not on Catholic evidence, nor on Irish evidence, but it is on English Protestant authority. The Duke of Berwick, an Englishman, declares,—and he was in command at the battle of the Boyne,—that James—(you all know the name we give him)—King James had brought all the French veteran troops around him, to guard his person; and he left the brunt of the battle to fall upon his Irish regiments. King James on that day,—between the French and Irish and all,—was only able to put twenty-three thousand men into the field; whereas the muster-roll of William of Orange totted up to fifty thousand men, and fifty pieces of artillery. King James had only twenty-three thousand men, all told, and twelve pieces of cannon; but he sent away six of them the night before the battle; so that there were only six left. William crossed the Boyne; and the Duke of Berwick tells us that the Irish infantry and cavalry charged that entire army *ten times*, before they re-

tired from the field. Ten distinct times, he says, the Irish
infantry charged,—flung themselves upon them, like lions or
tigers. And it was only when they found that it was not
in the power of human beings, for so small an army, reduced
to a few thousand men, to make an impression upon the
ranks of fifty thousand veterans—it was only then that they
retired from the field. But we have the list of killed and
wounded, which is the surest test, whether men behave well
in a battle or not. We find that the Irish gave more than
they got; for we find that the list of killed and wounded in
the Irish army did not come up to that of the English army
by nearly a thousand men.

Take the siege of Athlone. Mr. Froude tells us that, at
Athlone, the Irish made no stand, but gave up a position
which, in the hands of brave men, would be impregnable.
Did they? At the first siege of Athlone,—for there were
two sieges, as at Limerick,—in the first siege of Athlone,
Colonel Richard Grace, with eight hundred men, held the
town against the whole English army, and drove them back.
In the second siege of Athlone, Colonel Fitzgerald commanded four hundred men, on the Leinster side of the Shannon; and held the "English town," as it was called, with
these four hundred men. There was an army of from fifteen
to eighteen thousand against him; and he held that town,
until, out of the four hundred men, there were only two
hundred of the garrison left. Every man of them saw his
fellow-soldier fall by his side; and still they fought. And
when they did retreat, they cut down an arch of the bridge
that spanned the Shannon between them and the Connaught
side of the town of Athlone. When the whole English be-
sieging army brought their tremendous artillery to cover
their troops as they flung planks across, that they might fall
upon that handful of two hundred Irish soldiers, then a
party,—some twenty men,—came out from Fitzgerald's garrison, and in spite of the English artillery, in spite of
their musketry, and under their very eyes, they tore the
planks up again, and flung them into the stream. And out
of the twenty men only two returned into the city. If Mr.
Froude calls this cowardice, I do not know what he understands by courage. . I think it would be time enough for the

learned gentleman to accuse the men of Ireland of being cowards, when he finds that he can accuse the women of Ireland of being cowards. When William of Orange laid siege to Limerick,—in the first siege,—he battered down the walls, until he made a breach thirty-six feet wide. He then picked out twelve thousand of his best soldiers, and sent them to enter the city through the broken walls. And when they climbed the ruined ramparts, they found the women of Limerick,—the pure-minded, holy maidens and glorious mothers of Limerick,—standing side by side and shoulder to shoulder with their brothers, their husbands, and their fathers. And the women of Limerick beat back the twelve thousand Englishmen; so that when they withdrew, they left two thousand of their dead before the walls of the grand old city.

Moreover, the learned gentleman—(I declare I am beginning to doubt whether he is a learned gentleman at all)—says that, when James the First confiscated six counties of Ulster,—oh! he says, it was all a piece of good nature on the part of James to turn the Irish out of their land; for he let them all in again. It is true, he says, that he confiscated two millions five hundred thousand acres of Irish land; but he gave two millions of it back, and kept only five hundred thousand acres for the Scotch and English that he brought over. Well, first of all, I do not understand the good-natured playfulness of turning men out of their property. Even if he did let them back again, I think it was a great inconvenience. How would you like it yourselves? Suppose the United States Marshal came to your door, and ordered you out of your store, or premises, and had soldiers to oblige you to go out, and kept you walking about the streets three or four days, and then came and said: "Oh, my fine fellow, you can go back again;" how would you like it? The learned gentleman (as they call him) glosses over the real state of this business. According to him, the Irish got back two millions of acres out of two millions and a half. May I ask, even if this were true, (and it is not true,)—what right had James to keep the other half million? If a man had twenty dollars, and a pickpocket took that twenty dollars out of his pocket, and then gave him back fifteen, the first thing he would ask him is to give back the other five. But, according to Mr. Froude, the Irish were benevolently treated. They were robbed of two millions and a half acres of choice land; but they got back two millions; and so they ought to be happy and contented. James, he says, did not absolutely take away those two million and a half acres. According to Mr. Froude, the Irish got them back, provided they took the oath of allegiance? and the oath of allegiance was simply an oath to be good and peaceful citizens! But there was another oath that they were expected to take, and were obliged to take; and that was the "Oath of Supremacy," by which they abjured the Catholic religion; and, in any case, a man could not get his land back until he declared his disbelief in the religion of his fathers,—until he practically became an infidel or a Protestant. Mr. Froude does not mention it; but I will tell you who mentions it. Cox, the historian, mentions it;—the man who wrote the history of the times tells us, and gives authority for it;—he tells us that it was in the written instructions to the Protestants and Presbyterians that they were not to let the Irish back, unless they took the "Oath of Supremacy." And when they had swallowed the pill, had become Protestants,—perjured themselves,—when the tempter had bribed them to stain their souls with sin,—in what capacity were they let back? That is the question. The English settlers found that the land was too much for them; they found that they could not till it, and work it; and that they could not get the Irish to do as the slaves and serfs of England did. So they turned to the King, and said: "Where is the use of giving us all this land, unless you allow us to employ the Irish people who are here to work it?" Then he gave them leave to get the Irish to work it; and let them build their mud-cabins, and to be *cottiers* or *tenants* on their own inheritance, provided that they would first swear away their religion. This is the real state of the case. Nevertheless Mr. Froude says James was so good, and so kind, and so benign, that when he took away two millions and a half of acres, he gave them all back again, only asking the original owners to take the oath of allegiance! There are two ways of telling a story; and I am beginning to think there are more than two ways of writing history.

Then Mr. Froude comes to the question of the Parliament,—the "Irish Parliament," he says;—and he gives his argument; on which I take him up, because it is the back-bone of his whole case. He says to the American people: "Please give me your verdict, and say, once for all, to the Irish in America, to stop their nonsense about the independence of Ireland; and, as to the Irish at home, tell them to be quiet,—to be good and peaceful,—and let us, English, make their laws for them; because, when they had the power to make their own laws, they did not know how to make them. They made bad laws; and the proof lies here:—In 1782, England granted a total and complete independence to the Irish Parliament." That is quite true; but how did she grant it? She granted it when the "Volunteers" drew up their cannon,—had them loaded,—had their torches lighted, and around the mouth of each cannon a label with these words written on it:—"Freedom for Ireland or else—" So, my learned friend says: "England granted Ireland her independence in 1782," just in the same way as you would give up your purse to a man you met on the street, who might draw out of his pocket a Derringer revolver, and put it to your throat, so that you felt the cold steel, and might say to you: "Give me that purse, or take the contents of this!" You might give it up, and then say: "What a fine liberal fellow I was to give that man my purse!" Ireland brought the cannon right to the heart of England in '82, and said: "Come, now, the question at issue between us is this: I want free trade; I want the power of making my own laws. Give it to me; or take the contents of this." England gave it; and then Mr. Froude comes over to America and says: "We were so good,—we gave them their independence; but they made a bad use of it." It was only sixteen years from '82 to '98; and Mr. Froude says the Irish, being allowed to make their own laws, went "from anarchy to conspiracy, and from conspiracy into rebellion." I answer: First, Mr. Froude is wrong when he says that it was the independence of '82 and the political agitation of the time, that sprang up with it, that occasioned the Rebellion of '98. I answer, secondly, that the independent Parliament of '82 did not represent the Irish people. In that Irish Parliament there were three hundred members of the Irish House of Commons; and out of this three hundred, there were only seventy-two elected by the people. All the rest were the nominees of the " pocket boroughs," or " rotten boroughs," so called ; because, really, all the landlords of the land, that owned them, picked up every fellow that they thought would vote according to their wishes and desires. There were only seventy-two elected by the people. Who were the people, may I ask ? There were, in that year, verging up to three millions of Catholics in Ireland, and between five hundred and six hundred thousand Protestants. Whom did the Irish Parliament represent? Here you have, on one side, half a million of comparative strangers,—men who came into Ulster under James the First; Cromwellites, who were settled in Leinster and Munster, and protected in their occupation by Cromwell and by his successors. Were these men the Irish nation? No; there was not a drop of Irish blood in their veins. They had no Irish sympathies with them. Who were the Irish nation ? Three millions of the Irish people, who remained firm as a rock: first, to the religion of their fathers, and secondly, to the love that they bore the green old land, that was their mother? They were the Irish people—the nation; and that Parliament of '82 represented only five hundred thousand strangers. Not a single Catholic in Ireland sat in that Parliament; not a single Catholic in Ireland had even a vote to return a member to that Parliament. They might as well have been wild Indians; they might as well have been brute beasts. They had no recognition; and I deny that the Parliament of 82,—free and independent, and in a great measure, patriotic as it was,—I deny that it was a representative of the Irish nation. Grattan himself seems to have felt remorse when he was claiming the independence of the representation of so paltry a faction ; for he said, " I never will ask the independence of six hundred thousand Irishmen, while I leave three millions of them in slavery." If that Parliament failed ;—even if the experiment *was* a failure ;—I deny that it was " Home Rule " at all. I deny that it was an *Irish* Parliament; and I hold that Mr. Froude has no business to tell us, because a few Protestants and Orangemen, in 1782, did not know how to govern Ireland, that, therefore, the Irish people do not know how to elect members and make their own laws. But, my friends, bad as that Parliament was,—corrupt as it was,—I deny that it was the cause of the Rebellion of '98. I deny that "political agitation, leading to conspiracy," was the cause of that Rebellion. No ; no ! So long as the Muse of History writes, so long will it go down to future generations, that it was the premeditated design of the Prime Minister of England to precipitate the action of the Government, and to drive the Irish people into the Rebellion of '98. It was done calmly and coolly and for a purpose. William Pitt resolved to pass the bill of Union, and rob the Irish people of their Parliament; and he could not do it unless he disturbed the country by anarchy and war. He deliberately goaded the Irish people into rebellion. He sent over troops to Ireland, and fanatics from England. He brought from Germany the ferocious Hessians, who were quartered on the people, and committed such ravages amongst them,—burning their houses, killing their men, and worse than killing their women,—that the Irish were maddened into rebellion. Here is the proof of it,—here, from the gallant Sir Ralph Abercrombie, who was made Commander-in-Chief in Ireland, the Spring before the Rebellion. He found the army that he came to command in such a state, that, after reproaching them for their wickedness and insubordination, he gave up the command, and washed his hands clean out of it. Sir John Moore, the hero of Corunna, gives his testimony to the same effect. Lord Moira, an Englishman, who gave evidence before the House of Lords, deposes deliberately to the cruelty and ferocity of the Hessian soldiers, who were let loose upon the Irish people, and maddened them into rebellion. Take the case of the celebrated Father John Murphy, who headed the rebels in '98. He was a quiet, unpretending priest, saying his "office," visiting the sick, going about among the people, taking care of his chapel and chapel-house, and going through all the duties of an ordinary, hard-working parish priest in the country. He was at a sick call, attending at the bedside of a dying person; and, when he came back, he found his chapel burned to the ground, and the poor people gathered about the ruined sanctuary, huddled together in fear and terror; for the soldiers, or "the army," as they used to call them, had come down upon them. They asked him: "In the name of God! what are we to do? It is impossible to live in this country. It would be better to be dead!" And he answered, like a true man: "It would *not* be better to be dead; but it would be better to take up the pikes and, in the name of God, strike a blow for Ireland!" My friends, I am not a warrior, I am not a man of war, nor of blood, nor a man of revolution. I am the quietest and most peaceable of men; but, I declare to you, I do not know what I should have done, in Father John Murphy's position, except what Father John himself did.

But, after all, all these things are questions of the past, my friends; and we are more interested in questions of the present, and of the future, than we are in things of the past. The question, after all, is—is this thing to be continued?—is all this injustice, all this coercion, all this aggravation of a nation, and keeping it down,—all these assertions that the people have no right, no title to govern themselves,—all this justification of tyranny and spoliation,—is all this to continue? Well, according to Mr. Froude, it is; and he is an authority, because he has said, in one of his essays, "I don't see any way out of the Irish difficulty, except one of two things: first, let all the Irish go to America, and let us lose sight of them altogether, and have the island to ourselves; or, secondly, let them go on in their old ways, and we will have to coerce them into submission." Either exile or coercion, my friends, according to Mr. Froude. Well, I answer: I may tell Mr. Froude,—and I think with truth,—I do not like bragging or boasting; but, I am not blind to the signs of the times; and I may tell Mr. Froude, and I think with truth, that the Irish are not prepared to emigrate altogether. I am not sure but it may be a pleasant thing to cross the Atlantic:—I did not find it pleasant. It may be a fine thing, and a pleasant thing, to find a home, and freedom, and everything that the heart can desire, in America. Many of you have found a home; and if you all have found it, the better pleased I will be. But, after all, there is such a country as Ireland on the face of the earth; and a sweet old country I have always found her to be. There are such a people as the Irish people, who have held that land for ages and ages, in weal and in woe. That land God gave to the Irish people; and, with the blessing, and under the hand of that God, that land will belong to the Irish people until the day of judgment. Mr. Froude's scheme of universal emigration is a wild dream. I knew him to be a philosopher; I suspected him to be a historian; but I did not think or imagine that he was a poet, until I heard him talk of the universal emigration of the Irish race. Well, then there remains nothing more except to coerce us into submission; by which he means that, if the agitation for "Home Rule" continues, England will meet it in the old style, by a Coercion Bill. This was the old legislation for Ireland. I remember, in my own days, if the people wanted anything,—if the Catholics wanted their emancipation,—if the people wanted municipal or parliamentary reform,—the way that they were treated by the English Government was to pass a coercion bill;—that is to say, if any meetings were held, all the people attending them were to be fined, and the place was put under martial law. The people were to be ground to the very earth; and no man was to be allowed to speak his opinion. This is Mr. Froude's second remedy. I may as well tell him that the time for coercion bills has gone by. We will have no more of them; and I will tell you what has assisted in passing them away forever. You will be surprised to hear it from me; I may as well speak my sentiments and my convictions; and I verily believe that the National Schools of Ireland, with all their faults, have put an end to coercion bills forever. You may as well try to stop the sweeping of the hurricane by putting up your feeble hands against it; you may as well try to stop the lightnings of heaven by holding up your fingers against them, as try to stop by coercion the expression of the minds and desires of an educated people. It will never be done. The Irish people to-day are, at an average, as well educated as any other people in the world. You rarely meet in Ireland, to-day, a man or woman who does not know how to read and write; and you will rarely meet a man who does not feel a mixture of joy and pride and anger when he reads or hears of the wrongs and glories of his old country. "England," says

Mr. Froude, "is greatly afraid she will have to go back to measures of coercion again." I tell him, let England make her mind easy; she never will have to go back to them again; for the simple reason that she never will be able.

What future is before Ireland? Oh, my friends, what can I say? Before me lies the past of my native land: I can weep over her wrongs. Before me lies the Ireland of to-day, and I can sympathize with her sorrows. I believe I can see the dawning of her hopes. Of the future it becomes me not specifically to speak. I am a man of peace, not of war. It only remains for me to say that, next to the duty that I owe to God and His holy altar, is the duty that I owe to thee, oh! land of Ireland; to pray for thee; to sigh for thy coming glory; and to be ready—whenever the necessary conditions shall convince me that the fit hour has come—to take a man's part in the vindication of thy name.

APPENDIX.

PART I.

THE "BULL OF ADRIAN IV."

THE GREAT NORMAN FORGERY.

What Dr. Theiner said of it, and Froude suppressed.

[The annexed review of the controversy on the so-called "Bull" of Pope Adrian IV., purporting to cede Ireland to Henry II., was contributed to the "*Irish Ecclesiastical Record*" for November, 1872, by the Most Rev. P. H. Moran, Bishop of Ossory.]

THERE was a time when it would be little less than treason to question the genuineness of the Bull by which Pope Adrian IV. is supposed to have made a grant of Ireland to Henry the Second; and, indeed, from the first half of the thirteenth to the close of the fifteenth century, it was principally through this supposed grant of the Holy See that the English Government sought to justify their claim to hold dominion in our island. However, opinions and times have changed, and at the present day this Bull of Adrian has as little bearing on the connection between England and this country as it could possibly have on the union of the Isle of Man with Great Britain.

On the other hand, many strange things have been said during the past months in the so-called Nationalist journals, whilst asserting the genuineness of this famous Bull. I need scarcely remark that it does not seem to have been the love either of our poor country or of historic truth that inspired their declamation. It proceeded mainly from their hatred to the Sovereign Pontiff, and from the vain hope that such exaggerated statements might in some way weaken the devoted affection of our people for Rome.

Laying aside such prejudiced opinions, the controversy as to the genuineness of Adrian's Bull should be viewed in a purely historical light, and its decision must depend on the value and weight of the historical arguments which may be advanced to sustain it. The following is a literal translation of the old Latin text of Adrian's Bull :—

" ADRIAN, Bishop, servant of the servants of God, to our most dear Son in Christ, the illustrious King of the English, greeting and the Apostolical Benediction.

" The thoughts of your Highness are laudably and profitably directed to the greater glory of your name on earth and to the increase of the reward of eternal happiness in heaven, when as a Catholic Prince you propose to yourself to extend the borders of the Church, to announce the truths of Christian Faith to ignorant and barbarous nations, and to root out the weeds of wickedness from the field of the Lord ; and the more effectually to accomplish this, you implore the counsel and favor of the Apostolic See. In which matter we feel assured that the higher your aims are, and the more discreet your proceedings, the happier, with God's aid, will be the result ; because those undertakings that proceed from the ardor of faith and the love of religion are sure always to have a prosperous end and issue.

" It is beyond all doubt, as your Highness also doth acknowledge, that Ireland, and all the islands upon which Christ the Sun of Justice has shone, and which have received the knowledge of the Christian faith, are subject to the authority of St. Peter and of the most Holy Roman

Church. Wherefore we are the more desirous to sow in them an acceptable seed and a plantation pleasing unto God, because we know that a most rigorous account of them shall be required of us hereafter.

"Now, most dear Son in Christ, you have signified to us that you propose to enter the island of Ireland to establish the observance of law amongst its people, and to eradicate the weeds of vice; and that you are willing to pay from every house one penny as an annual tribute to St. Peter, and to preserve the rights of the Church of that land whole and inviolate. We, therefore, receiving with due favor your pious and laudable desires, and graciously granting our consent to your petition, declare that it is pleasing and acceptable to us, that for the purpose of enlarging the limits of the Church, setting bounds to the torrent of vice, reforming evil manners, planting the seeds of virtue, and increasing Christian faith, you should enter that island and carry into effect those things which belong to the service of God and to the salvation of that people; and that the people of that land should honorably receive and reverence you as Lord; the rights of the churches being preserved untouched and entire, and reserving the annual tribute of one penny from every house to St. Peter and the most Holy Roman Church.

"If, therefore, you resolve to carry these designs into execution, let it be your study to form that people to good morals, and take such order both by yourself and by those whom you shall find qualified in faith, in words, and in conduct, that the Church there may be adorned, and the practices of Christian faith be planted and increased; and let all that tends to the glory of God and the salvation of souls be so ordered by you that you may deserve to obtain from God an increase of everlasting reward, and may secure on earth a glorious name throughout all time. Given at Rome," etc.

Before we proceed with the inquiry as to the genuineness of this letter of Pope Adrian, I must detain the reader with a few brief preliminary remarks.

First: Some passages of this important document have been very unfairly dealt with by modern writers while purporting to discuss its merits. Thus, for instance, Professor

Richey, in his "Lectures on Irish History," presenting a translation of the Latin text to the lady pupils of the Alexandra College, makes the Pontiff to write:

"You have signified to us, our well-beloved son in Christ, that you propose to enter the island of Ireland *in order to subdue the people*, etc. . . . We, therefore, regarding your pious and laudable design with due favor, etc., do hereby declare our will and pleasure, that for the purpose of enlarging the borders of the Church, etc., you do enter and *take possession of that island.*"

Such an erroneous translation must be the more blamed in the present instance, as it was scarcely to be expected that the ladies whom the learned lecturer addressed would have leisure to consult the original Latin text of the document which he professed to translate. This, however, is not the only error into which Professor Richey has been betrayed regarding the Bull of Adrian IV. Having mentioned in a note the statement of Roger de Wendover, that the Bull was obtained from Pope Adrian in the year 1155, he adds his own opinion that "the grant appears to have been made in 1172." However, at that date, Pope Adrian had been for about thirteen years freed from the cares of his Pontificate, having passed to a better world in the year 1159.

Second: Any one who attentively weighs the words of the above document will see at once that it prescinds from all title of conquest, whilst at the same time it makes no gift or transfer of dominion to Henry the Second. As far as this letter of Adrian is concerned, the visit of Henry to our island might be the enterprise of a friendly monarch, who, at the invitation of a distracted state, would seek by his presence to restore peace and to uphold the observance of the laws. Thus, those foolish theories must at once be set aside, which rest on the groundless supposition that Pope

Adrian authorized the invasion and plunder of our people by the Anglo-Norman adventurers.

Third: There is another serious error which must also be set at rest by the simple perusal of the above document. I mean that opinion which would fain set forth the letter of Pope Adrian as a dogmatical definition of the Holy See, as if the Sovereign Pontiff then spoke *ex cathedra, i.e.,* solemnly propounded some doctrine to be believed by the Universal Church. Now it is manifest from the letter itself that it has none of the conditions required for a definition *ex cathedra:* it is not addressed to the Universal Church; it proposes no matter of faith to be held by all the children of Christ; in fact, it presents no doctrine whatever to be believed by the faithful, and it is nothing more than a commendatory letter addressed to Henry, resting on the good intentions set forth by that monarch himself. There is one maxim, indeed, which awakens the suspicions of the old Gallican school, viz., that "all the islands are subject to the authority of St. Peter." However, it is no doctrinal teaching that is thus propounded; it is a matter of fact admitted by Henry himself, a principle recognized by the international law of Europe in the middle ages, a maxim set down by the various states themselves, the better to maintain peace and concord among the princes of Christendom. To admit, however, or to call in question the teaching of the civil law of Europe, as embodied in that maxim, has nothing whatever to say to the great prerogative of St. Peter's successors, whilst they solemnly propound to the faithful, in unerring accents, the doctrines of Divine faith.

Fourth: To many it will seem a paradox, and yet it is a fact, that the supposed Bull of Pope Adrian had no part whatever in the submission of the Irish Chieftains to Henry the Second. Even according to those who maintain its genuineness, this Bull was not published till the year 1175, and certainly no mention of it was made in Ireland till long after the submission of the Irish Princes. The success of the Anglo-Normans was mainly due to a far different cause, viz., to the superior military skill and equipment of the invaders. Among the Anglo-Norman leaders were some of the bravest knights of the kingdom, who had won their laurels in the wars of France and Wales. Their weapons and armor rendered it almost impossible for the Irish troops to meet them in the open field. The cross-bow, which was made use of for the first time in this invasion, produced as great a change in military tactics as the rifled cannon in our own days. When Henry came in person to Ireland his numerous army hushed all opposition. There were 400 vessels in his fleet, and if a minimum of twenty-five armed men be allowed for each vessel, we will have an army of at least 10,000 men fully equipped, landing unopposed, on the southern shores of our island. It is to this imposing force, and the armor of the Anglo-Norman knights, that we must in great part refer whatever success attended this invasion of the English monarch.

To proceed now with the immediate matter of our present historical inquiry, the following is the summary of the arguments in favor of the authenticity of Pope Adrian's letter, inserted in the *Irishman* newspaper of June the 8th last, by J. C. O'Callaghan, Esq., editor of the "Macariæ Excidium," and author of many valuable works on Irish history:

"We have, firstly, the testimony of John of Salisbury, secretary to the Archbishop of Canterbury, and one of the ablest writers of his day, who relates his having been the envoy from Henry to Adrian, in 1155, to ask for a grant of Ireland, and such a grant having then been obtained, accompanied by a gold ring, containing a fine emerald, as a token of investiture, with which grant and ring the said John returned to Henry. We have, secondly, the grant or Bull of Adrian, *in extenso*, in the works of Giraldus Cambrensis and his contemporary, Radulfus de Diceto, Dean of London, as well as in those of Roger de Wendover and Matthew Paris. We have, thirdly, several Bulls of Adrian's successor, Pope Alexander III., still further to the purport of Adrian's, or in Henry's favor. We have, fourthly, the recorded public reading of the Bulls of Adrian and Alexander, at a meeting of Bishops in Waterford, in 1175. We have, fifthly, after the liberation of Scotland from England, at Bannockburn, and the consequent invitation of Bruce's brother, Edward, to be King of Ireland, the Bull of Adrian prefixed to the eloquent letter of remonstrance, which the Irish presented to Pope John XXII., against the English; the same Bull, moreover, referred to in the remonstrance itself, as so ruinous to Ireland; and a copy of that Bull, accordingly, sent back by the Pope to Edward II. of England, for his use under those circumstances. We have, sixthly, from Cardinal Baronius, in his great work, the 'Annales Ecclesiastici,' under Adrian IV., his grant of Ireland to his countryman, in full, or, as is said, 'ex codice Vaticano diploma datum ad Henricum, Anglorum Regem.' We have, seventhly, the Bull in the Bullarium Romanum, as printed at Rome in 1739. The citations and references in support of all the foregoing statements will be found in the 'Notes and Illustrations' of my edition of 'Macariæ Excidium' for the Irish Archæological Society in 1850, given in such a manner as must satisfy the most sceptical."

Examining these arguments in detail, I will follow the order thus marked out by Mr. O'Callaghan.

1.—We meet, in the first place, the testimony of John of Salisbury, who, in his "*Metalogicus*" (lib. iv., cap. 42), writes, that being in an official capacity at the Papal court, in 1155, Pope Adrian IV. then granted the investiture of Ireland to the illustrious King Henry II. of England.

I do not wish in any way to detract from the praise due to John of Salisbury, who was at this time one of the ablest courtiers of Henry II. However, the words here imputed to him must be taken with great reserve. Inserted as they are in the last chapter of his work, they are not at all required by the context: by cancelling them the whole passage runs smoother, and is more connected in every way. This is the more striking, as in another work of the same writer, which is entitled "*Polycraticus*," we meet with a detailed account of the various incidents of his embassy to Pope Adrian, yet he there makes no mention of the Bull in Henry's favor, or of the gold ring and its fine emerald, or of the grant of Ireland, all of which would have been so important for his narrative.

We must also hold in mind the time when the "*Metalogicus*" was written. The author himself fixes its date; for, immediately before asking the prayers of "those who read his book, and those who hear it read," he tells us that the news of Pope Adrian's death had reached him a little time before, and he adds that his own patron, Theobald, Archbishop of Canterbury, though still living, was weighed down by many infirmities. Now, Pope Adrian departed this life in 1159, and the death of Archbishop Theobald happened in 1161. Hence, Gale and the other editors of John of Salisbury's works, without a dissentient voice, refer the "*Metalogicus*" to the year 1159.

Now, it is a matter beyond the reach of controversy, that if Henry the Second obtained the investiture of Ireland from Adrian IV., he kept this grant a strict secret till at least the year 1175. For twenty years, *i.e.*, from 1155 to 1175, no mention was made of the gift of Adrian. Henry did not refer to it when authorizing his vassals to join Diarmaid, in 1167, when Adrian's Bull would have been so opportune to justify his intervention; he did not mention it when he himself set out for Ireland to solicit and receive the homage of the Irish Princes; he did not even refer to it when he assumed his new title and accomplished the purpose of his expedition. The Council of Cashel, in 1172, was the first episcopal assembly after Henry's arrival in Ireland; the

Papal Legate was present there, and did Adrian's Bull exist, it should necessarily have engaged the attention of the assembled Fathers. Nevertheless, not a whisper as to Adrian's grant was to be heard at that famous Council. Even the learned editor of "*Cambrensis Eversus*," whilst warmly asserting the genuineness of Adrian's Bull, admits "there is not any, even the slightest, authority, for asserting that its existence was known in Ireland before the year 1172, or for three years later"—(vol. ii., p. 440, note z.) It is extremely difficult, in any hypothesis, to explain in a satisfactory way this mysterious silence of Henry the Second, nor is it easy to understand how a fact so important, so vital to the interests of Ireland, could remain so many years concealed from those who ruled the destinies of the Irish Church. For, we must hold in mind, that throughout that interval Ireland numbered among its Bishops one who held the important office of Legate of the Holy See; our Church had constant intercourse with England and the Continent, and, through St. Laurence O'Toole and a hundred other distinguished prelates, enjoyed in the fullest manner the confidence of Rome.

If Adrian granted this Bull to Henry at the solicitation of John of Salisbury, in 1155, there is but one explanation for the silence of this courtier in his diary, as set forth in the "*Polycraticus*," and for the concealment of the Bull itself from the Irish bishops and people, viz., that this secresy was required by the state policy of the English monarch. And, if it be so, how then can we be asked to admit as genuine this passage of the "*Metalogicus*," in which the astute agent of Henry, still continuing to discharge offices of the highest trust in the court, would proclaim to the world as early as the year 1159, that Pope Adrian had made this formal grant of Ireland to his royal master, and that the solemn record of the investiture of this high dignity was preserved in the public archives of the kingdom?

It must also be added, that there are some phrases in this passage of the "*Metalogicus*" which manifestly betray the hand of the impostor. Thus, the words, "*usque in hodiernum diem*," imply that a long interval had elapsed since the concession was made by Pope Adrian, and surely they could not have been penned by John of Salisbury, in 1159. Much less can we suppose that this writer employed the words "*jure hæreditario possidendam.*" No such hereditary right is granted in the Bull of Adrian. It was not dreamt of even during the first years of the Anglo-Norman invasion, and it was only at a later period, when the Irish Chieftains scornfully rejected the Anglo-Norman law of hereditary succession, that this expedient was thought of for allaying the fierce opposition of our people.

Thus we are forced to regard the supposed testimony of John of Salisbury as nothing more than a clumsy interpolation, which probably was not inserted in his work till many years after the first Anglo-Norman invasion of our island.

2.—I now come to the second and main argument of those who seek to defend the authenticity of Pope Adrian's Bull. We have *Giraldus Cambrensis*, they say, a contemporary witness, whose testimony is unquestionable. He inserts in full this letter of Adrian IV., and he nowhere betrays the slightest doubt in regard to its genuineness.

Some years ago, we might perhaps have accepted that flattering character of Giraldus Cambrensis, but at the present day, and since the publication of an accurate edition of his historical works, it is impossible for us to do so.

It was not till many years after the death of Pope Adrian that Gerald de Barry, better known by the name of Giraldus Cambrensis, entered on the stage of Irish history. Twice he visited Ireland after the year 1183, and on both occasions he discharged those duties which, at the present day, would merit for him the title of special court correspondent with the invading army. The *Expugnatio Hibernica*, in which he inserts Adrian's Bull, may justly be said to have been written to order. Hence, as a matter of course, Giraldus adopted in it as genuine every document set forth as such by his royal master, and any statements that strengthened the claim or promoted the interests of his brother Welsh adventurers were sure not to be too nicely weighed in the scales of criticism by such a historian. The editors of the works of Giraldus, just now published under the direction of the Master of the Rolls, have fully recognized this special feature of the historical writings of Giraldus. The official catalogue describing the "*Expugnatio Hibernica*," of which we treat, expressly says:

"It may be regarded rather as a great epic, than a sober relation of facts occurring in his own days. No one can peruse it without coming to the conclusion that it is rather a poetical fiction than a prosaic, truthful history."

In the preface to the fifth volume of the "Historical Treatises of Giraldus," the learned editor, Rev. James F. Dimock, enters at considerable length into the inquiry, whether the *Expugnatio Hibernica* was to be accepted as genuine and authentic history. I need do no more than state the conclusions which he enunciates:—

"I think I have said enough to justify me in refusing to accept Giraldus's history of the Irish and of their English invaders as sober, truthful history."

And again he writes: "My good friend and pre-laborer in editing these volumes of Giraldus's work" (Mr. Brewer) "says of the '*Expugnatio*,' that Giraldus would seem to have regarded his subject rather as a great epic, which undoubtedly it was, than a sober relation of facts occurring in his own days. . . . This is a most true and characteristic description of Giraldus's treatment of his subject: the treatise certainly is, in great measure, rather a poetical fiction than a prosaic, truthful history."

I must further remark as another result from Rev. Mr. Dimock's researches, that the old text of Giraldus in reference to Pope Adrian's Bull, from which Mr. O'Callaghan's citations are now made, is now proved to be singularly defective. I will give the pithy words of that learned editor, which are stronger than any I would wish to use :—

"*No more absurd or nonsensical muddle was ever blundered into by the most stupid of abbreviators.*"

It is of course from the ancient MSS. of the work that this corruption of the old text is mainly proved; but it should indeed be apparent from an attentive study of the very printed text itself; for, as Mr. Dimock remarks, being accurately translated, its words "marvellously contrive to make Henry, in 1172, apply for and procure this privilege from Pope Adrian, who died in 1159! And with equally marvellous confusion they represent John of Salisbury, who had been Henry's agent in procuring this privilege in 1155, as sent, not to Ireland, but to Rome, for the purpose of publishing the Bull at Waterford, in 1174 or 1175!"

I will only add, regarding the testimony of Giraldus Cambrensis, that in the genuine text of the "*Expugnatio Hibernica*" he places on the same level the Bull of Adrian IV. and that of Alexander III. Nevertheless, as we will just now see, he elsewhere admits that there were many and grave suspicions that the supposed Bull of Alexander had never been granted by the Holy See.

The other names mentioned together with Giraldus will not detain us long. They are all writers who only incidentally make reference to Irish matters, and in these they naturally enough take Giraldus for their guide.

Ralph de Diceto wrote about 1210, and like Giraldus received his honors at the hands of Henry the Second. Irish historians have not yet accepted him as a guide in reference to matters connected with our country. For instance, the Synod of Cashel, of 1172, which was one of the most important events of that period of our history, is described by him as held in Lismore.

Roger de Wendover was a monk of St. Albans, who died 6th of May, 1237. His "*Flores Historiarum*" begins with the creation of the world, and ends two years before his death in 1235. He merely compendiates other sources down to the beginning of the thirteenth century. It is only the subsequent portion of his work which is held in esteem by our annalists.

Matthew Paris was a brother religious of Roger de Wendover, in St. Albans, where he died in 1259. Mr. Coxe, who edited a portion of the "*Flores Historiarum*" for the English Historical Society (1841–1844), has proved that, down to the year 1235, Matthew Paris only compendiates the work of Wendover. At all events his "*Historia Major*" is of very little weight. A distinguished German historian of the present day, Schrodl, thus conveys his strictures on its merits:—

"Se trompe a chaque instant, et, entraine par son aveugle rage de critique, donne pour des faits historiques des anecdotes piquantes qui n'ont aucune authenticite, des legendes deraisonnables et toutes sortes des details suspects, exageres et calomnieux."

To the testimony of such writers we may well oppose the silence of Peter de Blois, secretary of Henry the Second, though chronicling the chief events of Henry's reign, and the silence of all our native annalists, not one of whom ever mentions the Bull of Adrian.

3.—But it is time to pass on to the third argument which is advanced by our opponents. It is quite true that we have some letters or Bulls of Pope Alexander III. connected with the Irish invasion. Three of these, written in 1172, are certainly authentic. They are preserved in the "*Liber Niger Scaccarii*," from which they were edited by Hearne, and in later times they have been accurately printed by Mr. O'Callaghan and Rev. Dr. Kelly. They are addressed respectively to the Irish bishops, King Henry, and the Irish Princes. So far, however, are these letters from corroborating the genuineness of Pope Adrian's Bull, that they furnish an unanswerable argument for wholly setting it aside as groundless and unauthentic. They are entirely devoted to the circumstances of the invasion of our island and its results, and yet the only title that they recognize in Henry is "that monarch's power, and the submission of the Irish Chieftains." They simply ignore any Bull of Adrian, and any investiture from the Holy See.

There is however another Bull of Alexander III., preserved by Giraldus Cambrensis, which is supposed to have been granted at the request of King Henry, in 1172, and is confirmatory of the gift and investure made by Pope Adrian: and Mr. O'Callaghan holds that this Bull of Alexander III. sets at rest forever all doubt as to the genuineness of the grant made by Adrian IV.

The question at once suggests itself:—Is this Bull of Alexander III. to be itself admitted as genuine and authentic? If its own authority be doubtful, surely it cannot suffice to prop up the tottering cause of Adrian's Bull. Now its style is entirely different from that of the three authentic letters of which we have just spoken. Quite in opposition to these letters, " the only authority alleged in it for Henry's right to Ireland is the Bull of Adrian," as Dr. Lanigan allows. The genuine letters are dated from Tusculum, where, as we know from other sources, Alexander actually resided in 1172. On the other hand, this confirmatory Bull, though supposed to have been obtained in 1172, is dated *from Rome*, thus clearly betraying the hand of the impostor. Such was the disturbed condition of Rome at that period that it was impossible for His Holiness to reside there, and hence we find him sometimes holding his Court in Tusculum, at other times in Segni, Anagni, or Ferrara. It was only when these disturbances were quelled that Alexander III. was able, in 1178, to return in triumph to his capital.

But there is still another reason why we must doubt of the authority of this confirmatory Bull. The researches of Rev. Mr. Dimock have proved that Ussher long ago remarked, that this Bull of Alexander originally formed part of the work of Giraldus Cambrensis, although later copyists, and the first editors, including the learned Camden, recognizing its spuriousness, excluded it from Giraldus's text. The matter is now set at rest, for the ancient MSS. clearly prove that it originally formed part of the "*Expugnatio Hibernica.*" Thanks, however, to the zeal and industry of Mr. Brewer, we are at present acquainted with another work of Giraldus, written at a later period than his Historical Tracts on Ireland. It is entitled "*De Principiis Instructionis,*" and was edited in 1846, for the "*Anglia Christiana*" Society. Now, in this treatise Giraldus refers to the Bull of Alexander III., of which we treat, but he prefixes the following remarkable words:—

"*Some assert or imagine that this Bull was obtained from the Pope: but others deny that it was ever obtained from the Pontiff.*" "Sicut a quibusdam impetratum assertitur aut confingitur; ab aliis autem usquam impetratum fuisse negatur."

Surely these words should suffice to convince the most sceptical that the fact of the Bull of Alexander being recited by Giraldus, in his "*Expugnatio Hibernica,*" is a very unsatisfactory ground on which to rest the arguments for its genuineness.

4.—As regards the Synod of Waterford, in 1175, and the

statement that the Bulls of Adrian and Alexander were published therein for the first time, all these matters rest on the very doubtful authority of Giraldus Cambrensis. We have no record in the Irish Annals that any general meeting of the Irish Bishops was held in Waterford in 1175. The circumstances of the country rendered such a Synod impossible; for war and dissensions raged throughout the length and breadth of our island. It was in that year, however, that the first Bishop was appointed by King Henry, to the See of Waterford, as Ware informs us; and, perhaps, we would not err were we to suppose that the Synod so pompously set forth by Giraldus, was a convention of the Anglo-Norman clergy of Waterford, under their newly appointed Prelate, all of whom would, no doubt, joyfully accept the official documents presented in the name of the King, by Nicholas of Wallingford.

Leland supposes that this Synod of Waterford was not held till 1177. The disturbed state of the kingdom, however, rendered a Synod equally impossible in that year, and all our ancient authorities utterly ignore such a Synod.

5.—In the "Remonstrance" addressed by the Irish Princes and people to John XXII., about the year 1315, repeated mention is made of the Bull of Adrian. But then it is only cited there as a conclusive argument *ad hominem*, against the English traducers of our nation, "lest the bitter and venomous calumnies of the English, and their unjust, and unfounded attacks upon us and all who support our rights, may in any degree influence the mind of your Holiness." The Bull of Adrian IV. was published by the English, and set forth by them as the charter-deed of their rule in Ireland; yet they violated in a most flagrant manner all the conditions of that Papal grant. The Irish Princes and people, in self-defence, had now made over the sovereignty of the island to Edward de Bruce, brother of the Scottish King; they style him their adopted monarch, and they pray the Pope to give a formal sanction to their proceedings. Thus, throughout the whole Remonstrance, the Bull of Adrian is used as a telling argument against the injustice of the invaders, and as a precedent which John XXII. might justly follow in sanctioning the transfer of the Irish crown to Edward Bruce. But in all this the historian will find no grounds for asserting the genuineness of the supposed Bulls of Adrian or Alexander. We will just now see that at this very time the Irish people universally regarded those Bulls as spurious inventions of their English enemies.

6.—Baronius, the eminent ecclesiastical historian, inserts in his invaluable *Annals* the Bull of Adrian IV., " from a Vatican Manuscript." This is the sixth argument advanced by Mr. O'Callaghan.

It is not my intention to question in any way the services rendered by Cardinal Baronius to the cause of our Church History; but at the same time no one will deny that considerable progress has been made in historical research during the past three hundred and fifty years, and many documents are now set aside which were then accepted as unquestioned on the supposed reliable authority of preceding chroniclers.

In the present instance we are not left in doubt as to the source whence Baronius derived his information regarding Adrian's supposed Bull. During my stay in Rome I took occasion to inquire whether the MSS. of the eminent annalist, which are happily preserved, indicated the special "Vatican Manuscript" referred to in his printed text; and I was informed by the learned archivist of the Vatican, Monsignor Theiner, who is at present engaged in giving a new edition, and continuing the great work of Baronius, that the

Codex Vaticanus referred to is a MS. copy of the History of Matthew Paris, which is preserved in the Vatican Library. Thus it is the testimony of Matthew Paris alone that here confronts us in the pages of Baronius, and no new argument can be taken from the words of the eminent annalist. Relying on the same high authority, I am happy to state that nowhere in the private archives, or among the private papers of the Vatican, or in the "*Regesta*," which Jaffe's researches have made so famous, or in the various indices of the Pontifical Letters, can a single trace be found of the supposed Bulls of Adrian IV. and Alexander III.

7.—The last argument advanced by Mr. O'Callaghan will not detain us long. The insertion or omission of such ancient records in the Bullarium, is a matter that depends wholly on the critical skill of the editor. Curious enough, in one edition of the Bullarium, as may be seen in the references of Dr. Lanigan, Adrian's Bull is inserted, whilst no mention is made of that of Alexander; in another edition, however, the Bull of Alexander is given in full, whilst the Bull of Adrian is omitted. We may well leave our opponents to settle this matter with the conflicting editors of the Bullarium. They, probably like Baronius, merely copied the Bull of Adrian from Matthew Paris, and erred in doing so. Labbe, in his magnificent edition of the Councils, also publishes Adrian's Bull, but then he expressly tells us that it is copied from the work of Matthew Paris.

We have thus, as far as the limits of this article will allow, examined in detail the various arguments which support the genuineness of the supposed Bull, and now it only remains for us to conclude that there are no sufficient grounds for accepting that document as the genuine work of Pope Adrian.

Indeed, the Irish nation at all times, as if instinctively,

shrunk from accepting it as genuine, and unhesitatingly pronounced it an Anglo-Norman forgery. We have already seen how even Giraldus Cambrensis refers to the doubts which had arisen regarding the Bull of Pope Alexander; but we have at hand still more conclusive evidence that Adrian's Bull was universally rejected by our people. There is, happily, preserved in the Barberini Archives, Rome, a MS. of the fourteenth century, containing a series of official papers connected with the Pontificate of John XXII., and amongst them is a letter from the Lord Justiciary and the Royal Council of Ireland, forwarded to Rome under the Royal Seal, and presented to His Holiness by William of Nottingham, Canon and Precentor of St. Patrick's Cathedral, Dublin, about the year 1325. In this important, but hitherto unnoticed document, the Irish are accused of very many crimes, among which is insidiously introduced the rejection of the supposed Bulls:

"*Moreover, they assert that the King of England, under false pretences and by false Bulls, obtained the dominion of Ireland, and this opinion is commonly held by them.*" "Asserentes etiam Dominum Regem Angliæ ex falsa suggestione et ex falsis Bullis terram Hiberniæ in dominium impetrasse ac communiter hoc tenentes."

This national tradition was preserved unbroken throughout the turmoil of the fifteenth and sixteenth centuries, and on the revival of our historical literature in the beginning of the seventeenth century, was registered in the pages of Lynch, Stephen White, and other writers.

It will be well also, whilst forming our judgment regarding this supposed Bull of Adrian, to hold in mind the disturbed state of society, especially in Italy, at the time to which it refers. At the present day it would be no easy matter indeed for such a forgery to survive more than a few weeks. But at the close of the twelfth century it was far otherwise. Owing to the constant revolutions and disturbances that then prevailed, the Pontiff was oftentimes obliged to fly from city to city; frequently his papers were seized and burned, and he himself detained as a hostage or prisoner by his enemies. Hence it is that several forged Bulls, examples of which are given in "*Cambrensis Eversus*," date from these times. More than one of the grants made to the Norman families are now believed to rest on such forgeries; and that the Anglo-Norman adventurers in Ireland were not strangers to such deeds of darkness, appears from the fact that a matrix for forging the Papal Seal of such Bulls, now preserved in the R. I. Academy, was found a few years ago in the ruins of one of the earliest Anglo-Norman monasteries founded by De Courcy.

The circumstances of the publication of the Bull by Henry were surely not calculated to disarm suspicion. Our opponents do not even pretend that it was made known in Ireland till the year 1175, and hence, though publicly granted with solemn investiture, as John of Salisbury's testimony would imply, and though its record was deposited in the public archives of the kingdom, this Bull, so vital to the interests of the Irish Church, should have remained dormant for twenty years, unnoticed in Rome, unnoticed by Henry's courtiers, still more, unnoticed by the Irish Bishops, and I will add, unnoticed by the Continental Sovereigns so jealous of the power and preponderance of the English Monarch. For such suppositions there is indeed no parallel in the whole history of investitures.

It is seldom, too, that the hand of the impostor may not be detected in some at least of the minor details of the spurious document. In the present instance more than one ancient MS. preserves the concluding formula of the Bull: "Datum Romæ," *dated from Rome*. Now this simple formula would suffice of itself to prove the whole Bull to be a forgery. Before the news of the election of Pope Adrian to the Chair of St. Peter could reach England, that Pontiff was obliged to seek for safety in flight from his capital. Rome was in revolt, and Arnold of Brescia sought to renew there a spectre of the old Pagan Republic. John of Salisbury, in his "*Polycraticus,*" faithfully attests that, on his arrival in Italy, the Papal Court was held not in Rome, but in Beneventum: it was in this city he presented to Pope Adrian the congratulations of Henry II.; and he mentions his sojourn there during the three months that he remained in Italy. This is further confirmed by the Italian chronicles. Baronius saw the inconsistency of the formula, *Datum Romæ*, with the date 1155, and hence, in his Annals, he entered Adrian's Bull under the year 1159; but if this date be correct, surely then that Bull could not have been brought to Henry by John of Salisbury, and the passage of the "*Metalogicus*" referring to it, must at once be admitted a forgery. Other historians have been equally puzzled to find a year for this supposed Bull. For instance, O'Halloran, in his History of Ireland, whilst admitting that the Irish people always regarded the Bull as a forgery, refers its date to the year 1167, that is, eight years after the death of Pope Adrian IV.

There is only one other reflection with which I wish to detain the reader. The condition of our country, and the relations between Ireland and the English King, which are set forth in the supposed Bull, are precisely those of the year 1172; but it would have required more than a prophetic vision to have anticipated them in 1155. In 1155 Ireland was not in a state of turmoil or verging towards barbarism; on the contrary, it was rapidly progressing and renewing its claim to religious and moral pre-eminence. I will add, that Pope Adrian, who had studied under Irish masters, knew well this flourishing condition of our country. In 1172, however, a sad change had come over our island. Four years of continual warfare, and the ravages of the Anglo-Norman filibusterers, since their first landing in 1168, had well-nigh reduced Ireland to a state of barbarism, and the authentic letters of Alexander III., in 1172, faithfully describe its most deplorable condition. Moreover, an expedition of Henry to Ireland, which would not be an invasion, and yet would merit the homage of the Irish princes, was simply an impossibility in 1155. But owing to the special circumstances of the kingdom, such in reality was the expedition of Henry in 1172. He set out for Ireland, not avowedly to invade and conquer it, but to curb the insolence and to punish the deeds of pillage of his own Norman freebooters. Hence, during his stay in Ireland he fought no battle and made no conquest; his first measures of severity were directed against some of the most lawless of the early Norman adventurers, and this more than anything else reconciled the native Princes to his military display. In return he received from a majority of the Irish Chieftains the empty title of *Ard-righ*, or "Head Sovereign," which did not suppose any conquest on his part, and did not involve any surrender of their own hereditary rights. Such a state of things could not have been imagined in 1155; and yet it is one which is implied in the spurious Bull of the much-maligned Pontiff, Adrian the Fourth.

† P. F. M.

PART II.

THE INSURRECTION OF 1641.

ANALYSIS OF THE LEGEND, AND EXPOSURE OF SIR JOHN TEMPLE'S FALSIFICATIONS.

[In his "*Vindiciæ Hibernicæ*," first published in Philadelphia, in 1819, Mathew Carey gives the story told by Sir John Temple of the pretended "Rebellion" of 1641, with an analysis of the legend, in which (even from English authorities) the contradictions and exaggerations of Temple and Borlase are exposed. The full text is appended.]

The Insurrection in 1641. *Was there a General Conspiracy of the Irish Catholics, in that year, to Murder the Protestants?*

"A perjur'd wretch, whom falsehood clothes,
Ev'n like a garment—
Who in the day's broad searching eye,
Makes God bear witness to a lie."—*Churchill.*

THE decision of this question is attended with far more difficulty than any of those hitherto presented to the view of the reader. The nature of the case does not admit of the same kind of evidence as I have been hitherto enabled to produce, and which, I flatter myself, has been found irresistible.

The tale of this conspiracy has been so universally credited; so large a portion of the possessors of confiscated property in Ireland have been for one hundred and eighty years interested in affording it support and countenance; so much art and talent have been, during that time, employed in giving it an air of plausibility; there is so much difficulty in proving a negative in any case, more particularly in the present one, which is naturally, and has been moreover artfully, involved in mystery; and it is so extremely arduous an undertaking to operate upon the public mind, when imbued with inveterate prejudices, that the task is truly Herculean, and I should have abandoned it as impracticable, but that the narrative itself is replete with so many incredible and incongruous circumstances, as to carry strong internal evidence of fraud.

In order to give the story fair play, and to enable the reader to form a correct opinion on the subject, with all the evidence before him, I shall give the whole account of the discovery of the plot, as it stands in Temple's History of the Irish Rebellion, the authority almost solely relied on by all the subsequent writers on the subject. Some slight extracts are added from Borlase, containing a few additional particulars.

To simplify the examination, the narrative is divided into short sentences, each containing perfect sense, to oblige the reader to pause and reflect, as he proceeds.

The discussion of this question being one of the main objects of the work, the reader's calm and candid consideration of it is earnestly invoked. It is hoped that, laying aside all preconceived opinions on the subject, he will revolve it in his mind, as if it were wholly new, and he had now, for the first time in his life, to form a decision on it.

There are, unfortunately, too many to whom a compliance with this request is impossible: and indeed a large proportion of mankind can never command independence of mind enough even to examine evidence that militates with their early, and, of course, inveterate prejudices; far less ever to abandon those prejudices. There are, therefore, thousands who would as soon doubt any of the demonstrations of Euclid, or the existence of the solar system, as the existence of the universality of the plot of "*the execrable rebellion of* 1641."

To this contracted class I do not address myself: with them I have no fellowship: "Even though one were to rise from the dead," his testimony would not convince them. Let them hug the chains of their bigoted prejudices. The appeal is to that respectable description of readers, whose minds, open to conviction, are at all times ready to yield to the force of evidence, how strongly soever it may militate against opinions which have "grown with their growth." The favorable decision of one such reader, with a clear head and sound heart, would outweigh the disapprobation of a whole army of the slaves of prejudice.

*Extracts from Temple's History of the Irish Rebellion.**

1. "Sir William Cole, upon the very first apprehensions of something that he conceived to be hatching among the Irish, did write a letter to the lords justices and council, dated the 11th of October, 1641.

2. "Wherein he gave them notice of the great resort made to sir Phelim O'Neal, in the county of Tyrone, *as also to the house of the lord Macguire*, in the county of Fermanagh, and that by several suspected persons, fit instruments for mischief;

3. "As also that *the said lord Macguire had of late made several journies into the Pale and other places, and had spent his time much in writing letters and sending despatches abroad.*

4. "*These letters were received* by the lords justices and council;

5. "And they, in answer to them, required him to be very vigilant and industrious to find out what should be

---

* The reader will please to observe, that these extracts are taken *verbatim* from the original work; and, unless where otherwise distinctly marked by a dash, form an unbroken consecutive series.

the occasion of these several meetings, and speedily to advertise them thereof, or of any other particular that he conceived might tend to the public service of the state."

6. "They [the lords justices] had not any certain notice of the general conspiracy of the Irish, until the 22d of October, in the very evening before the day appointed for the surprise of the castle and city of Dublin.

7. "The conspirators being, many of them, arrived within the city, and having that day met at the Lion tavern, in Copper alley, and there turning the drawer out of the room, ordered their affairs together, and drunk healths upon their knees to the happy success of the next morning's work.

8. "Owen O'Connally, *a gentleman of a mere Irish family*, but one that had long lived among the English, and been trained up in the true Protestant religion, came unto the lord justice Parsons, ABOUT NINE O'CLOCK THAT EVENING!!

9. "And made him a broken relation of a great conspiracy for the seizing upon his majesty's castle of Dublin.

10. "*He gave him the names of some of the chief conspirators!* assured him that they were come up expressly to the town for the same purpose; and that next morning they would undoubtedly attempt, and surely effect it, if their design were not speedily prevented;

11. "And that he had understood all this from Hugh Mac-Mahon, one of the chief conspirators, who was then in town, and came up *but the very same afternoon*, for the execution of the plot;

12. "And with whom indeed *he had been drinking somewhat liberally;* and as the truth is, did then make such a broken relation of a matter that *seemed so incredible in itself*, as that his lordship *gave very little belief to it at first!!!*

13. "In regard *it came from an obscure person*, and one, as he conceived, somewhat distempered at that time.

14. "But howsoever, the lord Parsons gave him order *to go again to Mac-Mahon!!! and get out of him as much certainty of the plot!!!* with as many particular circumstances, as he could!!! straitly charging him to return back unto him the same evening!!!

15. "And in the mean time, having by strict commands given to the constable of the castle, taken order *to have the gates thereof well guarded, as also with the mayor and sheriffs of the city to have* strong watches set upon all parts of the same, and to make stay of all strangers,

16. "He went *privately!!* about ten of the clock that night, to the lord Borlase's house *without the town*, and there acquainted him with what he understood from O'Conally.

17. "They sent for such of the council as they knew then to be *in the town.**

18. "But there came only unto them that night sir Thomas Rotheram and sir Robert Meredith, chancellor of the exchequer: with these *they fell into consultation what was fit to be done!!!!* attending the return of O'Conally.

19. "And finding that he staid somewhat longer than the time prefixed, they sent out in search after him;

20. "And found him seized on by the watch, and so he had been carried away to prison, and the discovery that night disappointed,

21. "Had not one of the lord Parson's servants, expressly sent, amongst others, *to walk the streets, and attend the motions of the said O'Conally*, come in, and rescued him, and brought him to the lord Borlase's house.

---

* Although I shall analyze this precious narrative at length, before this chapter is closed, I cannot refrain from calling the reader's attention to these two paragraphs, 16 and 17, as they alone would be sufficient with impartial men, to discredit the whole plot. Sir William Parsons, being *in the city of* Dublin, at nine o'clock at night, is informed of a plot to explode in thirteen hours.—Instead of at once seizing the conspirators, he sends a drunken man, whose absence must have excited suspicion, to make further discoveries—and at ten o'clock, he goes "*privately*" to lord Borlase's house "*out of town*"—and then sends for such of the council as he knew to be then "*in town.*" Was there ever a more Münchausen tale? It is hardly calculated to impose on an idiot. How far out of town sir John's house was, cannot be ascertained —suppose only a mile. Then he walked a mile—the messenger another—and such of the council as were found, had to walk a third mile, and for what? To be so far removed from the scene of action, and from the means of applying a remedy to the impending evils, as to give every opportunity to the conspirators to insure their success! Here was a most pernicious delay, when every moment was invaluable!! Had there been any reality in the plot, sir William would have remained "*in town*"— collected all of the council there at the time—sent a messenger "*out of town*" for sir John Borlase—and then collected the whole body at their posts, where they ought to be on such an emergency.

22. "O'Conally having somewhat recovered himself from his distemper, occasioned partly, as he said himself, by the horror of the plot revealed to him, partly by his too liberal drinking with Mac-Mahon, that he might the more easily get away from him, (he beginning much to suspect and fear his discovery of the plot,)

23. "Confirmed what he had formerly related, and added these further particulars set down in his examination, as followeth:

"*The examination of Owen O'Conally, gentleman, taken before us, whose names ensue, October 22, 1641.*

"Who being duly sworn and examined, saith:

24. "That he being at *Monimore*, in the county of Londonderry, on *Tuesday last!* he received a letter from colonel Hugh Oge Mac-Mahon, desiring him to come to Conaught, in the county of Monaghan, and to be with him on *Wednesday* or *Thursday* last!

25. "Whereupon he, this examinate, came to Conaught on Wednesday night last;

26. "And finding the said Hugh come to Dublin, followed him hither;

27. "He came hither about *six of the clock this evening!*

28. "And forthwith went to the lodging of the said Hugh, to the house near the Boat, in Oxmantown;

29. "And there he found the said Hugh, and came with the said Hugh *into the town,* near the pillory, to the lodging of the lord Macguire;

30. "Where they found not the lord within; and there they drank a cup of beer;

31. "And *then went back again* to the said Hugh his lodging;*

32. "He saith, that at the lord Maguire his lodging, the said Hugh told him that there were and would be this night great numbers of noblemen and gentlemen of the *Irish Papists,* from all the parts of the kingdom, in this town;

33. "Who with himself had determined to take the castle of Dublin, and possess themselves of all his majesty's ammunition there, *to-morrow morning,* being Saturday;

34. "And that they intended first to batter the chimnies

---

* Here again is a dodging "*into town*" and "*out of town.*"

of the said town; and if the city would not yield, then to batter down the houses;

35. "And so *to cut off all the Protestants* that would not join with them!

36. "He further saith, that the said Hugh then told him, that the Irish had prepared men in all parts of the kingdom, *to destroy all the English inhabiting there, to-morrow morning by ten of the clock!!*

37. "And that in all the sea-ports, and other towns in the kingdom, *all the Protestants should be killed this night!!* and that all the posts that could be, could not prevent it;

38. "And further saith, that he moved the said Hugh to forbear executing of that business, and to discover it to the state, for the saving of his own estate;

39. "Who said he could not help it; but said, that they did owe their allegiance to the king, and would pay him all his rights: but that they did this for the tyrannical government that was over them, and to imitate Scotland, which got a privilege by that course;

40. "And he further saith, that when he was with the said Hugh, in his lodging the second time, the said Hugh swore, that he should not go out of his lodging that night; but told him that he should go with him the next morning to the castle; and said, if this matter were discovered, some body should die for it;

$40\frac{1}{2}$. "Whereupon this examinate feigned some necessity for his easement; went down out of the chamber; and left his sword in pawn; and the said Hugh sent his man down with him; and when this examinate came down into the yard, and finding an opportunity, he, this examinate, *leapt over a wall and two pales!!!* and so came to the lord justice Parsons.

"October 22, 1641.

WILLIAM PARSONS,
THOMAS ROTHERAM,
ROBERT MEREDITH,
OWEN O'CONALLY."

41. "How it came to pass that *the other lord justice attested not the examination, (it being took in his house, he present,)* hath begot some doubts, evidencing how (since) counsels swerved into cabals."

42. "*Hereupon the lords took present order to have a watch privately set upon the lodging of Mac-Mahon, as also upon the lord Macguire!!!!**

43. "And so they sat up all that night in *consultation!!!* having far stronger *presumptions* upon this latter examination taken than any ways at first they could entertain.

44. "The lords justices, upon a further consideration, there being come unto them *early next morning!* several others of the privy council, *sent before day, and seized upon Mac-Machon, then with his servant in his own lodging.*

45. "They at first made some little resistance with their drawn swords; but finding themselves over-mastered, presently yielded.

46. "And so they were brought before the lords justices and council, still sitting at the lord Borlase's house.†

47. "Where, upon examination, he did without much difficulty confess the plot, resolutely telling them, that *on that very day, all the forts and strong places in Ireland, would be taken!!*

48. "That he, with the lord Macguire, Hugh Birn, captain Brian O'Neil, and several other Irish gentlemen, were come up expressly to surprise the castle of Dublin.

49. "That *twenty men out of each county in the kingdom!!!* were to be here to join with them. ‡

50. "That *all the lords and gentlemen in the kingdom, that were papists, were engaged in this plot!!!*

51. "That what was *that day to be done in other parts of the country*, was so far advanced by that time, as it was impossible for the wit of man to prevent it!

52. "And withal told them, that it was true they had him in their power, and might use him how they pleased, but he was sure he should be revenged."

---

* The lords justices have information of a plot to explode in a few hours, whereby they are to be murdered, and as a precautionary measure, "*set a watch privately upon the lodgings*" *of the chief conspirators!!*

† It appears, therefore, that the council was sitting all night "*at lord Borlase's house*," "*out of town*," so as to leave the conspirators free scope to carry their projects into execution "*in town*." Was ever an imposture so absurdly compacted?

‡ There are thirty-two counties in Ireland, some of them *one hundred and fifty miles from Dublin—and twenty men were to be marched from each county*, to execute a plot requiring the utmost secresy!! An admirable scheme!

53. Extract from "The lords chief justices' letter to the lord lieutenant, October 25, 1641, sent by Owen O'Conally, the first discoverer. *

"May it please your lordship,

54. "On Friday, the 22nd of this month, *after nine o'clock at night*, this bearer, Owen O'Conally, SERVANT TO SIR JOHN CLOTWORTHY, KNIGHT, came to me, the lord justice Parsons, to my house,

55. "And in great secresie (as indeed the cause did require,) discovered unto me a most wicked and damnable conspiracy, plotted, contrived, and intended to be also acted by some evil-affected Irish Papists here.

56. "The plot was on the then next morning, Saturday, the 23d of October, being St. Ignatius's day, *about nine of the clock!* to surprise his majesty's castle of Dublin, his majesty's chief strength of this kingdom; wherein also is the principal magazine of his majesty's arms and munition.

57. "And it was agreed, it seems among them, that at the same hour, *all other his majesty's forts and magazines of arms and munition in this kingdom!!* should be surprised by others of those conspirators:

58. "And further, *that all the Protestants and English throughout the whole kingdom*, that would not join with them, should be cut off!! and so those Papists should then become possessed of the government and kingdom at the same instant.

59. "As soon as I had that intelligence, I then immediately repaired to the lord justice Borlase; and thereupon *we instantly assembled the council.*

60. "And *having sate all that night!!!* also all the next day, the 23d of October, in regard of the short time left us for the consultation of so great and weighty a matter, although it was not possible for us, upon so few hours' warning, to prevent those other great mischiefs which were

---

* Thus it appears that the lords justices did not think it necessary to write the lord lieutenant, then in London, till Monday the 25th, respecting a conspiracy for the destruction of "all the Protestants in Ireland that would not join it," which was to have exploded on the 23d!

to be acted, even at the same hour and at so great a distance, in all the other parts of the kingdom;*

61. "Yet such was our industry therein, *having caused the castle to be that night strengthened with armed men*, and the city guarded, as the wicked councils of those evil persons, by the great mercy of God to us, became defeated, so as they were not able to act that part of their treachery, which indeed was principal.

62. "And which, if they could have effected, would have rendered the rest of their purposes the more easy.

63. "Having so secured the castle, we forthwith laid about for the apprehension of as many of the offenders as we could, many of them having come to this city but that night, intending, it seems, the next morning, to act their parts in those treacherous and bloody crimes.

64. "The first man apprehended was one Hugh Mac-Mahon, Esq., (grandson to the traitor Tyrone,) a gentleman of good fortune in the county of Monaghan, who, with others, *was taken that morning* in Dublin, having, at the time of their apprehension, offered a little resistance with their swords drawn; but finding those we employed against them more in number, and better armed, yielded.

65. "He, upon examination before us, at first denied all; but in the end, when he saw we laid it home to him, he confessed enough to destroy himself, and impeach some others, as by a copy of his examination herewith sent, may appear to your lordship.

66. "We then committed him until we might have further time to examine him again, our time being become more needful to be employed in action for securing this place, than examining. This Mac-Mahon had been abroad, and served the King of Spain as a lieutenant colonel.

67. "Upon conference with him and others!!! *and calling to mind a letter we received the week before* from sir William Cole!!! a copy whereof we send your lordship here inclosed, we gathered, that *the lord Macguire was to be an actor in surprising the castle of Dublin !!!!!* †

---

* "Which were to be acted, even at the same hour, in all other parts of the kingdom"—but which were not acted, nor attempted.

† After having set a guard on his house the preceding night, they required all this variety of information, to "*gather that the lord Macguire was to be an actor in surprising the castle of Dublin :*"

68. "Wherefore we held it necessary to secure him immediately, thereby also to startle and deter the rest, when they found him laid fast."

Extracts from Borlase's "History of the Execrable Irish Rebellion."

69. "In the interim, the lord Parsons, (being touched with the relation,) repaired, about ten of the clock at night, to the lord Borlase, at Chichester house, without the town;

70. "And disclosed to him what O'Conally had imparted; which made so sensible an impression on his colleague, as (the discoverer being let go,) he grew infinitely concerned thereat, having none to punish, if the story should prove false, or means to learn more, were it true.

71. "In the disturbance of which perplexity, Owen O'Conally comes, (or, as others write, was brought,) where the lords justices were then met; sensible that his discovery was not thoroughly believed, professing that whatever he had acquainted the lord Parsons with, (touching the conspiracy,) was true:

72. "And could he but repose himself, (*the effects of drink being still upon him,*) he should discover more.

73. "Whereupon *he had the conveniency of a bed.*"

74. "In the interim, the lords justices summoned as many of the council as they could give notice to, to their assistance that night at Chichester house.

75. "Sir Thomas Rotheram, and Sir Robert Meredith, chancellor of the exchequer, came immediately to them.

76. "They then with all diligence secured the gates of the city,* with such as they could most confide in, and strengthened the warders of the castle, (which were a few inconsiderable men,) with their foot guard, † usually attending their persons, *charging the mayor and his brethren to be*

---

* "They secured the gates of the city." That is to say, the conspirators were "*in the town*"—and they "*out of town*"—they therefore must have shut themselves out.

† "The foot guard." Thus the safety of the city was confided, at a time of such imminent danger, to "*the warders*," "a *few inconsiderable men*," and "the foot-guard" of the lords justices, "*usually attending their persons*," which cannot be presumed to have been more than ten or a dozen at most !

watchful of all persons that should walk the streets that night!!!"

---

77. "Hugh Oge Mac-Mahon, Esq., grandson by his mother to the traitor Tir-Owen, a gentleman of good fortune in the county of Monaghan, who had served as a lieutenant-colonel in the king of Spain's quarters, was, after some little resistance, apprehended *before day in his own lodgings,* over the water, near the Inns, and brought to Chichester house;

78. "Where, upon examination, he did, without much difficulty, confess the plot, resolutely telling them, That ON THAT VERY DAY, (*it was now about five in the morning, the 23d of Oct.,* 1641 !!!) that all the forts and strong places in Ireland would be taken," &c., &c.

79. "Before Mac-Mahon was apprehended, O'Conally, having *on his repose* recovered himself, had his examination taken, in these words:" [as before.]

Analysis of the foregoing legend.

I. A Roman Catholic colonel is engaged in a plot, the object of which is "*to massacre all the Protestants in the kingdom,*" "except those who would join" in murdering their brethren.

II. This colonel, in want of a confederate, sends about fifty miles to O'Conally, *a Protestant,* to reveal to him this project.

III. O'Conally, who, in order to attach importance to his testimony, in some of the statements is styled "*a gentleman,*" is, in fact and in truth, merely *a servant* to Sir John Clotworthy, *one of the most envenomed enemies of the Roman Catholics,* and, of course, a very suitable person to be intrusted with such a secret, and very worthy to be sent for to a place distant forty-five miles.

IV. O'Conally receives a letter on *Tuesday,* the 19th of

October, at what hour is not known,—say nine o'clock; and, *wholly ignorant of the nature of the affair* which leads to the invitation, makes all his preparations at once, and commences his journey, we will suppose, about noon the same day.

V. He arrives *on Wednesday night*, the 20th, at Conaught, after a journey of about forty-five miles: and be it observed, *en passant*, that a journey of forty-five miles, at that period, was nearly as arduous an undertaking, and required almost as much preparation, as a journey of one hundred and fifty at present.

VI. Colonel Mac-Mahon, whose invitation had given O'Conally the option of coming on Wednesday OR *Thursday*, so far broke his engagement, that he had started, *on Wednesday*, for Dublin, previous to O'Conally's arrival, which took place on the night of that day.

VII. O'Conally, nothing discouraged by the breach of engagement on the part of the colonel, follows him to Dublin.

VIII. He arrives in that city on the memorable Friday, the 22d of October, " about six o'clock in the evening " ONE HOUR AFTER SUNSET.

IX. Conaught, in Monaghan, is not to be found on any map. I will therefore suppose it to have been in the centre of the county.

X. Monimore, by Pinkerton's map, is about forty miles in a direct line from the centre of the county of Monaghan —and this centre is about sixty miles also in a direct line from Dublin. The whole distance must, by the usual circuitous windings of the road, have been *at the very least one hundred and ten miles.*

XI. The climate of Ireland is very moist. Rains are generally abundant, particularly in autumn. Of course, *the roads at that season were very probably miry, and difficult to travel.*

XII. It thus appears, that O'Conally has performed a journey of about forty-five miles in a day and a half; that is, from mid-day on Tuesday, to Wednesday night: and a hundred and ten in three days and a half, at a season of the year, when THE SUN ROSE ABOUT SEVEN, AND SET ABOUT FIVE!! and this exploit was accomplished at a time when there were no diligences, post-coaches, post-chaises, or steam-boats, to insure expedition; and when, moreover, the roads were in all probability in very bad order.

XIII. Nothing discouraged by the fatigue of his journey of a hundred and ten miles, nor by his previous disappointment, nor by the darkness of the evening, he commences a search for the lodgings of an entire stranger, who had arrived that evening! Wonderful to tell, and impossible to be believed, he is said to have succeeded, and to have found out the stranger's lodgings! And let it not be forgotten, that on this night *the moon was invisible*,* a circumstance admirably calculated to aid his researches!

XIV. Although the colonel was engaged in a plot to explode *next day, at ten o'clock, A. M.*, O'Conally finds him alone, *between six and seven* † *o'clock on Friday evening, in the suburbs.* He appears to have seen none of his brother conspirators before nine, at which time O'Conally left him.

XV. The colonel takes him to the lodgings of a brother conspirator "*into town*," at the distance, probably, of a mile or two.

XVI. This conspirator not being at home, the colonel, after having taken a drink of beer with his new friend,

---

* *Extract of a letter from the Vice-Provost of the University of Pennsylvania.*

"DEAR SIR, January 6, 1819.

"I find that it was *New Moon*, at Dublin, at about two o'clock in the morning of the 24th of October, 1641, O. S. Consequently the moon must have been invisible on the whole night of the 22d–23d of that month.

"Yours, etc.,
"MR. M. CAREY. "R. M. PATTERSON."

† It must have required some time to find out Mac-Mahon's lodgings.

freely communicates "that there were and would be, this night, great numbers of noblemen and gentlemen of the Irish, from all parts of the kingdom," whose object was "*to cut off all the Protestants that would not join them.*"

XVII. And they then went back to "*the said Hugh his lodgings,*" in the suburbs, "near Oxmantown," where O'Conally drank till he was drunk.

XVIII. O'Conally notwithstanding this untoward circumstance, and that he was, two hours afterwards, unable to relate a consistent story, was alert enough "*to leap over a wall,*" and afterwards over "*two pales.*"

XIX. Notwithstanding his disordered state, he was able to find his way to sir William Parsons, *into the town*, to whom he communicated the whole affair.

XX. Here let us observe that this very sir William had received information of a plot, several days before, from sir William Cole, "*upon the very first apprehension of something he conceived to be hatching among the Irish.*"

XXI. And further, that this lord justice had written to sir William Cole, "to be very vigilant in inquiring into the occasion of those meetings;" whereby it appears that he had suspicions of a conspiracy.

XXII. Notwithstanding this information, sir William Parsons, who was jealous of some plot "hatching among the Irish;" who, of course, ought to be on the *qui vive,* and to take alarm on the slightest intimation of any scheme of that kind; when he received this "broken relation of a matter *so incredible in itself, gave very little belief to it at first,* in regard it came from an obscure person, and one, as he conceived, *somewhat distempered* at that time."

XXIII. "His lordship," with most wonderful sagacity, "hearing this broken relation" of a plot to explode in about twelve or thirteen hours, for the purpose of cutting the throats of all the Protestants, sends the informer!! between nine and ten at night!! with "order to go again to Mac-Mahon, and get out of him as much certainty of the plot as he could!!!"

XXIV. This informer who "*had been drinking somewhat liberally*"—and was "*somewhat distempered at the time*," was a most admirable spy to make further discoveries, and "to get out of Mac-Mahon as much certainty of the plot, with as many particular circumstances as he could!!!" His fitness for this employment at such a critical moment, was further proved by the circumstance that on his return he was so far intoxicated, "*the effects of drink being still upon him,*" that he could not give in his testimony, till he slept himself sober!!! Therefore, the "conveniency of a bed" being afforded him, "on his repose, having recovered himself, he had his examination taken."

XXV. After sending O'Conally to Mac-Mahon's lodgings, with strict orders "to return back unto him the same evening," sir William went "*privately*, at about ten of the clock that night, to Lord Borlase's house, WITHOUT THE TOWN," whereas O'Conally was directed to come to him at his house "IN THE TOWN."

XXVI. "They sent for such of the council as they knew then to be IN THE TOWN," to lord Borlase's house, "WITHOUT THE TOWN."

XXVII. There they fell into deep consultation "what was fit to be done, attending the *return* of O'Conally."

XXVIII. They then sent in search of him, and found that he had been taken by the watch, and rescued by the servants of sir William Parsons, "who had been sent, amongst others, to walk the streets, and attend his motions."

XXIX. "Sensible that his discovery was not thoroughly believed, he professed that whatever he had acquainted the lord Parsons with, was true; and could he but repose himself, (*the effects of drink being still upon him,*) he should discover more."

XXX. "*Whereupon he had the conveniency of a bed.*"

XXXI. "Having, (on his repose,) *recovered himself,*" he gave in his deposition.

XXXII. This is dated the 22d, and of course must have been made before twelve o'clock.

XXXIII. This deposition gave a full detail of a most murderous plot, whereby "*all the Protestants and English throughout the whole kingdom, were to be cut off the next morning.*"

XXXIV. Possessed of this deposition, which required the most decisive measures of precaution, it becomes a serious question, what did the lords justices do? On this point the whole merits of the question might be rested: and indeed the investigation of any other might be wholly omitted. The answer is, "*They took present order to have a watch privately set upon the lodgings of Mac-Mahon, as also upon the lord Macguire!!!*"

XXXV. In a plain simple case, in which a school-boy of ten years old could have at once pointed out the course to be pursued, they spend no less than *five precious hours,* "*in consultation,*" and in devising ways and means for the public safety, notwithstanding that the sword, not of Damocles, but of Mac-Mahon, and his bloody-minded associates, hung over them. "They sat up all that night in consultation," "having far stronger presumptions,* upon the latter examination taken, than any ways at first they could entertain."

XXXVI. The result of their long and painful consultation, from twelve o'clock at night till five in the morning,

---

* O'Conally swore positively that there was a conspiracy "to murder all the Protestants that would not join" with the conspirators. Yet the justices from this unequivocal testimony only derived "*presumptions*" of their danger!

was, that at that late hour, they at length adopted the resolution of apprehending Mac-Mahon!!!!!!

XXXVII. The lords justices had received the names of some of the principal conspirators from O'Conally, and, among the rest, of lord Macguire; had "*privately set a watch*," on Friday night," at his lodgings; they must of course have known that he was equally implicated with Mac-Mahon, and equally demanded the exercise of their vigilance; and yet they did not think of arresting him, until after the seizure of the latter, and "a conference with him and others, and *calling to mind a letter received the week before from sir William Cole*," they "gathered" that he "was to be an actor in surprising the castle of Dublin!"

XXXVIII. Owen O'Conally swears, that "in all parts of the kingdom, all the English inhabiting there," are to be "destroyed *to-morrow morning;*" but, in the very next sentence, he swears, "that all the Protestants, in all the seaports, and other towns in the kingdom, should be killed *this night*." It is not easy to conceive, how, after they were "*all killed*" on Friday night, they could be "*all destroyed*" on Saturday morning.

XXXIX. O'Conally's deposition states, that the massacre is to begin at "ten o'clock on the 23d;" to be general "in all parts of the kingdom;" that all the English inhabitants are to be cut off; and that "all the posts that could be, could not prevent it." As this is the cardinal point in the affair, on which the whole turns, if it can be proved to be so unequivocally false and groundless, as to be utterly destitute of even the shadow of truth, then is the entire story a fabrication, and O'Conally a perjurer.

XL. That this explosion did not take place; and that, of course, there could not possibly have been a general conspiracy, there is superabundant testimony, as will appear in the subsequent paragraphs.

XLI. I will first premise, that, as the arrest of Mac-Mahon and Macguire, in consequence of the pretended discovery of the sham plot, took place on the 23d of October, *at five o'clock in the morning,* just five hours before the time fixed for commencing the massacre, that circumstance could not have prevented an explosion in any other part of the kingdom, except in a very small portion of the circumjacent country.

XLII. Yet on Monday, the 25th of October, the lords justices wrote an elaborate and detailed account of the proceedings of the insurgents in the north of Ireland, with a prolix statement of various outrages, not only without the least hint or surmise, but even with an utter exclusion of every idea, of murder or shedding of blood.

XLIII. And further, I invoke the most earnest attention of the reader to this all-important fact—Notwithstanding the pretended generality of the plot, the lords justices, by public proclamation, on the 29th of October, declared that the insurrection was confined to "the mere old Irish of the province of Ulster, and others who adhered to them."

XLIV. These two strong facts prove that such parts of O'Conally's deposition as relate to the general extent of the conspiracy, and the plot to "cut off all the Protestants throughout the kingdom," are wholly false, and that he of course was an abandoned perjurer; and would decide the question on these vital points, beyond appeal or controversy. But much stronger evidence remains behind, derived from Temple, Borlase, Carte, Leland, and Warner, to which I now invite the attention of the reader.

XLV. Munster *continued tranquil for six weeks*, although, according to the testimony of Warner, *it contained but one troop of horse:** and of course, when defended by such an

---

* "In the province of Munster, of which sir William St. Leger was lord president, the English were very numerous, and ready to assemble in a body to preserve the

insignificant force, had there been any reality in the plot, the Irish could and would have totally overwhelmed their oppressors.*

XLVI. Connaught was in the same state for six weeks, principally owing to the influence of lord Clanrickarde, a Roman Catholic.†

---

peace and safety of the country. But they were utterly destitute of arms; and all the solicitations made by sir William, which were strong and numerous, could not persuade the lords justices and council to spare him any. He was a brave old soldier, of great experience and activity; and did everything that it was possible for a man to do *with one troop of horse, which was all his guard for the whole province;* a guard scarcely sufficient to repress the insolence of robbers, in a time of profound peace, much less in a time of such general spoil and disturbance. But, with the assistance of the noblemen and gentry of the province, *it continued quiet for above six weeks!!!* Indeed, no man of quality, or gentleman of English blood, either Papist or Protestant, had as yet joined the rebels."—*Warner*, 130.

* There is a discrepancy between Temple and Borlase as to the time when the insurrection commenced in Munster: the former stating it "the beginning," and the latter "the midst," of December. This does not, however, affect the disproof of O'Conally's deposition, which, in either case, is notoriously false.

"The flame having marched through Ulster and Leinster, it discovers its fury, *about the beginning of December,* 1641, in Munster, which province till that time, (by the moderation of the state,) had stifled its rage, then expressing its consent with the other provinces."—*Borlase*, 49.

"The whole province of Munster, *about the midst of this month of December,* BEGAN to declare themselves in open rebellion."—*Temple*, 155.

"In Munster, sir William St. Leger, the lord president, a soldier of activity and experience, and possessed even with an inveteracy against the Irish, could not obtain arms or soldiers sufficient for a time of peace, much less *for a juncture of distraction and disorder.* Yet the strength of the English Protestants, and *the loyalty of the Irish gentry, as yet preserved this province from any material disorder.*"—*Leland*, iii., 158.

† "The lord Ranelagh was president of Connaught: and all that province, except a few pillagers in the county of Sligo, had, owing in a great measure to the forward zeal and activity of lord Clanrickarde, though a Roman Catholic, till this time, continued quiet."—*Warner*, 157.

"The infection of the Pale having spread in the remoter parts, *about the middle of December,* the whole province of Connaught in a manner revolted, the county of Galway, of which lord Clanrickarde was governor, excepted."—*Ibid.*, 158.

"The peace and security of Connaught were equally neglected by the chief governors, although *the English power was inconsiderable in this province,* and the Irish natives kept in continual alarm for twenty-five years by the prospect of a general plantation, which, though suspended, had not been formally relinquished. *Yet here, too, the good affections of the principal inhabitants stemmed the torrent of rebellion.*"—*Leland*, 158.

XLVII. Leinster was likewise tranquil, except some outrages of small importance, until the beginning of December; as the summons to the lords of the Pale to come to Dublin, to consult on the affairs of state, was dated the 3d of that month, at which time there was no appearance of serious disturbance; and the butchery at Santry, by the sanguinary and merciless ruffian, sir Charles Coote,* which was obviously intended to provoke, and actually led to, the insurrection in that province, took place on the 7th.

XLVIII. And further, we have the testimony of Warner and Carte,† that the insurrection was *for about six weeks* confined almost wholly to the province of Ulster.

XLIX. That the original views of the insurgents did not comprehend a general massacre, or even single murders, we have further testimony, clear and decisive, derived even from Temple, as well as Warner, and Leland, which, independent of all other proof, would be sufficient to settle this question forever, and utterly overwhelm O'Conally's perjured legend.‡

L. Moreover, if there had been a plot for a general insur-

---

* "The town being left at his [sir Charles Coote's] mercy, *to which he appears to be a stranger*, he put to death several persons, *without distinction of age or sex!!!* in revenge of the several spoils committed on the English in those parts."—*Warner*, 165.

"In revenge of their depredations, he [sir Charles Coote] committed *such unprovoked, such ruthless, and indiscriminate carnage* in the town, as rivalled the utmost extravagancies of the Northerns."—*Leland*, iii., 169.

† "Had the lords justices and council acquitted themselves like men of probity and understanding, there was time enough given them to suppress an insurrection *which for six weeks was confined almost to the province of Ulster*, without any chief that was so considerable as sir Phelim O'Neal."—*Warner*, 130.

"*No one nobleman of the kingdom, nor any estated gentleman of English race*, engaged in the rebellion, or joined with the rebels in action, *till the month of December;* for as to those gentlemen of the county of Louth, who submitted to them before, being unable to defend themselves or to make resistance, they had not yet appeared in action. *The rebellion till then had been carried on by the mere Irish*, and CONFINED TO ULSTER, *to some few counties in Leinster, and that of Leitrim in Connaught*."—*Carte*, i., 243.

‡ '"It was resolved" by the insurgents "*not to kill any*, but where of necessity they should be forced thereunto by opposition."—*Temple*, 65.

rection, and such a massacre as 'O'Conally swore to, there would have been evidence produced from some of the conspirators: but notwithstanding the lords justices had recourse to the execrable aid of the rack, and put Mac-Mahon and others to the torture, there is not, in the examinations of the former, a single word to corroborate the sanguinary part of O'Conally's deposition. The examinations of the rest were never published.

LI. There is not to be found in Temple, Borlase, Carte, Warner, Leland, Clarendon, nor, as far as I have seen, in Rushworth, the examination of a single person engaged in a conspiracy which was said to have extended throughout the whole kingdom, except those of Mac-Mahon and lord Macguire!!!! That of the latter was not taken till March, 1642.

Perhaps the preceding analysis of this miserable legend might supersede the necessity of adding anything further on the subject. But its great importance, and a deep solicitude to dispel the thick mists with which prejudice and fraud have overspread it, induce me to place it in a new form, and bring it more home to the mind of the reader. The reasons for adopting this measure, which might otherwise appear a work of supererogation, will probably so far satisfy the reader, as to preclude the necessity of an apology.

Queries.

Is there a man in the world who can seriously believe:

I. That a *Catholic* COLONEL, engaged in a plot to murder the *Protestants*, would send forty-five miles for a *Protestant*, SERVANT to a *Protestant* gentleman, an inveterate enemy to the Roman Catholics, as an accomplice?

II. That a journey of a hundred and ten miles could be performed in three days and a half, *the sun rising about seven, and setting about five,* at a season of the year when the rains, then usually prevalent, must have rendered the roads almost impassable; and by a man who knew nothing of the business which led to the summons he had received, and who, of course, had no temptation to make any extraordinary exertion?

III. That a stranger, arriving in the suburbs of a city *an hour after sunset,* and fatigued with a long journey, should, *without any aid from the moon,* immediately commence a search for and actually find out the lodgings, of another stranger, who had arrived a few hours before?

IV. That sir William Parsons, who had, at nine in the evening, received intelligence of a plot, to explode at ten the next morning, and the names of some of the principal conspirators, should be so misguided, as to send back the drunken informer, "to get out of Mac-Mahon as much certainty of the plot as he could," instead of immediately apprehending the conspirators?

V. That being "*in town,*" he would have gone "*without the town*" and sent there for such of the council as lived "*in town,*" when such an awful explosion was likely to take place?

VI. That when the informer returned to the lords justices, he would be allowed to go to bed, before taking his examinations?

VII. That the lords justices would have remained all night, and until five o'clock in the morning, at lord Borlase's house, *without the town,* and closed the gates, thus shutting themselves out from the defence of the castle?

VIII. That when O'Conally had slept himself sober, and made circumstantial deposition of such alarming particulars, the council would have been such idiots as to take no other precaution than merely "to have a watch set privately upon the lodgings of Mac-Mahon, and also upon lord Macguire," as if they had been plotting to rob orchards or hen-roosts, to bar out a schoolmaster, break lamps in a midnight frolic, or attack the watchmen, instead of plotting to seize the castle, subvert the government, and cut the throats of one or two hundred thousand people?

IX. That the privy council would not, under such circumstances, have instantly apprehended the conspirators, instead of "sitting all night in council," upon one of the simplest points ever discussed, and which could have been decided in five minutes, as well as in five hours, five weeks, or five years; on which the most prompt and decisive measures were imperiously necessary; and at a moment when, if there were any truth in the statement of O'Conally, the salvation or destruction of the state might depend on a single hour?

X. That having taken the precaution, on Friday night, of "setting a watch privately upon the lodgings of lord Macguire," thereby establishing their belief that he was an accomplice in the plot, they would not have arrested him at the same time they arrested Mac-Mahon, but waited "till conference with the latter and others, and calling to mind sir William Cole's letter," which led them to " gather that the lord Macguire was to be an actor in surprising the castle of Dublin?"

XI. That a conspiracy, which was to explode throughout the whole kingdom on the 23d of October, should be arrested in Leinster, Connaught, and Munster, by the detection of it, in Dublin, a few hours before the appointed time?

XII. That if it had been intended to murder "all the Protestants *throughout the kingdom*," who " would not join the conspirators," there would have been no intelligence of a single murder on the 25th, or that, on the 29th, the lords justices should explicitly declare, that the insurrection was " confined to the mere old Irish in the province of Ulster, and others who had joined them?"

XIII. That though the lords justices had recourse to the execrable expedient of putting Mac-Mahon and others to the rack, they should not have extorted a word from any of them, to support the charge of murderous intentions, if any conspiracy had existed, for "cutting off all the Protestants and English throughout the kingdom?"

XIV. That no examinations should have ever been taken of any other of the conspirators?

XV. That if there were a general conspiracy, and of course a large assemblage of people in Dublin, for the purpose of seizing the castle on the 23d, the lords justices would not have been able, on the morning of that day, to apprehend more than two of the leaders and a few common servants?

XVI. That to execute an enterprise of which the success absolutely depended on promptitude and secresy, people would be collected from all the thirty-two counties of Ireland, at various distances, ten, twenty, thirty, fifty, one hundred, and one hundred and fifty miles from the scene of operations?

XVII. And finally, whether, the deposition of O'Conally being incontrovertibly established as false, and he of course perjured, in the two vital points,—

I. The universality of the plot, and

II. The determination to massacre all who would not join in it,

—there can be any credit whatever attached to the remainder of his testimony? And whether it does not necessarily follow, that the whole was a manifest fraud and imposture, designed to provoke insurrection, and lead to its usual and inevitable result,—confiscation?

Before the reader decides on answers to these queries, it is hoped he will bear in mind the strong facts adduced in

Chapter XX. to prove that the seventeenth century was, in the fullest sense of the word, the age of perjury, forgery, and fabricated plots. He will there see, that in London, the boasted courts of justice were at that period mere slaughter-houses, where the depositions of men, stained and covered over with crimes of the most atrocious nature, as the leopard is covered with spots, were received without hesitation in cases where the lives of innocent men were at stake, and were finally immolated. He will likewise behold the horrible fact, that the testimony of a man *whose perjury was detected in open court, and there confessed by himself*, was afterwards admitted, and was the means of consigning innocent persons to the ignominious death of the gallows.

Let him also bear in mind, that forged plots, supported by perjury, had been one of the regular and uniform machines of the government of Ireland, from the invasion to that period; and steadily from the Restoration in 1660, till the Revolution in 1688; and had produced the forfeiture of millions of acres.

And further, let it not be forgotten, that all the writers, Clarendon, Carte, Warner, Leland, Gordon, etc., agree, that the grand object of the lords justices was, in the beginning, to extend the flames of civil war; and, when the insurrection had by these means become general, to prevent a cessation of hostilities, for the purpose of producing extensive confiscations.

With all these strong facts taken into view, I then invite a decision; and entertain no doubt of a favorable verdict.

On this subject I have no hesitation in pledging myself, that if any independent and upright judge or lawyer of any court in France, Germany, England, Scotland, Ireland, or the United States, will pronounce affirmative answers to the above queries, so as to imply a belief in the reality of the conspiracy, as deposed to by the "Protestant gentleman," alias "*servant*," I will cheerfully suppress this work, and consent to have it burned by the hands of the common hangman.

[In the 28th chapter of his "*Vindiciæ Hibernicæ*" (2d edition, 1823), Mr. Carey proceeds, in the annexed manner, to dispose of the question, whether there was any massacre of Protestants in 1641.]

Was there really a Massacre of the Protestants in 1641? *Unparalleled Exaggeration. More Protestants pretended to be killed than there were on the Island. Conclusive Evidence drawn from Sir William Petty. Carte's and Warner's Refutation of the Legend.*

> "Falsehood and fraud grow up in every soil,
> The product of all climes."—*Addison*.

ALTHOUGH I have already in the first chapter incidentally touched on the numbers said to be massacred by the Irish in the insurrection of 1641, I think it proper to resume the subject, and go into it somewhat more at length, as it is a cardinal point in the vindication I have undertaken.

In order to proceed correctly in the investigation, I shall let the accusers narrate their own tales, in order to ascertain what is the sum and substance of the allegations:—

"*The depopulations in this province of Munster do well near equal those of the whole kingdom ! ! !*"—*Temple*, 103.

"There being, since the rebellion first broke out, unto the time of the cessation made Sept. 15, 1643, which was not full two years after, above 300,000 *British and Protestants cruelly murdered in cold blood*, destroyed some other way, or expelled out of their habitations, according to the strictest conjecture and computation of those who seemed best to understand the numbers of English planted in Ireland, *besides those few which fell in the heat of fight during the war.*"—*Ibid.*, 6.

"Above 154,000 Protestants were massacred in that kingdom from the 23d October to the 1st March following."—*Rapin*, ix., 343.

"By some computations, those who perished by all these cruelties are supposed to be 150,000 or 200,000. By the most moderate, and probably the most reasonable account, they are made to amount to forty thousand! if this extenuation itself be not, as is usual in such cases, *somewhat exaggerated!*"—*Hume*, iii., 545.

"A general insurrection of the Irish spread itself over the whole country, in such an inhuman and barbarous manner, that there were forty or fifty thousand of the English Protestants *murdered, before they suspected themselves to be in any danger*, or could provide for their defence, by drawing together into towns or strong houses."—*Clarendon, E.,* II.

That "Saul slew his thousands, and David his tens of thousands," was, in "olden time," sung by the women of Israel. Every Philistine was magnified into ten; every ten into a hundred; and every hundred into a thousand. But the amplifying powers of the Jewish women fade into insignificance, when compared with those of the Anglo-Hibernian writers. Every Englishman that fell in battle, or otherwise, was murdered. Every man was magnified into a hundred; every ten into a thousand; and every hundred into ten thousand.

Such a spirit of exaggeration has prevailed, in a greater or less degree, in all ages. Even in common occurrences, hardly calculated to excite any interest, we find, every day of our lives, that the statements of current events are so highly colored, as to differ full as much from the reality, as the countenance of a meretricious courtesan, who has exhausted her stores of carmine and white lead, differs from the undisguised countenance of an innocent country damsel, who depends wholly on the pure ornaments of beneficent Nature. This being undeniably the case, on topics where no temptation to deception exists, how dreadful must be the falsehood and delusion in the present case, where ambition, avarice, malice, bigotry, national hatred, and all the other dire passions that assimilate men to demons, were goaded into activity!

In all other cases, but that of the history of Ireland, to convict a witness of gross, palpable, and notorious falsehood, would be sufficient to invalidate the whole of his evidence; but such has been the wayward fate of that country, that the most gross and manifest forgeries, which carry their own condemnation with them, are received by the world as though they were

"Confirmation strong as proofs of Holy Writ."

Or, when some are found too monstrous to be admitted, their falsehood and absurdity do not impair the public credulity in the rest of the tales depending on the same authority.

The materials for Irish statistics, at that early period, are rare; a deficiency which involves this subject in considerable difficulty. Were correct tables of the population of Ireland to be had, the task would be comparatively easy; and I could put down all those tales, with as much ease as I have stamped the seal of flagrant falsehood on the many impostures already investigated.

But I avail myself of a sound rule,—to employ the best evidence that the nature and circumstances of the case will admit; and there are fortunately, some important data, on which to reason, in the present instance, and to shed the light of truth on this intricate question, and dispel the dense clouds with which it has been environed by fraud and imposture.

Sir William Petty, the ancestor of the Lansdowne family, laid the foundation of a princely fortune in the depredations perpetrated on the Irish, after the insurrection of 1641. Of course, he had no temptation to swerve from the truth in their favor; on the contrary, it was his interest, equally with the other possessors of the estates of the plundered Irish, to exaggerate their real crimes, and to lend the countenance of his reputation to their pretended ones. Hence, his testimony, on this ground, and as a cotemporary, cannot, so far as it tends to exonerate those upon whose ruin he raised his immense estate, be excepted against by the enemies of the Irish. I shall therefore freely cite him in the case: and the reader will at once perceive to what an extent delusion has been carried on this subject.

He states the aggregate number of the Protestants who perished in eleven years, to have been 112,000; of whom "two-thirds were cut off by war, plague, and famine." It is obvious to the meanest capacity,—if, of 112,000, the whole number that fell in that space of time, two-thirds were cut off " by war, plague, and famine,"—that those who fell, *out of war*, in *eleven years*, were only 37,000! I hope to prove, that even this statement, so comparatively moderate, is extravagantly beyond the truth.

Sir William Petty confutes himself, beyond the power of redemption.

"Mark how a plain tale shall put him down."

He bequeathed to posterity some statistical tables, which throw considerable light on this subject. They are very meagre, it is true; but, meagre as they are, I believe there are no others; at all events, I know of none: and must therefore avail myself of them.

He informs us, that the population of Ireland, in 1641, was, 1,466,000;* and that the relative proportion of the Protestants to the Catholics was as two to eleven:† of course, it follows, that the population was thus divided:—

---

* "This shows there were, in 1641, 1,466,000 people."—*Petty.*

† For the present I admit this proportion; as, however exaggerated the number of the Protestants may be, it does not affect the point at issue. But, from various circumstances, it is doubtful whether there was one Protestant to eleven Roman Catholics.

about 1,241,000 Roman Catholics, and 225,000 Protestants. From this conclusion there is no appeal.

The supplies of people from England and Scotland, until after the final defeat, capture, condemnation, and death of Charles I., were inconsiderable:* and surely it is impossible for a rational being to believe, that out of 225,000, there could have been 112,000 destroyed, and the residue have been able to baffle and defeat the insurgents, who comprised the great mass of the nation. It will therefore, I trust, be allowed, as an irresistible conclusion, that Sir William Petty's calculation, although, so far, more moderate than any of the "tales of terror" quoted at the commencement of this chapter, is most extravagantly overrated, probably trebled or quadrupled; and must, of absolute necessity, be false.

But even admitting it to be correct, what an immense difference between 37,000 *in eleven years*—and the numbers so confidently stated by the various writers of Irish history! What astonishment must be excited by Burton's 300,000, in a few months; Temple's 300,000, in less than two years; May's 200,000, in one month; Warwick's 100,000, in one week; or Rapin's 40,000, in a few days! Surely there is not, in the history of the world, any parallel case of such gross, palpable, shocking, and abominable deception. Can language be found strong or bold enough to mark the dishonor of those who knowingly propagated such falsehoods, or the folly or neglect of those who adopted and gave them currency? Their names ought to be held up, as "a hissing and reproach," to deter others from following in their foul and loathsome track of calumny and deception.

On the subject of the number of victims of the pretended massacre, the observations of Carte are so judicious and unanswerable, that they would be sufficient, independent of

---

* More Protestants, it is highly probable, removed from Ireland during the progress of the war, than the number of soldiers who were sent thither from England.

the other evidence I have produced, to put down forever those miserable legends about so many hundreds of thousands of the Protestants cut off in a few weeks, or months or years, and to stamp on the foreheads of their authors the broad seal of imposture. He states that the extravagant numbers, asserted to be massacred, were "*more than there were of English, at that time, in all Ireland.*"

"It is certain, that the great body of the English was settled in Munster and Leinster, *where very few murders were committed;* and that in Ulster, which was *the dismal scene of the massacre*, there were above 100,000 Scots, who, before the general plantation of it, had settled in great numbers in the counties of Down and Antrim: and new shoals of them had come over, upon the plantation of the six escheated counties: and they were so very powerful therein, that the Irish, either out of fear of their numbers, or some other politic reason, spared those of that nation, *making proclamation, on pain of death, that no Scotsman should be molested in body, goods or lands*, whilst they raged with so much cruelty against the English."—*Carte*, I., 177.

To these facts, he adds the following reflections:

"It cannot therefore reasonably be presumed, that there were at most above 20,000 English souls, of all ages and sexes, in Ulster at that time; and of these, as appears by the lords justices' letter, there were *several thousands got safe to Dublin, and were subsisted there for many months afterwards; besides* 6,000 *women and children*, which Captain Mervyn saved in Fermanagh; and others that got safe to Derry, Coleraine, and Carrickfergus, and went from these and other ports into England."

It is impossible to reconcile the latter part of these quotations with the rest; a case, as we have repeatedly stated, that incessantly occurs in Irish histories. The author informs us, on rational grounds, that there were "*not more than* 20,000 *English in Ulster;*" that "*several thousands got safe to Dublin;*" that "6,000 *women and children were saved* in Fermanagh;" and that " others *got safe* to Derry, Coleraine, and Carrickfergus." These all-important and conclusive facts he connects with a statement of "the *extreme cruelty* with which the insurgents raged against the English," and with a notice of the "*dismal scene of the massacre*," the subjects of which massacre are not very easily found, and, at all events, could not have been very numerous: for, let us add together "several thousands," and "6,000," and the "others" who "got safe" into the specified towns, where there were numerous garrisons; where, of course, in a time of violence and commotion, the inhabitants of the circumjacent country would naturally seek refuge; and where, it is not extravagant to suppose, that "the others," who thus "got safe," might have amounted to some thousands: let us then deduct the aggregate from 20,000, the total number of English, and we shall find a slender remainder. But the plain fact is, that the writers on this subject are so haunted by the idea of a massacre, that although it rests on the sandy foundation of forgery and perjury, as shall be fully proved in the sequel, and although many of their own statements, in the most unequivocal manner, give it the lie direct, their minds cannot be divested of the terrific object. These passages from Carte furnish a strong case in point. The most ardent friend of Ireland could not desire a much more complete proof of the fallacy of the accounts of the pretended massacre than is here given by this author himself, who, nevertheless, wonderful to tell! appears to resist the evidence of his own facts, and to be blind to the obvious inference to which they inevitably lead.

Ferdinando Warner, a clergyman of the Church of England, appears to have been the only writer who has gone into any elaborate investigation of the legendary tales of the pretended massacre; and his views of the subject will deserve the most serious attention of the reader. After stating the uncertainty of the accounts, and the consequent difficulty of making an exact estimate, he pronounces a strong and unequivocal sentence of condemnation on the Münchausen tales we are combating; and avers, that

"*It is easy enough to demonstrate the falsehood of the relation of every Protestant historian of this rebellion.*"

He proceeds to render a satisfactory account of the grounds on which this statement rests:

"*To any one who considers how thinly Ireland was, at that time, peopled by Protestants, and the province of Ulster particularly, where was the chief scene of the massacre,* THOSE RELATIONS, UPON THE FACE OF THEM, APPEAR INCREDIBLE.'

"Setting aside all opinions and calculations in this affair, which, besides their uncertainty, are without any precision as to the space of time in which the murders were committed, the evidence from the depositions in the manuscript above mentioned stands thus:—The number of people killed, upon positive evidence, collected in two years after the insurrection broke out, adding them all together, amounts only to *two thousand one hundred and nine;* on the reports of other Protestants, *one thousand six hundred and nineteen more;* and on the report of some of the rebels themselves, a further number of *three hundred;* the whole making *four thousand and twenty-eight.* Besides these murders there is, in the same collection, evidence, on the report of others, of eight thousand killed by ill-usage: and if we should allow that the cruelties of the Irish out of war, extended to these numbers, which, considering the nature of several of the depositions, *I think in my conscience we cannot,* yet to be impartial we must allow, that *there is no pretence for laying a greater number to their charge.* This account is also corroborated by a letter, which I copied out of the council books at Dublin, written on the fifth of May, sixteen hundred and fifty-two, ten years after the beginning of the rebellion, from the parliament commissioners in Ireland to the English parliament. After exciting them to further severity against the Irish, as being afraid ' their behavior towards this people may never sufficiently avenge their murders and massacres, and lest the parliament might shortly be in pursuance of a speedy settlement of this nation, and thereby some tender concessions might be concluded,' the commissioners tell them that it appears ' *besides eight hundred and forty-eight families, there were killed, hanged, burned, and drowned, six thousand and sixty-two.*' " — *Warner,* 297.

Thus I close this subject with stating, that these hundreds of thousands are reduced by Carte to 20,000, less " several thousands " and " 6,000 women and children," and " others; " and by Warner to about 12,000, of whom only 4,028 were murdered; a large portion of which detail, " in his conscience," he cannot allow! Would it not be an insult to the reader, to offer another word, to prove the utter falsehood of all the terrific statements given of the subject, whereby the world has been so long and so grossly deceived?

[In a subsequent notice of these statements, Mr. Carey (chap. xxix., second edition) still further exposes the falsehoods and exaggerations of the English writers.]

To establish the falsehood of these hideous portraits of cruelty, a few lines might suffice. Those lines would carry conviction. It would be enough to state the simple fact, that the originals were drawn by the miserable and abandoned falsifiers, who have so long deluded the world with a belief that there were 100,000 persons massacred in one week, 200,000 in a month, and 300,000 in two years; (whereas sir William Petty, as I have stated, makes *the whole number that fell in eleven years, by war, plague, famine, and massacre,* 112,000, which I have proved extravagantly overrated; and Warner, who had no partiality for the Roman Catholics, and who took more pains to investigate the subject than any other writer, either of the seventeenth or eighteenth century, reduces the number *killed out of war* to 4,028; with which Carte's account appears to correspond;) —who have recorded, that a general insurrection and massacre took place throughout the kingdom, on the 23d of October, 1641, whereas three-fourths of it was, for entire weeks afterwards, in a state of perfect tranquillity;—who have also recorded the falsehood, that Ireland enjoyed a sort of millennium for forty years previous to the insurrection, whereas she suffered, during that period, every species of the most revolting tyranny; in a word, who are in almost every page of this work convicted of a total disregard of truth. All these stories were dictated by the same spirit of imposture; penned by the same writers; rest, of course, on the same authority; and the falsehood of those already discussed being unanswerably proved, the residue must share the same sentence of condemnation.

. . . .

Temple, of all the writers whom I have quoted, *is the only original author. His book is one unvaried tissue of fables*, of which he was himself so much and so justly ashamed, that *he endeavored to suppress it; and actually refused permission to the booksellers of London to print a second edition.** But his endeavors were in vain; it too much flattered the existing prejudices,—too much favored the views of those who unjustly possessed the estates of which the Irish were plundered, to hope that it would be allowed to sink into oblivion.

---

* *Extract of a letter from the earl of Essex, lord-lieutenant of Ireland, to Mr. Secretary Coventry.*

DUBLIN CASTLE, JAN. 6, 1674-5.

"I am to acknowledge the receipt of yours of the 22d of December, wherein you mention a book that was newly published, concerning the cruelties committed in Ireland, at the beginning of the late war. Upon further inquiry, I find sir J. Temple, master of the rolls here, author of that book, was this last year sent to by several stationers of London, to have his consent to the printing thereof. But *he assures me that he utterly denied it;* and whoever printed it, did it without his knowledge. Thus much I thought fit to add to what I formerly said upon this occasion, *that I might do this gentleman right, in case it was suspected he had any share in publishing this new edition.*"

Carte's account affords a most striking display of the infatuation that prevails on this topic. The reader, in page 378, will find that he states, that the English were principally settled in Leinster and Munster; that there were few murders committed in those provinces; that the insurgents spared the Scotch, who composed the great mass of the Protestant population of Ulster; that there were not in that province more than 20,000 English; that of this number " several thousands" escaped to Dublin; that "6,000 were saved in Fermanagh;" that "others," not improbably thousands, found an asylum in three fortified towns: and yet this same historian, in the very same page, and at the distance of a few lines, pathetically and feelingly informs his readers, that *rivers of blood were shed! ! and massacres perpetrated, which it would be shocking to humanity to repeat! !*

While stating these particulars, mixed sensations of astonishment and indignation are excited, which the reader may conceive, but which language cannot express. One is lost in the mass of reflections excited by this stupendous delirium of the human mind. It affords another instance of the gross and glaring contradictions so constantly found between the different parts of the same history of Irish affairs. It is an extraordinary fatality, from which even the very few whose intentions appear correct have not escaped.

. . . .

Of all the writers on this subject, *there is none deserving of more unqualified censure than Hume.* He was under the influence of none of the dire passions that actuated some of the others. With a powerful mind and keen penetration, it was his duty to have examined carefully the credibility of his authorities; and it required a very cursory examination, indeed, of Temple's history, to be satisfied that to quote it was an ineffable disgrace. Yet, astonishing to tell, out of forty-eight references, in his account of the pretended massacre of 1641, there are no less than thirty-three to Temple, eleven to Rushworth, and only two each to Nalson and Whitelock. How utterly unworthy this procedure was of the talents and reputation of Hume; how indelible a stain it attaches to his memory; and how far, as respects this individual case, he is reduced to a level with the common race of historians, may be readily conceived, from the extracts which I shall produce from Temple's history. A large portion of the most horrible passages, for which he quotes that work, *are grounded on hearsay testimony;* which is distinctly stated in the depositions, and which therefore could not have been unknown to Hume, and ought to have forbidden him to place the least dependence on their authority.

But his offence is not confined to the original use of those "tales of terror." No: a much higher and more inexpiable one remains behind. Dr. John Curry published a work of transcendant merit, of which the title is "Historical and Critical Review of the Civil Wars of Ireland," in which he fully displayed the falsehood, and completely overthrew the narrative, of Temple. The peculiar characteristic of this work is, that almost every important fact it contains is supported by the most indisputable authority, not merely in the form of reference, but generally by exact quotation. It may be safely asserted, that a more valuable historical work was never published. The author, in 1764, sent a copy of it to David Hume, then at Paris, with a request that he would give it a candid consideration, and correct the errors that he had committed, by his dependence on such a deceptious guide as Temple. To this letter Hume sent an "*evasive answer,*" * in which he declined committing himself by any promise; and never, in any subsequent edition, corrected a single error in this part of his work. On this conduct, there can, among upright men, be but one sentence pronounced,—a most unqualified sentence of reprobation.

MR. FROUDE'S "RELIABLE AUTHORITIES."

In a little volume, entitled a "Historical Memoir of the Irish Rebellion of 1641," (which O'Connor assigns to Dr.

---

* Hume's "answer" was as follows:—"I am here at such a distance from my authorities, that I cannot produce all the arguments which determined me to give the account you complain of, with regard to the Irish massacre. I only remember I sought truth, and thought I found it. The insurrection might be excused as having liberty for its object. The violence also of the puritanical parliament struck a just terror into all the Catholics. But the method of conducting the rebellion, if we must call it by that name, was certainly such, and you seem to own it, as deserved the highest blame, and was one of the most violent efforts of barbarism and bigotry united. D. H."

John Curry,) published in London, as a reply to Harris's attack on Henry Brooke's "Trial of the Cause of the Catholics," the author in his "Introduction" records his opinion, as given below, as to the credibility of Temple, Borlase, and Clarendon, all of whom are cited by Mr. Froude as "reliable authorities" on the subject of the "rebellion" of 1641 :—

"The last of these writers breathes nothing but loyalty to the King, and indignation against both the English and the Irish rebels; the first plainly intimates his affection to the rebels in England, and suffers just so much seeming loyalty to drop from his pen, as was necessary to *his main design of blackening most effectually the Irish rebels;* and as for Borlase, who has botched up what he calls a history, *from pilfered parcels out of both,* he is a perfect mongrel, sometimes of one party, and sometimes of another; but always inconsistent with himself."

In another part of the same Introduction the author of the "Memoir" says :—

"In order to show upon what goodly authority those slanderers have grounded their dreadful charge of cruelties, *pretended* to have been committed by the Irish rebels, . . . I will more particularly exhibit the characters of the original relators of them; namely, Sir John Temple, Roger, first Earl of Orrery, and Dr. Edward Borlase, as they have been impartially drawn by that eminent *Protestant* historian, the Rev. Dr. Nalson [author of the 'Historical Collections']. That candid writer, after assuring us that 'the then Lords Justices of Ireland, Parsons and Borlase, did by their authority command many things which did not only exasperate, but render the Irish desperate,' adds : 'It is no less notorious that Sir John Temple, in writing the history of this rebellion, *was bound by confederacy* to assert the proceedings of these Lords Justices; and I cannot (says he) find him highly in reputation with the usurpers of the Parliamentarian faction, and by them empowered as a commissioner *to impose, upon the Protestant subjects of Ireland,* that traitorous, disloyal, and solemn league and covenant, which was a direct oath of confederacy, not only against, but purposely to ruin and destroy the king, the church, and the loyal party; I cannot observe *his book to be printed in London, by public allowance,* in the year 1646, at a time when no books were licensed, but such as made court to the prevailing faction of the usurpers, or which might be helpful to support these calumnies against his Majesty, especially as to the Irish Rebellion,—without a too just suspicion of his integrity.

"'The late Earl of Orrery cannot escape the like suspicion; . . . nor is it possible to regard him as an impartial writer, who in the blackest of times rendered himself, by his services to the usurper (Cromwell), so notoriously conspicuous to the three kingdoms; being, during that gloomy scene, Lord President of Munster. And to instance another of his titles, though not so illustrious, he was agent for the fanatics established by Cromwell in the estates of those Irish, who, repenting of their folly, had served his Majesty against the English rebels.

"'As for Dr. Borlase, besides the nearness of his relation to one of the Lords Justices, and his being openly and avowedly a favorite of the faction, and the men and actors of those times, he is an author of such strange inconsistency, that his book is rather a paradox than a history; and it must needs be so; for (I know not by what accident,) the copy of the manuscript written by the Rt. Hon. the Earl of Clarendon, happening to fall into his hands, he has very unartfully blended it with his own rough and unpolished heap of matters; so that his book looks like a curious embroidery, sewn with coarse thread upon a piece of sack-web; and, truly, had he no other crime but that of a plagiary, it is such a sort of theft to steal the child of another's brain, that may very well render him suspected *not to be overstocked with honesty and justice, so necessary to the reputation of an unblemished historian.* But it is far more unlawful to alter the lawful issue of another man's pen, and thereby disable it from propagating truth, and to teach it to speak a language which the parent never intended. And yet this is the case in Dr. Borlase's history, *in which he has taken great pains to expunge some and alter many passages.*'" *

---

* "Nalson's "Historical Collections." Introduction.

The character of the "evidence" on which the stories of Temple and Borlase rest is thus detailed by the same writer:—

"Let us, therefore, by a word or two, try the depositions in Temple and his copier, Borlase, by the touchstone of Lord Anglesey and Dr. Pett. And, first, are the matters sworn in these depositions credible? So far from it, that they are forced to have recourse to a miracle—(the apparition of hundreds of *ghosts*, crying for vengeance on the Irish!) to save some of them from appearing incredible and absurd! Secondly—were the persons swearing credible? They were, many of them, weak women and illiterate men: not capable of reading or subscribing their own depositions, and therefore apt to be imposed upon and deceived by those who read to them. A great number of them swore on mere hearsay. Some of them, afterwards, touched with remorse, solemnly declared the contrary of what they had sworn; and they were all, at the time of making their depositions, either interested or malicious enemies to those against whom they made them.

"Accordingly, at the trial of qualifications, at Athlone, (a court held by the regicides,) where the book called the 'black-book,' which contained these examinations, was produced, the same was so falsified in most particulars, as well by the witnesses themselves, who were pretended to have been duly sworn, as also by the persons said to have been murdered, *who were then, and are yet* (says my author, 1662) *living; that the said book was, for shame, laid aside as no evidence.* And several persons who had taken examinations touching these murders, have frequently since acknowledged the falsity of the matters published by them, as being had from the information of those who, by the hurry of the times, and their own frights, were so transported, that they swore all their neighbors, whom they left behind them, were murdered; whereas all, or most of them, were afterwards found living."

Of the bloodthirsty readiness with which Sir Charles Coote entered upon the work of plundering and slaughtering the defenceless people, the evidence is given in a letter addressed by the Lords of the Pale "to the nobility and gentry of the County of Galway." This document, the author of the "Historical Memoir" states, was dated December, 1641, and received the 2d of February following, showing that previously that part of Ireland had taken no share in the insurrection; while the manner in which those who did rise were goaded on is shown in the context. The writers say:

"You, we are confident, with the same affliction, took notice with us to how little purpose we sat in Parliament; when redress of our grievances must not only move first from, but receive the approvement of those who, commonly, were the authors of them. These, with the late demeanors of some ministers of the State, since this commotion, by cruelly putting to death some of his Majesty's subjects in the county of Wicklow, as also at Santry, and burning several gentlemen's houses and haggards, and taking away all their goods *without any other cause than that they were Catholics ;* as also the inhuman advice of Sir Chárles Coote to the Lord Justices, to execute a general massacre upon all of our religion, *which he offered to perform*, had the Council consented thereto, having induced us to enter into an association, wherein we desire you will be pleased to join, that, with an unanimous consent, we may vindicate the honor of our sovereign, assure the liberties of our consciences, and preserve the freedom of this Kingdom, under the sole obedience of his sacred Majesty, whom God long preserve," etc.

THE MASSACRE IN "ISLAND-MAGEE."

In his "Review of the Civil Wars in Ireland," the learned Dr. John Curry gives the following particulars regarding the massacre of the Irish at "Island-Magee," by the English and Scotch Puritans of Carrickfergus:—

"The report that his Majesty's Protestant subjects first fell upon and murdered the Roman Catholics, got credit and reputation, and was openly and frequently asserted," says

Jones, Bishop of Meath, in a letter to Dr. Borlase, in 1679. And Sir Audley Mervyn, Speaker of the House of Commons, in a public speech to the Duke of Ormonde, in 1662, confesses, "that several pamphlets then swarmed, *to fasten the rise of this rebellion upon the Protestants;* and that they drew the first blood." And, indeed, whatever cruelties may be charged upon the Irish, in the prosecution of this war, "their first intention, we see," says another Protestant voucher, (Warner, "*Hist. Irish Rebellion,*" p. 47,) "went no further than to strip the English and the Protestants of their power and possessions, and, unless forced to it by opposition, not to shed any blood." Even Temple confesses the same; for, mentioning what mischiefs were done in the beginning of this insurrection, he says: "Certainly, that which these rebels mainly intended at first, and most busily employed themselves about, was the driving away the Englishmen's cattle, and possessing themselves of their goods." (Temple's "*Irish Rebellion.*")

In a MS. journal of an officer in the King's service, quoted by Mr. Carte ("*Life of Ormonde,*" vol. i.), wherein there is a minute and daily account of everything that happened in the North of Ireland during the first weeks of this insurrection, there is not even an insinuation of any cruelties committed by the insurgents, on the English or Protestants, although it is computed by the journalist "that the Protestants of that province had killed near a thousand of the rebels, in the first week or two of the rebellion." And, on the 16th of November, 1641, "Mr. Robert Wallbank came from the North, and informed the Irish House of Commons, that two hundred of the people of Coleraine fought with one thousand of the rebels, slew six of them, and not one of themselves hurt. That, in another battle, sixty of the rebels were slain, and only two of the others hurt; none slain." (*Journals of the Irish Commons,* Appendix.) Nor do we find, in this account, the least mention of cruelties then committed by the Irish; but much of the success and victory of his Majesty's Protestant subjects, as often as they encountered them.*

---

* Leland, in his "*History of Ireland,*" vol. iii., p. 101, says: "It was determined (by the insurgents, in the beginning of the insurrection) that the enterprise should be conducted, in every quarter, with as little bloodshed as possible."

APPENDIX.

That a great number of unoffending Irish were massacred in Island-Magee, by Scottish Puritans, about the beginning of this insurrection, is not denied by any adverse writer that I have met with. An apology, however, is made for it by them all, which, even if it were grounded on fact, as I shall presently show it is not, would be a very bad one, and seems, at least, to imply a confession of the charge. Those writers pretend that this massacre was perpetrated on those harmless people, in revenge of some cruelties before committed, by the rebels, on the Scots, in other parts of Ulster. But as I find this controversy has been already taken up by two able Protestant historians, who seem to differ about the time in which that dismal event happened, perhaps by laying before the reader the accounts of both, with such animadversions as naturally arise from them, that time may be more clearly and positively ascertained.

A late learned and ingenious author of a history of Ireland (Leland) has shifted off this shocking incident from November, 1641 (in which month it has been generally placed), to January following, many weeks after horrible cruelties (as he tells us) had been committed by the insurgents on the Scots in the North. "The Scottish soldiers," says he, "who had reinforced the garrison of Carrickfergus, were possessed of an habitual hatred of Popery, and inflamed to an implacable detestation of the Irish, by multiplied accounts of their cruelties. In one fatal night they issued from Carrickfergus, into an adjacent district called Island-Magee, where a number of the poorer Irish resided, *unoffending and untainted with the rebellion.* If we may believe *one of the leaders of this party,* THIRTY FAMILIES *were assailed by them, in their beds, and massacred with calm and deliberate cruelty.* As if," proceeds the historian, "the incident were not sufficiently hideous, Popish writers have represented it with shocking aggravation. They make the number of the slaughtered, in a small and thinly inhabited neck of land, to amount to three thousand, a wildness and absurdity into which other writers of such transactions have been betrayed; they assert that this butchery was committed in the beginning of November, 1641, that it was the first massacre committed in Ulster, and the great provocation to all the outrages of the Irish in this quarter. Mr. Carte seems to favor this assertion; had he carefully perused the collection of original depositions now in the possession of the University of Dublin, he would have found his doubts of facts and dates cleared most satisfactorily; and that the massacre at Island-Magee, as appears from several unsuspicious evidences, was really committed in the beginning of January, when the followers of O'Nial had almost exhausted their barbarous malice." * (*Hist. of Ireland*, vol. iii.)

Before I examine the several particulars of the foregoing account, I must observe that the objection taken from the smallness of the place, as if it were incapable of containing three thousand inhabitants, is grounded on a misapprehension of some circumstances in this event. For the Irish that were destroyed consisted not only of the inhabitants of the place, but also, and for the greatest part, of the country people residing in its neighborhood, who, upon the invitations of Colonel Chichester and Sir Arthur Tyrringham, had fled to Carrickfergus for protection, on the first eruption of these tumults. "The town of Carrickfergus," says Mr. Carte, "was then the place of the greatest strength in the North; and as Colonel Chichester and Sir Arthur Tyrringham had, on the evening of the 23d of October, received intelligence of the insurrection, they immediately, by beat of drum and kindling of fires, apprised all the country people round them of their danger; so that the poor country people, who had not yet stirred, flocked to that place continually, with all they could carry of their substance" (another temptation to commit the massacre), "in such multitudes of men, women, and children, that the town was overthronged." The same author also informs us, that "Colonel Chichester and Sir Arthur Tyrringham invited several of the most eminent of the Irish thereabouts, who yet remained quiet in

---

* Sir Phelim O'Neil. This assertion has no other foundation than the depositions in the University of Dublin. What credit is due to these we shall just now see; but if any regard at all is to be had to such of them as have been carefully selected from the rest and published by Temple and Borlase, in their histories of this rebellion, we shall find some of them vouching the contrary of this relation, viz., that Sir Phelim O'Neil did not order the cruelties he is *charged* with ordering till many weeks after January, 1641. For by Captain Parkin's examination, "Sir Phelim began his massacres *after* his flight from Dundalk." (Temple, p. 85.) Now his flight from Dundalk, according to Carte, did not happen till about the latter end of March following. ("*Life of Ormonde*," vol. i.)

their houses, to come to Carrickfergus for security; who accordingly went thither, *but 'were made prisoners on their arrival.*"

And because it is allowed that Mr. Carte seems to favor the assertion " that near three thousand innocent Irish were massacred in Island-Magee, in the beginning of November, 1641," it is but just to produce the reasons which appear to have inclined him to that way of thinking, by inserting the passage at large, wherein they are contained :—

" On the 15th of November," says this well-informed writer, " the rebels, after a fortnight's siege, reduced the castle of Lurgan ; Sir William Bromlow, after a stout defence, surrendering it on the terms of marching out with his family and goods; but such was the unworthy disposition of the rebels, that they kept him, his lady, and children, prisoners, rifled his house, plundered, stripped, and killed most of his servants, and treated all the townsmen in the same manner. This," adds he, " was the first breach of faith which the rebels were guilty of in these parts (there was then no other insurrection in any of the other parts of Ireland), in regard of articles of capitulation; for, when Mr. Conway, on November the 5th, surrendered his castle of Bally-aghie, in the county of Derry, to them, they kept the terms for which he stipulated, and allowed him to march out with his men, and to carry away trunks with plate and money in them. Whether," proceeds Mr. Carte, " *the slaughter made by a party from Carrickfergus, in the territory of Magee,* a long narrow island, in which, it is affirmed, that *near three thousand harmless Irish men, women, and children were cruelly massacred,* happened before the surrender of Lurgan, is hard to be determined ; the relations published of facts, in those times, being very indistinct and uncertain, with regard to the time they were committed, though it is confidently asserted that the said massacre happened in this month of November."

Let us now try these different accounts by the only sure test of dates and facts. It is confessed on all hands that the chiefs of the insurgents, through fear of the Scots in Ulster, (" who," as the Earl of Clanrickarde informs us, " were forty thousand well-armed men, when the rebellion commenced," at the same time that the rebels were, at least, by half less numerous, and furnished with few better weapons than "staves, scythes, and pitchforks,") published a proclamation "forbidding their followers, on pain of death, to molest any of the Scottish nation, in body or goods." Temple acknowledges that "this proclamation was, for a time, observed;" and from Mr. Wallbank's report, already mentioned, to the House of Commons, of the constant success of his Majesty's forces in defeating the insurgents in different parts of Ulster, from the 23d of October to the 16th of November following, we may reasonably suppose that it was at least observed till that day, for it is surely in the highest degree improbable that these chiefs would, at any time before, have wantonly provoked the resentment of so formidable a body of men, by any cruel outrage or hostile act. But it is unquestionably evident, that the Scots in Ulster did some remarkable execution on the Irish, several days before the 15th of November, the day on which Lurgan was surrendered. For Sir William Parsons, in a letter from Dublin, of the 13th of that month, to the Earl of Clanrickarde, acquaints him, as with a welcome piece of news, that "the Scots did hold the northern Irish hard to it, having killed some of them." And Sir William St. Ledger, grudging, as it were, the Scots the honor of that action, told the Earl of Ormonde, on the 14th, that, "had it pleased God that his lordship had been there with his hundred horse, and himself to wait upon him, the Scots should never have had the honor to put such an obligation on Ireland."

From hence, I think, may fairly be deduced the only reason, why the behavior of the insurgents to Sir William Bromlow, on the 15th of November, was so very different from that which they had before shown to Mr. Conway, on the 5th of the same month, viz.: because the massacre in question was perpetrated on their innocent, unoffending people, in that interval of time; which, no doubt, provoked them to the above-mentioned breach of articles at the surrender of Lurgan, and to several other acts of injustice and cruelty in the prosecution of this war.

The deduction now made is so agreeable to dates and facts, that I am surprised to find this first breach of articles by the insurgents ascribed to any other cause; especially to one which appears manifestly repugnant to both. This cause, we are informed, was the repulse, defeat, and slaughter of a considerable body of the rebels at the siege of Lisburn, by a Scottish garrison stationed there; for thus the before-cited history relates the immediate effects which that disaster produced in these rebels: " But such success " (of the Scots) " was attended with consequences truly horrible; the Irish, incensed at resistance, carried on their hostilities without faith or humanity. Lurgan was surrendered by Sir William Bromlow, on terms of security to the inhabitants, and permission of marching out with his family, goods, and retinue; but all were instantly seized, and the whole town given up to plunder." Thus have we a cause plausibly assigned, which did not exist until many days after its supposed effect was produced. For the defeat and slaughter of the rebels at Lisburn, or, as it was then called, Lisnegarvy, did not happen, according to Borlase, till the 28th November; but Lurgan, as we have seen, was surrendered to them on the 15th of that month, thirteen days before.

Let us now see upon what grounds this massacre in Island-Magee is transferred from November, 1641, to the beginning of January following. One would expect to find an assertion so singular supported by some solid, or at least plausible proof; but instead of meeting with any such, in the place before quoted from this history, we are only there directed to look out for it (where certainly it never can be found) in the collection of original manuscript depositions now in the possession of the University of Dublin. But we shall presently demonstrate the insufficiency, not to say futility, of proofs drawn from these depositions.* And, in truth, if they were to be admitted as proofs, or evidence in any degree, there is hardly anything so incredible or absurd, that might not, with equal reason, be obtruded upon us for genuine history. Every suggestion of frenzy and melancholy; miraculous escapes from death, visions of spirits chaunting hymns; *ghosts*, rising from rivers, brandishing

---

* " Any one (says Mr. Carte) who has ever read the examinations and depositions here referred to, which were generally given upon hearsay, and contradicting one another, would think it very hard upon the Irish, to have all those, without distinction, to be admitted as evidence."

swords, and shrieking revenge, would have a just and rational title to our belief, *having, all of them, received the sanction of these vouchers.*

*The original depositions in the possession of the University of Dublin considered.**

I shall now briefly consider the nature of that evidence which has hitherto induced so many people, learned and unlearned, to give, or at least seem to give credit to those horrible relations of murders and massacres which have been imputed to these insurgents;—evidence that, in itself, is so manifestly futile, contradictory, or false, that I am persuaded every person of common sense would be ashamed to produce the like upon any ordinary occasion.

The evidence I mean is that huge collection of manuscript depositions (consisting of thirty-two folio volumes) which are said to have been sworn, on the subject of the outrages and depredations committed by the insurgents, in this war, and are now in the possession of the University of Dublin. *From this enormous heap of malignity and nonsense, Temple and Borlase have selected such examinations as appeared to them the least exceptionable, and consequently the most likely to obtain credit to their horrible narrations.* To these, therefore, I shall refer the reader *as a select specimen of the rest:* after I have submitted to his consideration what Dr. Warner (who, it seems, underwent the drudgery of perusing and examining the whole collection) has left as his opinion of it. "Besides the examinations," says he, "signed by the commissioners, there are several copies of others, said to be taken before them, which are, therefore, of no authority; and there are many depositions *taken ten years after, which are still less authentic.* As great stress," adds the Doctor, "has been laid upon this collection, in print and conversation, among the Protestants of Ireland; and as the whole evidence of the massacre turns upon it, I spent a great deal of time in examining these books; and I am sorry to say, that they have been made the foundation of much more clamor and resentment than can be warranted by truth and reason."

---

* Curry's "Review of the Civil Wars in Ireland" (1810), Chap. IV.

" There is one circumstance in these books, not taken notice of by any before me, which is, that though all the examinations signed by the Commissioners are said to be upon oath, yet in infinitely the greater number of them, the words ' being duly sworn,' have the pen drawn through them, with the same ink with which the examinations are written; and in several of those where such words remain, many parts of the examinations are crossed out. This is a circumstance which shows, that the bulk of this immense collection is parole evidence; and what sort of evidence that is, may be easily learned by those who are conversant with the common people of any country, especially when their imaginations are terrified, and their passions heated by sufferings. Of what credit are depositions worthy," adds he, " (and several such there are,) that many of the Protestants, that were drowned, were often seen in erect postures in the river, and shrieking out revenge?"*

At the same time that Dr. Warner rejects the depositions now in the possession of the University of Dublin, he informs us, " that he has, in his own possession, a choice and duly attested copy of such of these examinations only, as were taken on oath ; which," says he, " *demonstrates the falsehood of the relation in every Protestant history of this rebellion.*" Had the Doctor favored the world with a publication of these choice examinations, or even an abstract of them, we should then be in some measure able to judge of their authenticity; whereas at present we have only his bare word for it. However, from an anecdote which he himself has related, concerning the first real and original examinations, we may fairly conclude that his favorite copy of them, however well attested, deserves not a jot more credit than those which he has already so justly condemned. That anecdote imports, " that soon after the Restoration, when the claims in favor of innocents were canvassed, and the House of Commons desired, that none of those whose names could be found in the depositions, might be heard, relating to such

---

* " Hundreds of ghosts of Protestants " (says Temple, from these depositions), " that were drowned by the rebels at Portnadown bridge, *were seen in the river bolt-upright, and were heard to cry out for revenge on these rebels.* One of the ghosts was seen with hands lifted up, and standing in that posture, *from the 20th of December to the latter end of the following Lent!*"

claims of innocency; the Duke of Ormonde, though no friend to the Irish, for good reasons rejected the proposal. The Duke," adds he, " probable knew too much of these examinations, and the methods used in procuring them, to give them such a stamp of authority; or otherwise it would have been the clearest and shortest proof of the guilt of such as were named in them."

Upon this occasion, I submit it to the consideration of every candid and intelligent reader, whether depositions found insufficient to convict the persons, or confiscate the properties of the Irish then living, ought to be now deemed proper and competent evidence to impeach the characters or principles of their innocent descendants, at that time unborn? or whether any person now existing can be thought to be so well qualified, either by want of partiality to the Irish, or by the knowledge of their case, to judge of the weight or futility of that evidence, as the Duke of Ormonde was, at that juncture? And, conscious of this material defect in the original examinations, with what probability of success could Dr. Warner rely on his own copy of them, how well soever attested, as capable of ascertaining the facts, which he has so confidently related out of it? *

[The able and painstaking author of " The Cromwellian Settlement of Ireland" (Mr. John P. Prendergast), whom Mr. Froude himself quotes as a most reliable historian, in the second edition of his work (London, 1870) makes the following observations on the evidence relied on by the English fabricators of the massacres of 1641.]

" The proper evidences to prove or disprove this dreadful massacre are, of course, authentic contemporaneous documents—not compilations of a later age, like Hume's ' History of England,' or even the ponderous pamphlets of party writers of the day, like Milton and Clarendon, strangers to Ireland and its transactions.

---

* Warner himself confesses, "that so many of the rebels' sayings to their Protestant and English prisoners, which are recorded even in the choice manuscript collection of depositions in his custody, are so ridiculous, incredible, or contradictory to one another, as show plainly, that they spoke what their own or different passions of their leaders prompted them to."

"There is one document that ought to be decisive in this case and it would have been so if the English of Ireland were not interested enough, and the English of England prejudiced enough, to propagate and perpetuate any calumny, to the damage of the fame and national character of the people of Ireland. It is the following: Just two months after the outbreak, the Government issued a Commission under the Great Seal, to seven despoiled Protestant Ministers, to take evidence upon oath ' to keep up the memory of the outrages committed by the Irish to posterity.'

"The Commission, dated 23d of December, 1641, was, in its original form, to take an account of losses. It was amended, *on the 18th of January*, 1642, *to include murders.* So that this was an after-thought; a thing scarce possible, if there had been a general massacre. The first Commission recites ' that many British and Protestants have been separated from their habitations, and others deprived of their goods;' the Commissioners are accordingly to examine upon oath, concerning the amount of loss, the names of the robbers, and what traitorous speeches were uttered by the robbers or others. The second adds, ' And what violence was done by the robbers, and how often, and what numbers have been murthered, or have perished afterwards, on the way to Dublin or elsewhere.' And the remonstrance shows that the outrages, in spite of the Commissioners' attempt to present the most terrible pictures, were, for the most part, only such as necessarily followed the stripping the English and driving them from their possessions, as these planters had driven the Irish from theirs, thirty years before; and that the murders were fewer than have occurred in similar insurrections, where of course some would be slain resisting the pillagers of their homesteads. The Commissioners seem unconscious of any general massacre. The murders they record are the occurrences of four months, collected from different parts of Ulster. In the few instances where any numbers were slain, some of them at least were plainly acts of war,—though the Commissioners would have them supposed to be cold-blooded murders,— and occurred late in December. So far therefore from warranting the supposed extensive massacre of the English, this official account disproves it, and shows how baseless is

Clarendon's story of forty thousand or fifty thousand English murdered before they knew where they were, or of an incredible number of men, women, and children promiscuously slaughtered in ten days, as he elsewhere has it; or of one hundred and fifty-four thousand, or three hundred thousand, massacred in cold blood. The letters of the Lords Justices during the first months of the rebellion are equally silent concerning any massacre; and their Proclamation of 8th February, 1642, while it falsely charges the Irish with the design, says *it had failed*. All the accounts of the time are full of the crowds driven out, not murdered. . . . . .

"Bishop Bedel, of Kilmore, remained in his palace unharmed, his flocks untouched, surrounded by crowds of English that fled thither as to a port of safety, and lay in his barns and stables, and even on hay in the churchyard. Thither fled the Bishop of Elphin and a train of Roscommon exiles, and there he enjoyed such a heaven upon earth for three weeks, that he would willingly have endured another Irish stripping to enjoy again such holy converse. For the Irish never hindered these two Bishops and their poor flocks from using their religious exercises,* though their own was made a crime; and seven priests, reprieved by the King, were hanged in England at this time, at the angry demand of the House of Commons, simply for saying Mass. In November, an Irish priest arrived at Bishop Bedel's to conduct them to Dublin. The Bishop of Elphin and the rest departed, leaving Bedel and his family behind. Bedel died there in February, 1642, and the Irish paid him honor by firing over his grave. His family continued there unmolested until the 15th of June, 1642, when they joined a party of 1340 English, that, by treaty with the Irish, were escorted safely to Sir Henry Tichborne's garrison at Drogheda. Of the Bishop of Elphin's company not one miscarried, nor was a thread of the garments that Bedel gave the stripped English touched by the rebels on their way. . . . . Bedel is always represented to have died a prisoner, though he was only removed for a fortnight to the neighboring Castle of Cloughouter, by order from Kilkenny, on the advance of an English force, and

---

* Life of Bishop Bedel, by his son-in-law, Alexander Clogy, Minister of Cavan. London, 1862.

then restored to his son-in-law's house. In like manner Sir Phelim O'Neil is handed down by history as the murderer of Lord Caulfield, his neighbor in the country, and friend in Parliament. Yet he treated him and his family with great care when he surprised the fort of Charlemont, on the 23d of October, 1641; and there Lord Caulfield was kept until the 14th of January, 1642, when he was sent with an escort towards Cloughouter Castle, by a similar order, (probably from Kilkenny,) to that which brought Bishop Bedel thither. They were to rest the first night at Sir Phelim O'Neil's Manor of Kynard (now Calledon); but as Lord Caulfield was entering the gate, he was shot in the back by Edmund O'Hugh, a foster-brother of Sir Phelim, and thus murdered in the absence and without the knowledge of Sir Phelim. That Sir Phelim had no part in this murder is certain; for he was sorely distressed at it, and had O'Hugh committed to Armagh jail for trial for the murder: but he escaped; whereupon Sir Phelim had the sentry hanged for his connivance or neglect."

FROUDE'S FALSITIES.

WHAT THE AUTHOR OF "THE CROMWELLIAN SETTLEMENT OF IRELAND" SAYS OF THEM.

[In the annexed letters, addressed to the press of Ireland and America, by Mr. Prendergast, author of "The Cromwellian Settlement of Ireland," that gentleman convicts Mr. Froude not only of circulating historical falsehoods long since proved to be such,—but even of suppressing facts which have been distinctly brought under his (Mr. Froude's) notice; in order to present to his readers a false and distorted view of the action of the English (and in particular of Cromwell) towards the Irish people and their clergy.]

SANDYMOUNT, DUBLIN, *Nov.* 5, 1872.

SIR,—Mr. Froude, I believe, is lighting a fire that he has little conception of. Deep as our hatred has hitherto been, at our unparalleled historic wrongs, it is as nothing to the intense detestation we shall hereafter hold the English in. Though the vile English press are unwilling to commit themselves to the support of Mr. Froude's crusade against the exiled Irish until they see the success of it, it is easy to perceive how they sympathize with it, and how gladly they would see the Americans hate us as deeply as they do themselves. For, in truth, the self-imposed mission of this friend and lover of Ireland (God save us from our English lovers!) is to turn the Americans against us. With hypocritical flattery he pretends to seek American opinion. "We ourselves are at our wit's end," he says. "If America will counsel England what to do, she will listen gratefully. And if a time is ever to come when Celt and Saxon are to live side by side in peace and in quiet, it will be when America tells the Irish that they must depend for the future on their own industry." America has become the Supreme Court of Appeal, he says, with English hypocrisy; and he asks their judgment. But he has already renounced it! Suppose America should say: "Try our Constitution; give Ireland a Federal Union; make her a State like one of the States of our Union." Oh, no! Even if that be necessary to Ireland's happiness, England, he tells them beforehand, will not do it. "She will not commit political suicide by any measure that might tend to separation."

What he wants, then, is judgment in England's favor, and against Ireland.

His language is that of the hypocrite, and there is poison under that tongue. A more calumnious harangue than his lectures cannot be conceived.

He admits the brutal cruelties of the English, but represents them as called forth by the still greater crimes of the Irish. Witness his approval of Cromwell's massacre of the inhabitants of Drogheda, together with the flower of the English veterans fighting under the King's commission; I leave out the Irish soldiery. But is it come to this, that the killing of ladies, women, girls, and innocent children, which was the sport of Cromwell's soldiers for two whole days, is to be approved of by Englishmen at this time of day?

He (Mr. Froude) did not think it so cruel as the oppression and lawlessness which brought misery into every poor man's cabin. It is plain he knows little of the history of that time. But were what he states as true as it is false, would that justify such a deed?

It is such deeds that bring English power to be hated and finally overthrown everywhere. This very massacre of Cromwell's works at this day. It makes us loathe the name of Englishman as the incarnation of cruelty. It might terrify temporarily; but it fixed National hatred perpetually.

Look at the rebellion of 1798. The English intrusted the Orangemen with the bayonet, and that favorite instrument of theirs for spreading their power—the cat-o'-nine tails. The rebellion was put down, but they have left a hatred that will never be put down. So in India, in the late mutiny. Their floggings, killings, hangings, burnings, blowing away from guns, have left such hatreds that the English there live in anticipation of another outbreak, and the wounds made in 1857 will never heal.

Mr. Froude is now reopening every old wound, and England may perhaps have to curse the day when the cold-blooded hypocrite was born. Listen to him describing his love for the Irish. "They either," he says, "attract strongly or repel strongly." Him they attracted! During the last thirty years he has been thrown (that is, he has thrown himself) much amongst them. He has spent his college vacations, when a young man, wandering in the mountains. He has lived in peasants' cabins for months together. He was once overtaken by illness in the wilds of Mayo, and " the poor creatures," he adds, with English contemptuousness, " treated me with a tenderness I can never forget." And well this viper repays their kindness by slandering the nation; out-slandering, indeed, all our former maligners—and that is no easy task.

Who made this man our judge? He seems possessed of a devil that gives him a supposed dominion over Ireland. Ireland has put money into his purse. In his ten long volumes, his few chapters on Ireland have given the greatest charm to his work. The subject, though old, is ever new and fresh, like the people. He is still determined to make money of us. But now he advances beyond the domain of past history; he sets himself up as our censor, and the guide of America in her opinion of the Irish.

That he will rue his conduct I have no doubt. I have never yet seen any one undertake the running down of Ireland that did not bring his own reputation to ruin. The conscience of the world revolts secretly against the cruel injustice of the deed.

But, be this as it may, Mr. Froude has done what can never be undone.

No Irishman will ever rest satisfied till he is freed from the misery of living under a people who, though they know that the strongest feature in the character of the Irish is their national feeling, yet seek to depreciate the nation with a watchfulness that never sleeps and a malignity that never tires.

The reputation this man has acquired as a historian only serves him the better to slander the Irish. I do not believe he can have made any search into the original sources of any period but that period which his history treats of. If he has, nothing but reckless hatred of the Irish could induce him to represent them as cowards—to represent 200,000 well-drilled Irish, under Ormonde, as driven, like chaff, before Cromwell and 18,000 English !

The English of Ormonde's army refused to fight as comrades with the Irish. When Cromwell appeared before the walls of some towns held for the King, the English garrisons opened their gates and gave up their officers—their English officers—to be hanged. All the English garrisons of Munster revolted from Ormonde when Cromwell was at a distance, and kept them for Cromwell at his approach. At Rathmines, the treachery of some of the English regiments who went over to Col. Michael Jones, the Parliamentarian Governor of Dublin, in the middle of the battle, helped mainly to cause Ormonde's defeat. The Scottish

Presbyterians, another part of Ormonde's supposed 200,000 men, were equally indisposed to fight as faithful comrades of the Irish. And the troops of the late Catholic Confederates, —little else but a sudden levy of a mass of peasants,—had no heart to fight under commanders of English blood and interest, though Catholic in religion, who were ready to betray the cause rather than it should become a national conflict, the only thing that could have rallied the Irish.

The Ulster Irish, called "the Nunciotists," were the only body who maintained the cause of Ireland for Ireland's sake. Thus the discipline of these troops of Ormonde is as untrue as the numbers stated by Mr. Froude. Let us pass, then, from this slanderer's charge against the Irish of cowardice (and let all Irishmen, whether their coats be red or green, or blue or black, note it), to the equally false charge he makes against our fathers of a massacre. The Irish Catholics, it seems, rose and massacred an unarmed crowd of 38,000 confiding and unsuspecting Protestants! "The valet that helped to undress his master over night, stood with a pike by his bedside in the morning." This sensational drawing, when once indulged in (and Froude, Macaulay, and Carlyle have all sacrificed truth and honesty to this vicious taste), overpowers all the better feelings.

There was no massacre. It was not a rising of Catholics upon Protestants, but of an oppressed nation against their tyrants, in the interest of their rightful King. Mr. Froude defends us from the charge of murdering 150,000. On the best computation, says this friend of the Irish, it was only 38,000.

> "An open foe may prove a curse,
> But a pretended friend is worse!"

I have, in the Second Edition of the "Cromwellian Settlement," appealed to the collection of outrages and murders

APPENDIX. 305

made by order of the English House of Commons in March, 1642, under a Royal Commission, composed of seven despoiled Protestant ministers, for the purpose of damning us all to posterity, for disproof of this supposed massacre. And I confidently rest the case upon it. I have read, I think, all the papers of the time, and the result of all is the same.

But enough of this. The lie will be repeated—this and a thousand daily national insults will be our fate—until that which happened in the case of America happens in Ireland. I am old enough to remember when the insulting of the Americans (not long escaped from the yoke) was nearly as much the sport of the English as taunting the Irish (still under it) is now. But from the time of the success of the Americans in their war against the Mexicans, it ceased. As soon as they became weak again (or were supposed to be weak), during the late civil war, the insolence and brutality of the English burst forth again. Then it all subsided again when the Northern States were victorious, and the English became so mean as to submit to be judged by the three *ex post facto* rules of International Law, and to submit to an Award by Arbitrators, in order to cover their shame in paying that fine for their insolence which they saw the Americans were resolved to exact, and these once proud English did not dare to refuse.

As soon as the Irish are feared, they will be honored by this brutal, this repulsive people.—Your obedient servant,

JOHN P. PRENDERGAST.

SANDYMOUNT, DUBLIN, 17*th Nov.*, 1872.

SIR,—Some persons may think the language of my letter of the 5th of this month, concerning Mr. Froude, too strong. Perhaps they will deem it too weak, as I do, when they have read his book called "The English in Ireland in the Eighteenth Century." At the time I wrote I had only seen the account of his speech at Delmonico's, upon his reception, and the abstract of his first lecture. Since I have read his book I would wish to alter one phrase. I would withdraw the term "Cold-blooded hypocrite," and substitute "Blood-thirsty fanatic." His lectures give no measure of the malignity of his book. The man seems to be absolutely possessed, filled with demoniac hate. There is nothing in the world like his present effort except Peter the Hermit's preaching the Crusade. His thirst for the destruction of the Irish is only equalled by the zeal of the Crusaders against the Infidels. If he could, he would raise against the Irish the cry of "Hep! Hep!" to which thousands of Jews throughout Europe were massacred. He aims at agitating and rousing both England and America against us. He has laid the fuel here for rebellion and civil war, and he then crosses the Atlantic to secure, if he can, the assistance of America towards our subjection. Their acquiescence is all he asks. "It will be worth twenty batteries of cannon to the English," he says. If this is not his purport, words have no meaning. No Southern planter, infuriated at the prospect of his slaves acquiring their freedom, or the Spartans, maddened at the resistance of the helots, can be more demon-like than this Froude. "Cromwell!" "Cromwell!" "Cromwell!" is the beginning, middle, and ending of his book, his dream, his aspiration. "Leave them to us! oh, leave the Irish to our tender mercies, and the world shall see Cromwellian rule re-established in that accursed land!" This is his prayer. It is the old story of the Spartans seeking and getting the aid of the Athenians to keep the helots of Sparta in subjection. Twice did Athens help Sparta to bring back the helots under the Spartan cat-o'-nine-tails. And well was Athens repaid, when some years later Sparta reduced the Athenians to slavery. and the Spartan army surrounded

Athens with bands of music playing, for greater triumph to themselves and indignity to her, while they forced her own sons to take down the city walls. They even talked of sowing the ground where the city stood with salt! It remains to be seen what course the Americans will take. Let no one deem my language too heated till they have read Froude's book. If I mistake not, it will be translated into many languages. I trust it may. The world will then begin to form some notion of the character of the race the Irish have had to deal with. I shall fearlessly await the judgment of mankind. His book smells of blood. Every horrible dream of the enraged, the terrified English of 1641 is reproduced under pretence of an answer to my defence of the Irish against the false charge of the stupendous massacre of 300,000 or 38,000 Protestants, *or less*, as this kind friend and lover of the Irish suggests, by the Papists. The one number is as false as the other. It is nothing to the purpose (as an answer) to show that at Portadown numbers of Protestants, varying, according to different accounts, from 60 to 200, were butchered in December, 1641, or that many were massacred in the same month at Lisgool Castle, in the county of Fermanagh. The latter was a siege; those at Portadown were prisoners. The war of "no quarter," on the part of the English, had begun.

The killing of women and children by the Irish, where true, is horrible (in many instances the reports are perfectly false), but it is far less horrible than the same crime authorized by Sir Charles Coote and other English commanders in this war, as in the wars of Elizabeth's day, mentioned by Froude himself. But be the stories against the Irish in this respect true or false, it is no answer to my denial of the appalling account of the massacre, unless it were of numbers, amounting to thousands, which is not pretended. But it serves Mr. Froude's purpose of spreading war and blood again.

I remember well, the first time I appeared in the Four Courts Library after publishing the "Cromwellian Settlement," that one of her Majesty's counsel addressed me, "Why, Prendergast, I hear you deny *the Irish rebellion* of 1641!" Much of Mr. Froude's parade of murders is about as little to the point as my learned friend's idea of my argument—

> "Whose notions fitted things so well,
> That which was which he could not tell,
> But oftentimes mistook the one,
> For t'other, as great clerks have done."

Mr. Froude, however, is not so stupid. He knows well enough that the question is, "Was there a massacre in Ulster, of thousands, at or shortly after the outbreak of 23d of October, 1641?" It is remarkable that, often as the Irish had before been forced into rebellion or war, no such national crime was ever alleged against them. Mr. Froude makes the priests and the Catholic religion to be at the root of the massacre. He has been to the returns of the Commission of the seven despoiled ministers, made in March, 1642, for inflaming the English of that day, and reproduced now by Mr. Froude for the same purpose at this day. From thence he takes Bishop Jones's tale of a great meeting of monks at Multifarnam Abbey, in the county of Westmeath, where the project of a massacre was said to be debated. The tale is that of an informer, incredible to those who know the history of that time, and are familiar with the tales that were then coined and credited, or *pretended to be credited.* But, says Mr. Froude, the Irish priests themselves admitted that 150,000 Protestants had been murdered by their Popish parishioners. Froude, in his kind feeling for the Irish *whom he so loves,* does not believe in the numbers: he believes in 38,000 *or even less,* and finally says that the mind was incapable of making any rational computation because of the terror, but that the numbers were enormous; and the priests had themselves to blame for being the authors of this frightful tale. But suppose it should turn out that English Protestants and not Irish priests were the authors of this 150,000 Protestants massacred? Well, the tale will still pass current under Mr. Froude's brilliant painting, and the efforts of the poor defender of the defamed Irish and their priesthood will not be regarded or even heard. Now, what is the foundation of this tale? A passionate friar named O'Mahony urged the native Irish to continue the war with the English rather than accept the peace (afterwards known as the peace of '46) on terms he deemed derogatory and ruinous. Those terms their Catholic leaders, of English blood, were determined to accept, and they caused O'Mahony's book, called "Disputatio Apologetica," printed in Latin at Frankfort, in Germany, to be publicly burnt. "Fight on," said O'Mahony; "you have already slain 150,000 of your enemies, the heretics [*i.e.* English], in these four or five years, since 1641 to the time of my writing this work, in this present year, 1645. Your foes have publicly proclaimed it in their printed declarations; you yourselves do not dispute the fact, and as for myself, I believe they have lost even more. I only wish we could say, *all.*" There is no need of wasting time in comment on this piece of evidence. It is a sample of the kind of proofs used in every part of this controversy.

Sir John Temple is another witness of Mr. Froude's. "Sir John Temple," he says, "considered that 150,000 perished in two months (that is, by the end of December, 1641) and 300,000 in two years." This is from his "Irish Rebellion," a book published in 1646, for the purpose of pro-venting the peace then on the point of being signed, and to hinder any peace at any future time between the English and Irish, as Sir John Temple expressly declares. Yet Sir John's own letter of 12th December, 1641, to the King, given by Mr. Froude, because he thinks it will lead ordinary readers to accept it as proof of the astounding massacre, proves the contrary. He prints the passage he relies on in italics. It is this:—"Many thousands of our nation are already perished" (page 105 in note). Is this proof of a massacre? Does it not even contradict the statement in his book of 150,000 being dead at this time, not by massacre, but through fatigue, famine, disease, and in other ways.

But what are all these horrors, supposing them to be true, to the acts done by the orders of legitimate authority? The manner of English war in Ireland has ever been to massacre women and children.

"My manner of dealing" (says Sir Henry Gilbert) "was, I slew all those from time to time that did belong to, feed, accompany, or maintain any outlaws or traitors, and after summoning any fort or castle, if they did not immediately yield it, I would not afterwards take their surrender, but won it perforce, how many lives soever it cost, *putting man, woman, and child of them to the sword;* being of opinion that no conquered nation will ever yield willingly their obedience for love, but rather for fear."

This is from Mr. Froude's "Elizabeth," 10th volume, page 507. The year is 1569.

Are the acts of Irish peasants at all equal in atrocity to the murders done by order of the Parliament of England (only that "Parliament can do no wrong"), in drowning the King's Protestant soldiers, taken at sea coming at the King's orders to his aid in England? If they were Irish, even though Protestants and valiant servitors against the Confederate Catholics, they were to be thrown overboard; and 70 soldiers of Colonel Willoughby's regiment, all

Protestants, and many women, being taken by a Parliament ship on their passage to Bristol in 1644, were so dealt with (Proclamation of the Supreme Council of Confederate Catholics, July 6, 1644; Carte Papers, vol. xi., Public Record Office, Ireland). I should not venture to offer any Catholic document for proof (for it would not be believed by Mr. Froude), only that the fact is confirmed by the correspondence of Protestants who, of course, never tell lies (though Mr. Froude himself admits the magnifying 38,000 or less into 150,000), and that the fact is confirmed by the Marquis of Ormonde and the public and private correspondence of the day. The English made a boast of it. Captain Swanley (honor to the English navy!) tied the men in pairs, back to back, and flung them into the sea at Milford Haven. The weekly papers were merry over it. One said, "that Captain Swanley took six score" (they swelled the butchers' bill to make it more delightful to the English taste for blood) "English-Irish and sent them a-fishing to the bottom of the sea." Another said "that Captain Swanley made those Irish drink their bellies' full of salt water." Another "that Captain Swanley made those who would not take the Covenant take the water with their heads downward." Another, "that the Captain made trial if an Irish cavalier could swim without hands." (Mercurius Aulicus for May 16, 1644, p. 983.) And Captain Swanley received the thanks of Parliament and a chain of gold worth 200*l.*

There is here no mention of women, though they may have been drowned. For, after the defeat of the king at Naseby, more than 100 women, some of them the wives of English Royalist officers, were cut to pieces; and the excuse was, that they were believed to be Irishwomen, wives and followers of soldiers of the King's Irish army. But there is no time, no need for multiplying instances. I must pass to the massacre at Drogheda by Cromwell :—

"The Irish histories say" (says Mr. Froude) "that there was an indiscriminate massacre of men, women, and children. Cromwell's own account" (he continues) "mentions only men in arms, and priests, who, as having been the instigators of the worst crimes, were held less innocent than those who had committed them. It is possible, he adds, that in such a scene women and children may have been accidentally killed; but there is no evidence of it from an eye-witness, and only general rumors and reports at second-hand. Of authentic evidence," (he continues,) "in addition to Cromwell, two letters, one of them from a Royalist, disprove conclusively the story of a general massacre. A printed official list of the officers and soldiers slain at the storming of Drogheda, supplied to the Parliament, brings the number to nearly 3,000, *besides many inhabitants. These citizens*" (says Mr. Froude) "*fought by the side of the troops and shared their fate.*" ("English in Ireland in the Eighteenth Century," p. 124, note.)

The proofs, however, of a general massacre are only too numerous to quote. The Marquis of Ormonde, in the same work, says, "Cromwell outdid himself," that it recalled the "massacre and tortures of the early Christians, and the cruelties of Amboyna." I never heard it disputed by any one who had read history, except Carlyle, Mr. Froude's model. The great question in dispute is, "Did they massacre after promising quarter?" He says there is *no evidence of any massacring of women and children from an eye-witness.* So far is this from the truth, that there is an account by an eye-witness and actor in no less common a book—a book in constant use, namely, in Anthony Wood's "Athenæ Oxonienses." The account is to be found in the autobiography of Anthony Wood, given in the preface to Bliss's edition of the "Athenæ," in four volumes quarto. Anthony Wood's eldest brother, Thomas Wood, Master of Arts of the University of Oxford, was a captain in Colonel Henry Ingoldsby's troop at the siege of Drogheda, "and returned" (says Anthony Wood) "from Ireland to Oxford for a time to take up the arrears of his studentship at Christ Church." It was the winter after the siege. "At which time, being often with his mother and brethren," says Anthony Wood, "he was wont in the winter evenings to tell them of the most terrible assaulting and storming of Drogheda, wherein he himself had been engaged." He told them, continues Anthony, "that 3,000 at least, besides women and children, were, after the assailants had taken the town, put to the sword on the 11th and 12th of September, 1649." He told them "that when they (the soldiery) were to make their way up to the lofts and galleries in churches, and up to the towers whither the enemy had fled, each of the assailants would take up a child and use it as a buckler of defence as they mounted the steps to keep themselves from being shot or brained. After they had killed all in the Church of St. Laurence, they went into the vaults underneath, where all the flower and choicest of the women and ladies had hid themselves. One of these," he continues, "a most handsome virgin, arrayed in costly and gorgeous apparel, kneeled down to Thomas Wood with tears and prayers to save her life; and he being struck with a profound pity, took her under his arm and went out of the church with intentions to let her shift for herself, but a soldier perceiving his intentions, thrust his sword up her fundament." (Reason will be shown before I have done for using Anthony Wood's dreadful language.) What (it will be said) must have been Captain Thomas Wood's horror to find this beautiful, trembling creature, who trusted to his protecting arm, thus cruelly and inhumanly butchered by this brute of an Englishman, as she leaned upon him while getting up the steps of the vault? Of course he struck him, in horror and disgust, with the flat, if not with the edge, of his sword? Hear Anthony Wood's account of what his brother told him.

"Whereupon Captain Wood, seeing her gasping, took her money, jewels, etc., and flung her down over the works!" In other words, this English officer and gentleman, and Master of Arts of the University of Oxford, turned upon this poor tortured creature, robbed her, and flung her alive, over the walls of Drogheda! But "those citizens of Drogheda fighting beside the troops necessarily shared the fate of the Irish soldiery." "It is possible that in such a scene women and children may have been accidentally killed!" Was this lovely girl, whose beauty and elegance disarmed even her furious conqueror, accidentally killed? Was the trembling crowd of terrified ladies of the best quality, that, like a herd of hunted deer, had sought shelter in the vaults under St. Laurence's church, and were there massacred—were these ladies and their children citizens fighting beside the troops?

"There is no evidence of an indiscriminate massacre of men, women, and children from an eye-witness, only general rumors and reports at second hand." Is not Captain Thomas Wood's account the account of an eye-witness? And are the cotemporaneous printed letters of the Marquis of Ormonde to the King mere general rumor and report at second-hand? But what will be thought of Mr. Froude's candor and conscientiousness when it is known that he had in his hands, at the time of publishing his book, the evidence of Captain Thomas Wood and the letter of the Marquis of Ormonde, extracted in handwriting? For Mr. Froude having written to a friend of mine to know if there was anything beyond Irish rumor for the story of a general massacre, my friend sent the letter to me at Oxford, whence I furnished him with the extracts, and they were by him sent to Mr. Froude. I had quite forgotten it till after I had written the greater part of this letter. His high commendation is given to this massacre; for he not only adopts the language of his hero, but glories in the deed, and vaunts it at this hour. "I am persuaded," wrote Cromwell (it is from Froude I quote), "that it is a judgment of God upon these wretches who have imbrued their hands in so much innocent blood, and that it will tend to prevent the effusion of blood for the future, which are satisfactory grounds for such actions, which otherwise could not but work much remorse and regret." How utterly mistaken this infallible hero of Mr. Froude was, the tenor of Mr. Froude's whole book is enough to show. * * * * * * * *

There is not time nor space to show the reckless audacity of his statements of the prosperity he supposes to have followed Cromwell's rule in Ireland during that tyrant's lifetime. The whole is an argument for the restoration of the naked sword as the sole instrument of English rule in Ireland. The book, I say again, smells of gore, as if he were athirst for Irish blood. * * * * * * * *

Mr. Froude, in denying the massacre of women and children (with what truth and candor may be now left to the judgment of the unprejudiced), relies upon Cromwell's statement as mentioning among the slain only men in arms *and priests*. These Mr. Froude boldly states to have been the instigators of the worst crimes, and as less innocent than those that committed them, to have been justly massacred. That Mr. Froude will find plenty of charges against priests of having committed atrocities in the rebellion of 1641, I know. I have read more of their crimes in this rebellion, or war, than most men; far more than Mr. Froude ever has read, or will read. I am not of their religion; but this I can say, that I have never, to my recollection, found any of these charges substantiated. The more horrible the details of the imputed crime, the more quickly is the judgment made captive through the imagination; though the opposite ought to be the course. Yet, often have I found some terrible imputation against priests end in an act of benevolence, carefully screened by their adversaries behind a mass of horrid imputed details that are left imbedded, as it were, in the memory, the good deed so hid as to be forgotten. Let any one in search of instances read the lately published Life of "Bishop Bedel," by Alexander Clogy, the bishop's son-in-law, companion of his father-in-law in his so-called imprisonment, and the account written by Bedel's son, only published within the past year. I am probably, in this, doing a disservice to these ecclesiastics, for every vile imputation will be caught up to be repeated, their good deeds kept back.

This leads me naturally to a subject connected with the treatment of the Irish priesthood by the English at a later period, that can scarcely be handled without indelicacy. But I have made a covenant with myself that I will for the future be deterred by no personal considerations, by no misplaced modesty, in this great conflict with the tyrants and maligners of Ireland and the Irish. For have they not sent forth their standard-bearer (unless it be true that he has gone forth of his own demoniac design, as he says,) to the ends of the world to rouse the English race against us? Last year, when I had occasion to treat of Cromwell's massacre at Drogheda, modesty made me suppress the gross language of Anthony Wood in giving an account of the death of the tortured, murdered virgin. His plainer, coarser terms leave a never-to-be-forgotten image. I should hesitate now to touch what I *must* treat in plain language but for the necessity of the case, and because Mr. Froude has already done so. I now proceed. It is two or three years since I was applied to to know what authority there was for the story related by Plowden, that the same penalty that was inflicted on Abelard, had, in the year 1723, been actually decreed by both Houses of Parliament in Ireland (so far as their limited power enabled them) against every priest in Ireland who should not quit his country by a certain day. For many years I had searched in vain. I remember consulting Coxe's "Life of Walpole," as he was said by Plowden to have stopped the bill at the intercession of Cardinal Fleury. It was stated by Plowden that the Commons presented the bill to the Lord Lieutenant (the Duke of Grafton) on the 15th of November, at the Castle, and that they most earnestly requested his Grace to recommend the same in the most effectual manner, to his Majesty's goodness, and that by his Grace's "zeal for the Protestant interest the same might be permitted to pass into a law." As the public records have now been thrown open to the public by the intervention of Lord Romilly, the Master of the Rolls, so that what was previously accessible only at an enormous cost, and in many cases not at all, I determined to ascertain, if possible, the truth. Taking up the printed journals of the House of Commons of the year 1723, I found that a bill "To Prevent the Further Growth of Popery" had passed through all its stages, and that it was agreed that the Speaker, with the House, should attend the Lord Lieutenant and desire it might be transmitted to England, and effectually recommended by the Lord Lieutenant to be allowed to pass into a law, just as stated by Plowden. I forthwith (it was on the 23d February, 1869) proceeded to the Parliamentary Records, then under the care of Sir Bernard Burke, the keeper of State papers (they have since been removed to the public record office), and after some search among the draughts of Heads of Bills, I found the paper wanted. It was what lawyers call, in the case of depositions taken in Chancery, the "dominical"—that is to say, the rough original manuscript of the bill on paper, in the form of a barrister's brief. It was interlined, passages roughly scored out, and slips of paper containing stringent provisions were attached by black and red wafers here and there to the margin. Among the many provisions against unregistered priests, there was one making it death, without benefit of clergy, with forfeiture of lands and goods as in high treason, for any one to give a mouthful of bread or a glass of water to any unregistered bishop, priest, or monk returning into Ireland after he had once been banished!

There were also heavy penalties against unregistered priests saying Mass. Several persons had on examinations before justices of the peace, says the preamble, confessed that they had heard Mass by priests suspected to be unregistered, yet by the arts and contrivances of the priests, who frequently had a curtain drawn between them and their congregation, no discovery could be made of the person saying Mass, that it might appear whether he was duly qualified to say Mass. For the future, therefore, the officiating priest was to appear with his face bare, under heavy penalties, and the door of every chapel was to be kept open, that the Cromwellian squireen riding by might see the priest's face. If found shut, the chapel was to be shut up forever, and all persons present to be heavily fined. But I in vain looked for the enactment recorded by Plowden. I accordingly made a return to my inquirers that I was now satisfied, as I had long before suspected, that it was an invented tale. Just two years after, however, happening to take up a volume in manuscript containing entries of the letters of the Lord Lieutenant and Council for the year 1719, amongst the papers in the State Paper Department in Dublin Castle, I found that the whole was perfectly correct as stated by Plowden, except in two particulars, one that he had mistaken the year, the other that he supposed the penalty to be general for all priests, instead of being confined to unregistered priests. The following is the letter referred to:—

"COUNCIL CHAMBER, DUBLIN CASTLE,
"*27th of August*, 1719.

"MY LORDS—We herewith transmit to your Excellencies

the following bill:—' An Act for Securing the Protestant Interest of this Kingdom by further amending the several Acts of Parliament made against Papists, and to Prevent the Growth of Popery.' The heads of this bill arose in the House of Commons, who, being sensible (as the truth is) that there are now more unregistered Priests and Popish Archbishops, Bishops, Jesuits, Friars, and others exercising foreign ecclesiastical jurisdiction in this kingdom than ever heretofore, notwithstanding the many laws against the same, found it impossible to prevent that evil otherwise than by subjecting persons who should be convicted of being unregistered Popish Priests, Popish Archbishops, &c., to greater penalties than those they were liable to by the former acts. After the country had paid a sum of twenty pounds to the discoverer of every such offender, and been at great expense in prosecuting and convicting them of the offence, they are only liable to transportation, unless they return after being transported, but for so doing are punishable with death. Priests, Friars, &c., are no sooner transported but new ones come over from France, Spain, or Portugal, so that their number continues as great as ever. The common Irish will never become Protestant or well affected to the Crown while they are supplied with priests, friars, &c., who are the fomenters and disturbers here. So that some more effectual remedy to prevent priests and friars coming into this kingdom is perfectly necessary. The Commons proposed the marking of every person who shall be convicted of being an unregistered priest, friar, &c., and of remaining in this kingdom after the 1st of May, 1720, with a large P, to be made with a red-hot iron on the cheek. The Council generally disliked that punishment, and have altered it into that of castration, which they are persuaded will be the most effectual remedy that can be found out to clear the nation of those disturbers of the peace and quiet of the kingdom, and would have been very well pleased to have been able to have found out any other punishment which might in their opinion have remedied the evil. If your Excellencies shall not be of the same sentiments, they submit to your consideration whether the punishment of castration may not be altered to that proposed by the Commons, or some other effectual one which may occur to your lordships' consideration, but are fully convinced there is an absolute necessity of making the law against unregistered priests and friars more severe than it now is.

"There are several other good clauses and provisions in this bill, of which the nation will receive great benefit, and which are very needful to be enacted into law.

"We therefore desire your Excellencies will be pleased that it be returned in form under the Great Seal.—We are your Excellencies' most humble servants,

   "BOLTON." (Charles Paulet, Marquis of Winchester, Duke of Bolton.)
   "MIDDLETON." Canc, (Alan Broderick, Lord Middleton.)
   "JOHN MEATH." (John Evans, Bishop of Meath.)
   "JOHN CLOGHER." (John Sterne, Bishop of Clogher.)
   "SANTRY." (Sir JAMES BARRY, Lord Santry.)
   "(Sir) OLIVER ST. GEORGE.
   "E. WEBSTER.
   "R. TIGHE.

"To their Excellencies the Lords Justices of Great Britain, Whitehall.

"Under Cover—To Charles Delafoy, Secretary to their Excellencies the Lords Justices of Great Britain, Whitehall."

Now for Mr. Froude's treatment of this event. He knew he could not avoid it, or ignore it, or misstate it, as he has done so many other events. For, having met Mr. Froude shortly afterwards, making his searches in the State Paper Department, at Dublin Castle, I thought it right to tell him of my discovery. But he was already aware, so he told me, of the fact, having seen the original letter in the Public Record Office, London. There was something, however, so extraordinary in the man's demeanor that I had my misgivings that he intended to misdeal with the transaction in some way, so I published it in the FREEMAN'S JOURNAL of the 28th April, 1871. I confess I had great curiosity to see how he would treat the matter in these circumstances. In

"The English in Ireland in the Eighteenth Century," he gives a chapter to this subject, and it is worth a longer exposition (may I not say exposure?) than your limited space can grant me. Let me first take his divisions of the chapter. It is Book iv., chapter iv.:—

"Intended severities against the Irish Priests—Fiction and Fact—The Registered and Unregistered Clergy—Uncertain dealings with them by the Government—Need of more systematic methods—Alteration of the heads of a Bill by the Council—Singular character of that alteration—The Bill thrown out by the House of Lords—Further efforts in the Viceroyalty of the Duke of Grafton—Postponement of the question in England."

Let it be remembered that I had bound him with such strong cords by publishing the entire letter beforehand that there was no possibility of his misstating the terms or the scope of it; and then observe the writhings and twistings of this English viper, that, nursed in his youthful sickness by the poor peasantry of Mayo, and since that day a frequent visitor of Ireland, seeks to spit his venom against us at home by publishing this book, and then immediately rushes to America to endeavor to instill into the English race abroad the same hatred he and his colleagues are filled with at home, because we will not be their slaves.

"In the midst of the heat and dust of the Wood hurricane (Wood's halfpence) the heads of a bill—if we are to believe the standard Irish historian" (says Froude), "were introduced, carried, earnestly recommended to the Home Government, of so extraordinary a nature that, were the story true in the form in which it has come down to us, the attempt by an Englishman to understand the workings of Irish factions might well be abandoned as hopeless. 'In the year 1723, &c.,' says Plowden," (and then he gives the extract I have already given.) "A statement so positively made," (he continues,) "has passed into the region of acknowledged certainties. It has been beaten into the metal of the historical thoroughfare, and, being unquestioned, has been moralized over by repentant Liberal politicians as illustrating the baneful effects of Protestant ascendancy."

Any one would suppose from this opening that "the Irish historian" was the trickster and the cheat, and not the English historian the fraudulent knave. For it is nothing but knavery to try by the use of such terms to make the careless reader to believe beforehand that Plowden's statement differs as much as "fiction" does from "fact" (according to one of the headings in the table of this chapter), instead of being substantially true, though not in form, as he had no means of access to the original and authentic documents. There is something more than "some chrysalis of fact," as Mr. Froude calls it, underlying Plowden's statement. This punishment, this shocking outrage upon decency and humanity, was actually recommended from Ireland to the Government in England, though Plowden did not know that it was a substitute for another and scarcely less inhuman punishment, the branding of unregistered priests with a large "P" with a red-hot iron on the cheek.

Mr. Froude, with all the art of an orator, next introduces the priests, and divides them into two classes—the registered and the unregistered :—

"The registered, for the most part, orderly, and well-disposed, the unregistered being the Regulars, the Jesuits, the priests trained in Spain, France, and Flanders. These, he continues, fed continually on the recollection of their wrongs, and lived in constant hope of aid from the Catholic powers to root out the Protestants and shake off the yoke of Great Britain, receiving their instructions from Rome or Flanders, or the mock court of the Pretender. They were the persistent enemies of the English settlement, the recruiting sergeants, who gathered the thousands of eager Irish youths that were enlisted annually for the Catholic armies, the impassioned feeders of the dreams which were nourished in the national heart, of the recovery of the Irish race, the return of the Stuarts, and the expulsion of the detested Saxon. They were the originators of all the political troubles which continued to distract Ireland. In Kerry, where the cause needed thoroughgoing men, the registered priests were put out of their cures as too soft and malleable, and their places taken by others of stronger national type" (observe the insult, the taunt to the nation), "who were the encouragers of the hougher and the ravisher, the smuggler and the Rapparee—whose business was to render futile the efforts of the English settlers to introduce order, and enforce the law. If English authority was to be maintained, it was fair and reasonable to distinguish between the registered and unregistered priests."

The purpose of all this rhetorical abuse of the unregistered clergy is as a preface to the branding bill and its shocking substitute, as suggested by the Lord Lieutenant and Privy Council, a Castration Act. The number of prelates, friars, and unregistered priests was daily growing larger. There was no sufficient penalty to prevent their returning. A Committee of the House of Commons accordingly drew a bill, which they considered, says Mr. Froude, would keep such persons at a safe distance. And among other clauses it contained a provision, "that every unregistered priest found in the kingdom after the 1st of May, 1720, might" (says Mr. Froude) "be branded with a hot iron in the cheek, as a mark by which he might be identified." He does not say (according to the fact) to be marked with a large "P," made with a red-hot iron on the cheek. Now, hear this cynic on the necessity of the stronger penalty. "The Council," says Froude, "among whom was the Lord Lieutenant, the Chancellor, and two bishops, considered the branding both too mild, and that it would fail in its effects. The hot iron had been already tried, he says, for the Rapparees, but the Rapparees made it a common practice to catch and brand other innocent persons to destroy the distinction. These four or five noble lords, "says Froude, (as if they were not the Lord Lieutenant and the Privy Council, the government in a great measure of Ireland!) " did certainly recommend as a substitute for the iron a penalty, which was reported, rightly or wrongly, to have been used in Sweden with effect against the Jesuits." And here this brutal cynic pretends to relieve the priests of Ireland from its being supposed that this treatment was for the purpose of securing their chastity, by suggesting that this mutilation proceeded on another ground, and was for another end.

But let us have done with the disgusting subject and disgusting man, who seems to be as lost to all sense of modesty as of humanity. He it is, who, in an article in the Review he edits, in describing "A Fortnight in Kerry" (where, however, he spent two summers), foully and indecently libelled the memory of O'Connell, the Liberator, and was then surprised to find that the people of Kerry looked coldly upon him. Does he take us for dogs? That we are not men? Or else that we are sunk so low as not to dare to resent the insults any Englishman may put upon us? And this libeller of our name and nation, of all things, indeed, sacred and profane, except the "Royal Irish" Sepoys, and the Ulster Janissaries, talks of spending his days among us! Heaven forbid! Girls of Ireland, remember the outspoken approver of the murder of your poor tortured sister at Drogheda! Mothers, think of the children used by the English as shields while fighting their way up the stairs of the church-towers! Ladies, forget not the crowds of those of your own rank slaughtered in cold blood in the vaults beneath! He sanctions it all. He is guilty of it all. Make the country too hot with your indignation to hold him. Men of Ireland, treat him not to the penalty devised against your clergy, but brand him with the red-hot iron of tongue and pen on one cheek with a large "L" as liar, on the other, with an "S" as slanderer of this nation.—Your obedient servant,

JOHN P. PRENDERGAST.

www.ingramcontent.com/pod-product-compliance
Lightning Source LLC
Chambersburg PA
CBHW030741230426
43667CB00007B/793